# It Still Takes A Candidate

## Why Women Don't Run for Office
### Revised Edition

*It Still Takes A Candidate* serves as the only systematic, nationwide empirical account of the manner in which gender affects political ambition. Based on data from the Citizen Political Ambition Panel Study, a national survey of almost 3,800 "eligible candidates" in 2001 and a second survey of more than 2,000 of these same individuals in 2008, Jennifer L. Lawless and Richard L. Fox find that women, even in the highest tiers of professional accomplishment, are substantially less likely than men to demonstrate ambition to seek elective office. Women are less likely than men to be recruited to run for office. They are less likely than men to think they are qualified to run for office. And they are less likely than men to express a willingness to run for office in the future. This gender gap in political ambition persists across generations and over time. Despite cultural evolution and society's changing attitudes toward women in politics, running for public office remains a much less attractive and feasible endeavor for women than for men.

Jennifer L. Lawless is associate professor of government at American University, where she is also the director of the Women & Politics Institute. Her research focuses on gender, elections, and representation. Professor Lawless has published numerous articles in academic journals, such as *American Journal of Political Science, Perspectives on Politics, Journal of Politics, Political Research Quarterly, Legislative Studies Quarterly, Social Problems,* and *Politics & Gender.* She is a nationally recognized speaker, and her scholarly analysis and political commentary have been quoted in various newspapers, magazines, television news programs, and radio shows. In 2006, she sought the Democratic nomination for the U.S. House of Representatives in Rhode Island's second congressional district. Currently, she serves as the editor of *Politics & Gender.*

Richard L. Fox is associate professor of political science at Loyola Marymount University. His research examines how gender affects voting behavior, state executive elections, congressional elections, and political ambition. He is the author of *Gender Dynamics in Congressional Elections* (1997) and coauthor of *Tabloid Justice: The Criminal Justice System in the Age of Media Frenzy* (2007). He is also coeditor, with Susan J. Carroll, of *Gender and Elections* (2010). His work has appeared in *Political Psychology, Journal of Politics, American Journal of Political Science, Social Problems, PS,* and *Politics & Gender.* He has also written op-ed articles that have appeared in the *New York Times* and the *Wall Street Journal.*

# It Still Takes A Candidate

*Why Women Don't Run for Office*

Revised Edition

**JENNIFER L. LAWLESS**
*American University*

**RICHARD L. FOX**
*Loyola Marymount University*

CAMBRIDGE
UNIVERSITY PRESS

CAMBRIDGE UNIVERSITY PRESS
Cambridge, New York, Melbourne, Madrid, Cape Town,
Singapore, São Paulo, Delhi, Mexico City

Cambridge University Press
32 Avenue of the Americas, New York, NY 10013-2473, USA

www.cambridge.org
Information on this title: www.cambridge.org/9780521179249

© Jennifer L. Lawless and Richard L. Fox 2005, 2010

First published 2005
Revised edition published 2010
Reprinted 2011 (thrice), 2012

*A catalog record for this publication is available from the British Library.*

*Library of Congress Cataloging in Publication Data*

Lawless, Jennifer L., 1975–
It still takes a candidate : why women don't run for office / Jennifer L. Lawless,
Richard L. Fox. – Rev. ed.
    p.  cm.
Rev. ed. of: It takes a candidate. 2005.
Includes bibliographical references and index.
ISBN 978-0-521-76252-6 (hardback) – ISBN 978-0-521-17924-9 (pbk.)
1. Women – Political activity – United States.  2. Political participation – United States.
3. Women political candidates – United States.  4. Women – United States – Attitudes.
5. Sex role – United States.  I. Fox, Richard Logan.  II. Lawless, Jennifer L., 1975–
It takes a candidate.  III. Title.
HQ1236.5.U6L38  2010
320.082 – dc22        2009047364

ISBN 978-0-521-76252-6 Hardback
ISBN 978-0-521-17924-9 Paperback

# Contents

# List of Tables

# List of Figures

# Acknowledgments

We conducted the Citizen Political Ambition Panel Study because of our deep concern about women's political underrepresentation in the United States. Perhaps we are just impatient, but it seemed that women's broad inclusion in top elective offices was moving too slowly. And we sensed greater roadblocks to women's full political integration than had previously been identified. So, in an effort to uncover the degree to which gender interacts with the process by which people emerge as candidates, we went to work, surveying and speaking with thousands of women and men who are well suited to run for office. We believe that the first edition of this book – which was based on data from 2001 – went a long way in explicating the prominent role gender plays in the evolution of political ambition.

But after completing the first edition of the book, we knew there were several areas on which we were unable to elaborate. Although the first edition established the gender gap in political ambition and offered several explanations for it, we felt it was important to add greater empirical depth to the central findings, especially those dealing with the manner in which gender interacts with political recruitment and self-assessed qualifications. This edition does just that; we have substantially updated and revised the sections of the book that focus on the factors that contribute to the gender gap in candidate emergence.

We also felt it was important to write a revised edition of the book because of the significant changes to the U.S. political landscape that occurred after we completed our original survey in 2001. The past nine years have been particularly tumultuous: we have seen the waging of two wars, acrimonious partisan rancor in Washington, one of the most unpopular and polarizing presidents in recent history, a shift in congressional party control, and the government's ineffective handling of the Hurricane Katrina disaster. In terms of women and politics, we have seen the ascension of Nancy Pelosi as the first female Speaker of the House, the emergence of Hillary Clinton as the first serious female presidential contender (not to mention the recipient of 18 million votes), and the nomination of Sarah Palin as the first Republican vice presidential candidate. It is hard to imagine a more important time to study the intersection of gender and political ambition and assess whether the prognosis for women's political representation has changed. Surprisingly, the results reported in this book reveal almost no change in the gender gap in political ambition. In 2001, we uncovered a 16 percentage point gender gap; seven years later, the gap was almost identical at 14 percentage points. If women are ever to achieve electoral parity, then it is clear that the change will not occur on its own.

Identifying and explaining the persistent gender gap in political ambition is vitally important. But it is safe to say that when we began the project, we really did not know what we were getting into. The ramifications of what it would entail to administer – by ourselves – a multiwave national mail survey to seven thousand "eligible" candidates had not dawned on us. At the conclusion of a yearlong foray into data collection, we had signed, folded, sealed, and stamped almost twenty-five thousand pieces of mail. We fed every envelope into the printer, by hand. We wrote a personal note on each letter, encouraging the recipient to complete the survey. We affixed an actual stamp to each piece of mail. If nothing else, this endless procession of mind-numbing tasks proved our shared mania and self-loathing.

Then, of course, there was the obsessive monitoring of the mail. On a bad day, when only a few completed surveys would arrive, our hopes for the project's success would plunge. Our faith was almost always restored the following day, when hundreds of surveys would pour in. (As a pointer for those administering a mail survey, we learned that Mondays and Fridays are good mail days, but Tuesdays and Wednesdays are not.) Ultimately, the project was a great success; almost four thousand good-hearted souls violated the rational choice paradigm and took the time to fill out a lengthy survey with nothing to gain other than advancing social science (and getting us off their backs).

As proof of our insanity, we decided to do it all over again seven years later. This time, though, we had an additional step that required tracking down current address information for the respondents. Through our searches, we learned of exciting new marriages, new babies, new careers, and unfortunate tragedies. We learned that we could not follow up with one respondent because she had been moved into the Witness Protection Program. We learned that we could not contact another because he was standing trial, as were many of his colleagues in Enron's government relations department. Overall, through extensive Internet searches and phone calls, we managed to obtain current address information for nearly three thousand members (82 percent) of the original sample of respondents. We then commenced the mail survey process, which amounted to the signing, stuffing, sealing, and stamping of 11,904 pieces of mail. Ultimately, we were very gratified when more than two thousand women and men completed the second-wave survey.

Obviously, the completion of a project like this requires help and assistance from numerous people, and we would like to thank them all. We are particularly grateful to Walt Stone and Linda Fowler, both of whom offered extensive and insightful comments at various stages of this project. Kathy Dolan, who expressed support for the work even in its earliest stages, provided helpful feedback on the manuscript as well. We would also like to thank Dominique Tauzin, who joined us on many occasions to help put out the mail. In addition, she made numerous phone calls to badger people to complete the survey (something we did not have the nerve to do).

From a practical standpoint, our endeavor would have been impossible without Jonathan Ma and Eliana Vasquez. They provided invaluable assistance in assembling the initial sample and helping to track the flow of mail. We could not have executed the second wave of the study without logistical help from Carol Cichy and Dave Rangaviz. And we thank My-Lien Le, who constructed the index for the book in record time and with an obsessive-compulsive attention to detail.

We are also grateful to many people who provided feedback on the survey instruments and who read parts of the manuscripts. Cliff Brown, Barbara Burrell, Eric R.A.N. Smith, Terry Weiner, and Harriet Woods offered advice on the original survey. In addition, several individuals working in politics and at women's organizations offered suggestions for the second-wave survey. We thank Marya Stark (Emerge), Marcia Cone and Simone Joyaux (Women's Fund of Rhode Island), Ilana Goldman (Women's Campaign Forum), Susannah Shakow (Running Start), and Mary Hughes. Dave Brady, Dick Brody, Mo Fiorina, Brian Frederick, Amy Gangl, Claudine Gay, Simon Jackman, Kent Jennings, Terry Moe, Karen O'Connor, Zoe Oxley, Kathryn Pearson, Kira Sanbonmatsu,

Wendy Schiller, Keith Shaw, Sean Theriault, and Sue Tolleson Rinehart helped us tighten our analysis and offer a more compelling contribution. We would also like to thank Jane Mansbridge and Lori Marso, who took the time to tutor two empirically minded political scientists in some of the finer points of feminist theory.

We also could not have conducted the study without financial support from American University, Brown University, Cal State Fullerton, the Carrie Chapman Catt Center at Iowa State University, Stanford University, Union College, Hunt Alternatives Fund, and the Barbara Lee Foundation. Debbie Walsh and Sue Carroll at the Center for American Women and Politics at Rutgers University supported the project from the outset and also provided funding and a place to work. Norman Nie and the Stanford Institute for the Quantitative Study of Society helped fund part of one of the first waves of the survey. Darrell West, as the director of the Taubman Center for Public Policy at Brown University, helped issue a report based on our first survey; he then did the same for the second survey when he became vice president of governmental studies at the Brookings Institution. We are very pleased that women's organizations and public officials use these reports to encourage more women to run for office.

Several students also made important contributions to the project: Jinhee Chung, Shana Gotlieb, Ben Gray, Peter Jewett, Erik Kindschi, Marne Lenox, AnneMarie MacPherson, Ben Mishkin, Oriana Montagni, and Teresa Tanzi. Adam Deitch copyedited multiple versions of the second survey, promoted the book widely in 2005 and 2006, and assures us that, one day, he will actually read it.

We also want to thank our friends, as well as our colleagues at our former institutions, Brown University and Union College, and our current institutions, American University and Loyola Marymount University, for providing great camaraderie. And we would be remiss not to thank our editor at Cambridge, Ed Parsons, who encouraged and supported us through both editions of the book and who seems to share our need for immediate feedback.

Finally, we would like to thank our families, who put up with endless interruptions and listened to numerous complaint sessions about the progress of both editions of the book and the coauthor. Thank you Margie, John, Louis, Dominique, Lila, and Miles.

# Electoral Politics

## *Still a Man's World?*

Cheryl Perry made partner at a prestigious law firm in Hartford, Connecticut, when she was only thirty-three years old. She is active professionally, holding positions with the city's bar association and the Connecticut Trial Lawyers Association. In addition, Ms. Perry served on the coordinating committee for the 1996 Olympics. Several of her peers in the legal community have repeatedly urged her to consider running for elective office. But when asked if she considers herself qualified to run, Ms. Perry replies, "Absolutely not. I'd never run."[1]

Tricia Moniz also looks like an excellent candidate for public office. A sociology professor at a large university, she has won four campuswide teaching awards, is an authority in the areas of juvenile justice and diversity, and finds her expertise sought out by many state and city agencies. Because of her professional experience, Professor Moniz works closely with community and political party leaders who regularly consult her on public policy issues. When asked if she feels qualified to serve as an elected official, she laughs and says, "Lord no," elaborating that she does not feel qualified to serve even at the local level.

Randall White also seems to fit the bill for entering the electoral arena. A college professor in Pennsylvania, he has published numerous works on biblical interpretation. A dedicated teacher with a strong interest in local politics, he frequently attends and speaks at city council meetings. When

---

[1] To protect anonymity, we changed the names and modified identifying references of the women and men we surveyed and interviewed for this book. The backgrounds and credentials we describe, as well as the specific quotes we use, are taken directly from the surveys we administered and interviews we conducted.

asked if he feels qualified to seek elective office, Professor White immediately responds, "Yes; I am much smarter and a lot more honest than the people currently in office." He confidently asserts his qualifications to run for a position situated even at the state or national level.

Kevin Kendall lives outside of Seattle, Washington, and began practicing law in 1990. Since then, he has become a partner in his law firm. In addition to working as a full-time litigator, Mr. Kendall is active in several professional associations and nonprofit community organizations in and around Seattle. When asked whether he feels qualified to pursue an elective position, Mr. Kendall states, "I am a quick study. People tell me I should run all the time." Asked to name the level of office for which he thinks he is most suited, Mr. Kendall responds, "I could run for office at any level. I've thought about it a lot and, one day, probably will."

The sentiments of these four individuals exemplify the dramatic gender gap we uncovered throughout the course of investigating eligible candidates' ambition to seek public office. These four women and men all possess excellent qualifications and credentials to run for office. They are well educated, have risen to the top of their professions, serve as active members in their communities, and express high levels of political interest. Yet despite these similarities, the two women express little desire to move into the electoral arena. The two men confidently assert the ease with which they could occupy almost any elective position. Although the factors that lead an individual first to consider running for office and then to decide to seek an actual position are complex and multifaceted, we find that gender exerts one of the strongest influences on who ultimately launches a political career.

The critical importance gender plays in the initial decision to run for office suggests that prospects for gender parity in our political institutions are bleak. This conclusion stands in contrast to the conventional wisdom of much political science scholarship. Because extensive investigations of women's electoral performance find no discernible, systematic biases against women candidates, many scholars conclude that, as open seats emerge and women continue to move into the professions that precede political candidacies, more women will seek and occupy positions of political power. These circumstances are certainly prerequisites for women to increase their presence in elective offices. We argue, however, that it is misleading to gauge prospects for gender parity in our electoral system without considering whether well-positioned women and men are equally interested and willing to run for office.

As fundamental as political ambition is to women's emergence as candidates, there is a glaring lack of empirical research that focuses on gender and the decision to run for office.[2] This may be a result of scholarship following history; men have dominated the political sphere and U.S. political institutions throughout time. Writing in the late 1950s, for example, Robert Lane (1959, 97) remarked that political scientists have "always had to come to terms with the nature of man, the political animal." Fifteen years later, another prominent political scientist, David Mayhew (1974, 6), described politics as "a struggle among men to gain and maintain power." It is not surprising, therefore, that when we wrote the first edition of this book, none of the sixteen published academic books that concentrated predominantly on political ambition focused on gender.[3] A 2004 search of scholarly journals in the disciplines of political science, sociology, and psychology revealed a similar pattern. The only national study of the interaction between gender and political ambition appeared in 1982, when Virginia Sapiro reported that female delegates to the 1972 national party conventions were less politically ambitious than their male counterparts. Over the course of the two decades following Sapiro's study, eight articles have investigated gender and the candidate emergence process.[4] Six of the articles are based on samples of actual candidates and

[2] Consistent with its traditional use in most political science research, our definition of *political ambition* is synonymous with the desire to acquire and hold political power through electoral means. Some scholars offer a broader conception of political ambition; it can manifest itself in forms other than running for office, such as serving as a community activist, organizing letter-writing campaigns and protests, or volunteering for candidates or issue advocacy groups (e.g., Burrell 1996). Because holding elective office is the key to increasing women's representation, we focus on the conventional definition of the term and examine the reasons women are less likely than men to enter the electoral arena as candidates.

[3] Of the sixteen books, one includes a case study of a woman's decision to run for office (Fowler and McClure 1989), one includes a chapter that addresses the role that race and gender might play in the candidate emergence process (Moncrief, Squire, and Jewell 2001), and one includes a chapter that elaborates on the manner in which the scholarship has not sufficiently addressed the intersection between gender and political ambition (Williams and Lascher 1993). We conducted this search with WorldCat, which includes all books cataloged in the Library of Congress. We used "political ambition," "candidate emergence," and "decision to run for office" as the initial search terms and then narrowed the list to include only those books that focused on interest in pursuing elective office. We excluded single-person political biographies.

[4] A search of articles using PAIS International (1972–2004), Sociological Abstracts (1974–2004), PsycINFO (1887–2004), and JSTOR (including all volumes and issues of political science journal articles published after JSTOR's "moving walls") yielded more than two hundred results for "political ambition," "candidate emergence," and "decision to run

officeholders, all of whom, by definition, exhibited political ambition when they entered political contests. Further, they rely on data from the 1970s and 1980s, when women's candidacies were extraordinarily rare and cultural acceptance of women in politics was far less widespread than it is today. The two articles that focus on individuals who have not yet run for office rely on data from the single-state investigation that served as the pilot study for this book.[5] Several case studies and historical analyses chronicle women officeholders' decisions to run for office (e.g., Witt, Paget, and Matthews 1994; Kirkpatrick 1974). And political biographies written by women who have held elective office also shed light on the process by which they became candidates (Kunin 2005; Clinton 2003; Schroeder 1999; Boxer 1994). But no systematic, nationwide empirical accounts had attempted to explain the role gender plays in the candidate emergence process. We simply did not know the manner in which gender interacts with political ambition in contemporary society.

The first edition of this book went a long way in exploring the role gender plays in the initial decision to run for elective office. And now, in this revised and expanded edition, we add greater depth to our examination of the factors that lead people to make the move from politically minded citizens to candidates for public office. Beyond its more detailed account of the manner in which gender shapes political ambition, this edition allows us to examine these gender dynamics at a crucial point in time. Nancy Pelosi's rise to the position of Speaker of the House of Representatives, Hillary Clinton's push for the presidency, and Sarah Palin's emergence as a vice presidential nominee mark major advances for women in politics.

Our analysis is based on data from the Citizen Political Ambition Panel Study. The panel consists of national surveys we conducted in 2001 and 2008 with "eligible" candidates – successful women and men who occupy the four professions that most often precede a career in politics. We base much of our analysis on the survey responses of the nearly 3,800 women and men who completed the original survey in 2001. But throughout

---

for office." When we narrowed the list to articles that focused on interest in pursuing elective office, sixty-three remained. Since the first edition of this book was published in 2005, two articles related to women's candidate emergence appeared in political science journals (Deckman 2007; Fulton et al. 2006). Neither of the articles focuses on women and men who have not yet run for office.

[5] The pilot study was based on data collected from roughly two hundred eligible candidates from the state of New York. For a more elaborate description of that sample and a summary and analysis of the findings, see Fox and Lawless 2003; Fox, Lawless, and Feeley 2001.

each chapter, we supplement our analysis with data from the more than two thousand respondents who completed the 2008 survey; the second wave allows us to expand on and explicate many of the findings from the first edition of the book. This study provides a significant methodological advance in exploring candidate emergence and presents the first opportunity to examine broadly the manner in which gender influences the decision to run for office. At its core, this book is about political ambition: why men have it and why women don't.

### Representation, Equality, and the Study of Gender in Electoral Politics

Investigators who study women and electoral politics have fought to convince the political science community to take the subfield of women and politics seriously.[6] Nearly all of the research that addresses gender and U.S. politics, therefore, tends to begin with a justification for studying women and elections. Invariably, the normative underpinning to which scholars refer is women's underrepresentation. Although this justification has become almost cliché, it remains a potent reflection of reality; women's presence in our political institutions bears directly on issues of substantive and symbolic representation.

Most empirical research in the area of representation focuses on the different issues women and men bring to the forefront of the legislative agenda and the degree to which gender affects legislators' abilities to represent female constituents' substantive interests. At both the national and the state level, male and female legislators' priorities and preferences differ. Jessica C. Gerrity, Tracy Osborn, and Jeanette Morehouse Mendez's (2007) analysis of bill sponsorship and floor remarks in the 104th through 107th Congresses, for example, reveals that women who replace men in the same district are more likely to focus on "women's issues," such as gender equity, day care, flex time, abortion, minimum wage increases, and the extension of the food stamp program (see also Burrell 1996).[7] Further, both Democratic and moderate Republican women in Congress are more likely than men to use their bill sponsorship and cosponsorship

---

[6] For a compelling analysis of the theoretical, methodological, and empirical difficulties involved in fully integrating gender politics into the political science discipline, see Flammang 1997.

[7] For competing evidence, see Leslie Schwindt-Bayer and Renato Corbetta (2004), who argue that, controlling for party and constituency influences, member sex does not predict the "liberalness" of representatives' roll call behavior in the 103rd–105th Congresses.

activity to focus on women's issues (Swers 2002).[8] Debra Dodson (1998) highlights such behavior in her discussion of the Women's Health Initiative, which she explains was enacted only because women in Congress appealed to the General Accounting Office to fund the research. Before this initiative, even though women were twice as likely as men to suffer from heart disease, the majority of the medical research was conducted on male subjects. A recent study of state legislative behavior also uncovers female legislators' greater likelihood to champion women's interests (Bratton 2005).[9]

Substantive representation pertains not only to policy priorities and voting records; women's presence in the top tier of political accomplishment also infuses into the legislative system a distinct style of leadership. Sue Tolleson Rinehart's (1991) study of mayors finds that women tend to adopt an approach to governing that emphasizes congeniality and cooperation, whereas men tend to emphasize hierarchy. Because women mayors are more likely than men to seek broad participation and inclusion in the budget process, they tend to be more likely than men to admit to and address the fiscal problems facing their cities (Weikart et al. 2007).[10] A

---

[8] With the growth of party polarization, however, fewer moderate Republican women serve in Congress. Indeed, Brian Frederick's (2009) analysis of roll-call votes in the 108th and 109th Congresses reveals that Republican women are ideologically indistinguishable from their male counterparts. This finding holds even when the analysis focuses strictly on women's issues.

[9] Investigators have produced a wide array of empirical research that highlights the unique policy agenda women bring to elective office. For additional evidence of substantive representation at the congressional level, see Swers 1998; Paolino 1995. At the state level, see Thomas 1994; Berkman and O'Connor 1993; Carroll, Dodson, and Mandel 1991; Kathlene, Clarke, and Fox 1991; Thomas and Welch 1991; Saint-Germain 1989. And for a theoretical discussion of women's substantive representation, see Susan Moller Okin (1989), who argues that the presence of female legislators has finally allowed issues such as marital rape, domestic violence, and child custody – all of which have traditionally been deemed private matters – to receive public attention and debate.

[10] For more recent nonacademic accounts of how women's leadership styles affect process and deliberation, see Marie C. Wilson's (2004) *Closing the Leadership Gap* and Dee Dee Myers's (2008) *Why Women Should Rule the World*. For additional political science studies pertaining to gendered political styles and the public policy ramifications that ensue, see Fox and Schuhmann 1999; Rosenthal 1998; Thomas 1994; Alexander and Andersen 1993; Eagly and Johnson 1990; Flammang 1985. Not all studies uncover such gender differences, though (see, e.g., Duerst-Lahti and Johnson 1992; Blair and Stanley 1991; Dodson and Carroll 1991). According to Beth Reingold (1996, 468), the one factor that distinguishes the studies that find differences in leadership styles from those that do not is the presence of strong institutional norms of behavior. The successful rational actor is aware of the dangers of "ruffling feathers, stepping on toes, and burning bridges" (Reingold 1996, 483; see also Reingold 2000).

similar set of findings applies at the state legislative level. Lyn Kathlene
(1994) uncovers significant differences in the manner in which male and
female state legislature committee chairs conduct themselves at hearings;
women are more likely to act as facilitators, whereas men tend to use
their power to control the direction of the hearings. Women's likelihood
to conduct business in a manner that is more cooperative, communica-
tive, and based on coalition building than men's can directly affect policy
outcomes. Because they are more concerned with context and environmental factors when deliberating on crime and punishment, for instance,
women state assembly members are more likely than men to advocate
for rehabilitation programs and less likely than men to support punitive
policies (Kathlene 1995).

Political scientists also point to symbolic representation and the role
model effects that women's presence in positions of political power con-
fers to women citizens (Pitkin 1967). Lonna Rae Atkeson and Nancy
Carrillo (2007), for example, find that, as the percentage of a state's
female legislators increases, so do female citizens' levels of external efficacy (see also Atkeson 2003). David Campbell and Christina Wolbrecht's
(2006) cross-national study also uncovers a positive relationship between
the presence of highly visible female politicians and adolescent girls'
expectations of political engagement.[11] Although symbolic effects are
quite difficult to quantify – and, accordingly, this literature is much less
developed empirically – the logic underlying symbolic representation is
compelling. Barbara Burrell (1996, 151) captures the argument well:

> Women in public office stand as symbols for other women, both enhancing
> their identification with the system and their ability to have influence within
> it. This subjective sense of being involved and heard for women, in general,
> alone makes the election of women to public office important because, for
> so many years, they were excluded from power.

Together, the literatures on substantive and symbolic representation
suggest that the inclusion of more women in positions of political power
would change the nature of political representation in the United States.
Electing more women would substantially reduce the possibility that

---

[11] By contrast, Kathleen Dolan (2006) and Jennifer Lawless (2004a) find little empirical
evidence – based on National Elections Studies data – to support the assumption that
the presence of women candidates translates into any systematic change in women's
political attitudes or behaviors. For a discussion of the difficulties involved in studying
the potentially nuanced effects of symbolic representation, see also Schwindt-Bayer and
Mishler 2005.

politicians overlook gender-salient issues. Moreover, the government would gain a greater sense of political legitimacy, simply by virtue of the fact that it would be more reflective of the gender breakdown of the national population. As political theorist Jane Mansbridge (1999, 651) explains:

> Easier communication with one's representative, awareness that one's inter-
> ests are being represented with sensitivity, and knowledge that certain fea-
> tures of one's identity do not mark one as less able to govern all contribute
> to making one feel more included in the polity. This feeling of inclusion in
> turn makes the polity democratically more legitimate in one's eyes.

Because concerns surrounding representation are so fundamental, we situate our analysis on this foundation. If women are not as willing as men to enter the electoral arena, then large gender disparities in office holding will persist and continue to carry serious implications for the quality of political representation. Further, the degree of comfort women articulate regarding their entry into electoral politics serves as an impor-tant barometer of women's full integration into all aspects of life in the United States. Many enclaves of male dominance crumbled across the last half of the twentieth century, but high-level electoral politics was not one of them.

### Traditional Gender Socialization in the Context of U.S. Politics: The Central Argument and Its Implications

This study provides the first broad-based empirical documentation that women are less politically ambitious than men to seek elective office. We advance the central argument that the gender gap in political ambition results from long-standing patterns of traditional socialization that per-sist in U.S. culture. Gender politics scholars Pamela Conover and Virginia Gray (1983, 2–3) define traditional sex-role socialization as the "division of activities into the public extra-familial jobs done by the male and the private intra-familial ones performed by the female." These differ-ent roles and social expectations for women and men have permeated the landscape of human civilization throughout time. Historian Gerda Lerner (1986) persuasively links the origins of the gendered division of labor to tribal hunter-gatherer societies. She explains that the division was a "necessity" because women had to produce enough children (many of whom died in infancy) to maintain the very existence of the tribe. Politi-cal theorist Jean Bethke Elshtain (1981) attributes the first enunciation of separate spheres for women and men as a political concept to Aristotle, who delineated between the public world of the *polis* and the nonpublic world of the *oikos*. Not surprisingly, the gendered division of labor has historically resulted in men's entry into, and dominance of, the public world of politics and women's almost total exclusion from the political sphere. By hearkening back to tribal societies and the writings of Aristotle, we do not mean to diminish dramatic social and cultural change, especially that which has transpired during the past fifty years in the United States. But centuries – or even millennia – of socialized norms do die hard. It was not until 1975, for instance, that the U.S. Supreme Court discarded state laws that excused women from jury service on the grounds that it would interfere with their domestic duties (Kerber 1998).

Throughout this book, we employ the term *traditional gender socialization* within the context of U.S. politics to refer to the greater complexities of women's lives, in terms of both how society perceives them and the manner in which they perceive themselves as eligible candidates. More specifically, we propose three manifestations of traditional gender socialization to explain the gender gap in political ambition.

### Traditional Family Role Orientations

Gender-specific family roles and responsibilities serve as perhaps the most obvious manifestation of traditional gender socialization. Up through the mid-twentieth century, the notion of women serving in positions of high political power was anathema, in large part because of the expectation that women should prioritize housework and child care. The women's movement of the 1960s and 1970s advocated greater gender equity in household management, but the promise of egalitarian household dynamics never fully materialized. A 1995 UN study of two-career families in developed countries, for example, found that women continue to perform almost three times as much of the unpaid household labor as men (Freedman 2002). Even in the current era, the primary institutions of social and cultural life in the United States continue to impress on women and men that traditional gender roles constitute a "normal," "appropriate," and desirable set of life circumstances. Summarized well by feminist historian Estelle Freedman (2002, 131), "Women's domestic identities have proven to be quite tenacious."

Not only do women continue to bear the responsibility for a majority of household tasks and child care, but they also face a more complicated balancing of these responsibilities with their professions than do men. As a result, an increasing number of highly successful professional women

are "opting out" of their careers to fulfill traditional gender roles. A
2003 *New York Times Magazine* exposé highlighted this trend. The piece
focused on eight women graduates of Princeton University, most of whom
were in their thirties. Some earned law degrees from top universities, such
as Harvard and Columbia. Others garnered MBAs, started businesses, or
launched careers in journalism. All of these women found the balancing
act of career and family obligations too difficult, so all chose to leave their
careers.[12] Pamela Stone's 2007 book, *Opting Out: Why Women Really
Quit Careers and Head Home*, provides a more authoritative account of
this phenomenon. She concludes that many of the women who opt out
are actually responding to significant private and professional pressures
that ultimately force them out of the workplace.[13]

Debates about whether women can and/or should attempt to balance
their careers with their families, as well as the steps workplaces can take
to minimize women's departures, will likely continue into the foreseeable
future (Eagly and Carli 2007).[14] In the meantime, however, women's dual
roles carry important implications for their involvement in politics. The
traditional division of household labor and family responsibilities means
that, for many women, a political career would be a third job. Because
men tend not to be equal partners on the home front, entering politics
does not interfere as directly with their ability to fulfill their personal and
professional obligations.

### Masculinized Ethos

When individuals consider running for office and launching successful
campaigns, they must rely on the support of numerous political institutions. Most of these institutions are dominated by men and ultimately
embody a perpetually ingrained ethos of masculinity. International relations and feminist scholar Cynthia Enloe (2004, 4–5) explains:

> Patriarchy is the structural and ideological system that perpetuates the
> privileging of masculinity . . . legislatures, political parties, museums, news-
> papers, theater companies, television networks, religious organizations,

---

[12] Lisa Belkin, "Why Don't More Women Get to the Top?" *New York Times Magazine*,
October 26, 2003, 43.

[13] See Kathleen Hall Jamieson (1995) for a broader historical discussion of the manner in
which women struggle to strike a balance between their competing private and public
sphere roles.

[14] For a somewhat controversial account of the extent to which women benefit by leaving
the workforce and staying home with their children, see Linda Hirshman's (2006) *Get
to Work: A Manifesto for Women of the World*. For a response to Hirshman, see Katha
Pollitt, "Mommy Wars, Round 587," *Nation*, July 17, 2006.

corporations, and courts...derive from the presumption that what is masculine is most deserving of reward, promotion, admiration, [and] emulation.

In-depth analyses of the United States' central political institutions confirm Enloe's claim. Scholars have identified, to varying degrees, a type of masculinized ethos within the various components of the national government.[15] Further, state legislatures have been very slow to include women and their distinct policy agendas (Thomas 1994). Women's full integration into the Democratic and Republican parties has also been a long and difficult road; no woman has led either of the national party organizations in the last thirty years (Burrell 2006). Men are more likely than women to participate actively in political fundraising networks (Burns, Schlozman, and Verba 2001; Brown, Powell, and Wilcox 1995). And when we turn to television media, men are the leading faces of broadcast news. Granted, Katie Couric became the host of the *CBS Evening News* in 2006, which marked the first time a woman ever served as the lead anchor for any of the three major news networks.[16] Diane Sawyer assumed the anchor position for *ABC World News* in January 2010. But all of the top-rated cable news programs are still hosted by men. In addition, when *National Journal* recently asked a panel of "congressional and political insiders" to name the columnists, bloggers, and television or radio commentators who most shape their own opinions, the top five vote getters were men.[17]

Even if we assume that the men who occupy positions in these institutions no longer exhibit overt signs of bias against eligible women candidates (and this is a substantial assumption), years of traditional conceptions about candidate quality, electability, and background persist. As Georgia Duerst-Lahti (2006, 17) observes, electoral positions, especially

---

[15] Scholars have identified gendered and masculinized components of all three branches of the federal government. For insights into the gendered institution of the presidency, see Borelli and Martin 1997; for Congress, see O'Connor 2002; and for the judiciary, see Mezey 2003.

[16] For an amusing recounting of the masculine face of broadcast journalism, see Maureen Dowd, "It's Still a Man's World on the Idiot Box," *New York Times*, December 2, 2004, A39.

[17] Thomas Friedman, David Brooks, Charles Krauthammer, George Will, and Paul Krugman occupied the top five positions on the list. The only woman to appear in a top ten slot was Peggy Noonan, who placed ninth. "Congressional and Political Insiders Poll: Reading Lists and Viewing Habits Are as Divided as the Country's Politics," *National Journal Magazine*, August 19, 2009, http://www.nationaljournal.com/njonline/no_20090917_4420.php (accessed December 18, 2009).

at the highest levels, are "imbued with masculinity" and the conscious and subconscious perceptions that "masculine persons" should occupy these positions. In other words, the organs of governance were designed by men, are operated by men, and continue to be controlled by men; even if they want to be more inclusive of women, they often do not know how to do so.[18] As a result, women and men have different experiences and develop different impressions when dealing with the various arms of the political process. Whereas political institutions overtly and subtly facilitate and encourage men's emergence into politics, they often continue to suppress women's willingness to launch political careers.

### Gendered Psyche

The presence of traditional gender role expectations and the dominance of a masculinized ethos culminate to create and sustain the gendered psyche, a deeply embedded imprint that propels men into politics, but relegates women to the electoral arena's periphery. Cynthia Enloe's discussion of patriarchy highlights that part of the reason traditional systems endure involves the manner in which they lead women to overlook their own marginalization from the public sphere and its institutions. Instead, patriarchal systems make many women feel "secure, protected, [and] valued" (Enloe 2004, 6). The most dramatic political consequence of the gendered psyche, therefore, is that politics often exists as a reasonable career possibility for men, but does not even appear on the radar screen for many women.

The gendered psyche's imprint can also be far subtler. When women operate outside of their traditional and "appropriate" realms, they tend to express less comfort than men. Contemporary studies that assess psychological development uncover gender differences in levels of confidence, the desire for achievement, and the inclination to self-promote. Several studies of business executives, for example, find that, in salary negotiations, women often downplay their achievements. The net result is that women garner significantly lower salaries than equally credentialed men (Bowles, Babcock, and McGinn 2004, 20). Women, in essence, tend not to be socialized to possess the qualities the modern political arena demands of its candidates and elected officials. Whereas men are taught to be confident, assertive, and self-promoting, cultural attitudes toward

---

[18] An edited collection by Georgia Duerst-Lahti and Rita Mae Kelly (1995) builds on this theme and offers a broad collection of articles that consider the relationships among power, institutions, and gender.

women as political leaders, expectations of women's family roles, and the overarching male exclusiveness of most political institutions leave an imprint suggesting to women that it is often inappropriate to possess such characteristics. And when women do participate in historically masculine environments, they often come to believe that they have to be better than men to succeed. Congresswoman Grace Napolitano (D-CA) summarized this consequence of the gendered psyche when she speculated as to why an increasing number of women have been elected to local offices across the country: "Women are doing a better job because they have to work twice as hard."[19]

These sociocultural, institutional, and psychological manifestations of traditional gender socialization serve as the major source of the substantial gender gap in eligible candidates' political ambition. It is essential to recognize, however, that while traditional gender socialization makes it difficult for women to envision themselves as candidates for public office, the broader dimensions of electoral politics in the United States perpetuate and reinforce women's perceptions and reluctance. After all, women have made significant gains entering the formerly male-dominated professions of law, business, and medicine. Yet politics continues to lag far behind. Why does politics remain such a formidable arena for women to enter? Why do patterns of traditional gender socialization exert so powerful an impact on political ambition and candidate emergence? At least part of the answer lies in the structural barriers and electoral rules that define the U.S. political system.

Electoral competition in the United States is unique because it is dominated by candidates as opposed to political parties. Congressional politics scholar Gary Jacobson (2004, 23) notes a trend between the 1950s and 1980s: "The electoral importance of individual candidates and campaigns expanded, while that of party labels and national issues diminished." A weak party system exerts little control over who is nominated to run for office and provides only minimal financial and logistical support to candidates for most elective positions. Candidates, therefore, must be entrepreneurs. To compete for almost all top offices, candidates must raise money, build coalitions of support, create campaign organizations, and develop campaign strategies. In competitive electoral races, they often must engage in these endeavors twice – both at the primary stage and in the general election. Explicit linkages to political party organizations and

---

[19] Terry Neal, "As More Women Run, Gains in Congress Predicted," *Washington Post*, October 1, 1998, A16.

platforms, as well as other support networks, are entirely the candidates' responsibility to develop.

For fairly clear reasons, this system of competition makes running for public office a much more remote possibility for women than men. Although all candidates, regardless of sex, might face daunting hurdles in emerging as viable candidates in this entrepreneurial environment, women face one very significant additional obstacle. Navigating the candidate emergence process involves relying on and utilizing the types of backgrounds, experiences, and characteristics that have historically been impressed on men, but discouraged among women.

Exacerbating the difficulties women face in the entrepreneurial candidate emergence process are the rules that govern electoral competition. More specifically, the individualistic political culture that characterizes the United States eschews gender quotas. In other nations, when the rules of the electoral game include quotas, legislatures see substantial increases in women's political representation and the diffusion of public policies that benefit women (Krook 2009). Indeed, Eileen McDonagh (2008) argues that, at least in part because of quotas, other democracies are more likely than the United States to view women as well suited to govern. Even without quotas, though, other democracies with relatively patriarchal histories tend to see a greater proportion of women in politics because they do not have the winner-take-all and single-member district systems prevalent in the United States. Women candidates are more likely to emerge and succeed in proportional party list electoral systems (Matland 1998; Norris 1994; Rule 1987).[20] The candidate-centered system in the United States, therefore, hampers women's entrance into public office (Davis 1997; Darcy, Hadley and Kirksey 1993). Not only does the system serve as a barrier to women's full inclusion in politics; but it also exacerbates the consequences of traditional gender socialization.

## Organization of the Book

Why don't women run for office? The pages that follow answer this question by reporting and analyzing the results of the Citizen Political Ambition Panel Study, our unique nationwide survey of almost 3,800 eligible

---

[20] This is not to say that systems of proportional representation with party lists do not have costs of their own. Jane Mansbridge (1999, 652) explains that such systems often facilitate party collusion that leads to noncompetitive races and voter demobilization. Overall, however, she concludes that proportional party list systems are a "flexible" way to promote descriptive representation and women's candidacies.

candidates in 2001, and the more than 2,000 whom we resurveyed in 2008. We augment the data analysis with in-depth interviews of a representative sample of two hundred of these respondents. The extensive interviews add nuance and depth to the broader empirical findings we uncover from the surveys.

Before turning to the data analysis, we establish the theoretical and historical underpinnings of our investigation of the initial decision to run for office. Chapter 2 identifies and evaluates the leading explanations for the slow pace at which women move into elected positions. We establish political ambition as the critical missing link in the research that explores women's underrepresentation. In developing our theory of political ambition, we argue that it is essential to focus on the earliest stages of the candidate emergence process. Thus, we propose a two-stage conception of the process: considering a candidacy and deciding to enter an actual race. We end Chapter 2 with a description of the manner in which our research design and sample of eligible candidates allow us to examine the decision to run for office and assess prospects for increasing women's representation.

Our empirical investigation of eligible candidates' levels of political ambition begins in Chapter 3. Despite having similar levels of political activism and political interest, eligible women candidates are dramatically less likely than men to consider running for office and to launch an actual candidacy. A series of new questions pertaining to political proximity that we included in the 2008 survey allows us to rule out the possibility that the gender gap in political ambition is the result of women and men's differential levels of direct exposure to politics. In fact, we do not uncover any notable gender differences in political proximity. Yet the gender gap in political ambition we establish is virtually as large in 2008 as it was in 2001. We also uncover a gender gap in the levels of office in which eligible candidates express interest; women are less interested than men in high-level positions, which bodes poorly for women's inclusion on the highest rungs of the political career ladder.

Chapters 4 through 6 develop and test empirically the impact that traditional gender socialization exerts on political ambition. More specifically, Chapter 4 explores the manner in which political socialization, a politicized upbringing, and current family structures and responsibilities influence levels of political ambition across generations. We find that "traditional" upbringings and early political socialization affect the levels of political ambition eligible candidates express today. Unexpectedly, traditional family structures and responsibilities do not, in and of themselves, keep women from thinking about entering politics. They do, however, add to the complexity involved in women's decisions to run (or not to run) for office. By analyzing new data from the second wave of the study, we flesh out more fully how changes in family structures and responsibilities influence political ambition at different phases of the life cycle. Ultimately, the patterns we identify transcend generations, although the gender gap in political ambition is actually the largest among respondents younger than the age of forty.

In Chapter 5, we rely extensively on data from the 2008 survey to examine party and political recruitment as sources of the gender gap in ambition. We move well beyond the important findings from the first edition of the book and provide a detailed account of the depth and breadth of women and men's recruitment experiences. The results indicate that party identification does not affect levels of political ambition. But when we turn to the role of political parties as electoral gatekeepers, we find that they do play a vital role in the candidate emergence process. Highly qualified and politically well-connected women from both major political parties are less likely than similarly situated men to be recruited to run for public office by all types of political actors. They are less likely than men to be recruited intensely. And they are less likely than men to be recruited by multiple sources. Although we paint a picture of a political recruitment process that seems to suppress women's inclusion, we also offer the first evidence of the significant headway women's organizations are making in their efforts to mitigate the recruitment gap, especially among Democrats. The chapter concludes with a demonstration of the substantive importance of the gender gap in political recruitment. Receiving the suggestion to run for office significantly increases the likelihood that an eligible candidate – male or female, Democrat or Republican – has considered running for political office or has taken any of the concrete steps that tend to precede a candidacy.

Chapter 6 shifts the focus to eligible candidates' perceptions of the political environment and themselves as candidates. Drawing heavily on interview data and the survey results from the second wave of the study, this chapter presents one of the most important findings of this book: despite comparable credentials, professional backgrounds, and political experiences, highly accomplished women from both major political parties are more likely than men to underestimate their qualifications to seek and win elective office. The second-wave data, in particular, reveal that women are not only more likely than men to doubt that they have the skills and traits necessary to succeed in electoral politics, but also are more likely than men to perceive a competitive, biased electoral arena. Further, women are more likely than men to be influenced by their own self-doubts when considering a candidacy. The self-assessments we uncover are nuanced and complex, but they provide clear evidence that the gendered psyche affects political ambition.

Chapter 7, our final empirical chapter, presents a model of candidate emergence that significantly accounts for the gender gap in political ambition. The chapter then focuses on the more than three hundred respondents who actually decided to throw their hats into the political arena and seek elective office. Our results indicate that the gender gap in political ambition is reduced by the second stage of the candidate emergence process, but far fewer women than men reach this stage. Even here, though, women remain more likely than men to doubt their qualifications to run for office. When we turn to future interest in office holding, we find that men feel a greater sense of freedom than women do to pursue a political candidacy, and that the gender gap persists across both waves of the panel study.

In Chapter 8, we assess the implications of our findings. Our research debunks the literature that purports to explain women's underrepresentation on the grounds of structural impediments and institutional inertia alone. Because the gender gap in political ambition is rooted in patterns of traditional gender socialization, our findings temper the optimism that has come to surround broad assessments of prospects for gender equity in our governing institutions. We conclude by proposing a reasonable research agenda that will allow for a better understanding of the role gender continues to play in electoral politics, especially at the precandidacy stage of the candidate emergence process.

## 2

# Explaining Women's Emergence in the Political Arena

On Sunday, March 13, 2005, Secretary of State Condoleezza Rice appeared on *Meet the Press*. After answering questions about the war in Iraq, Iran's nuclear capability, and John Bolton's appointment as ambassador to the United Nations, the discussion turned to the 2008 presidential election. Tim Russert, the host of the program, alerted Secretary Rice to a website that featured songs and paraphernalia aimed to draft Rice to run for president. He then named six prior secretaries of state who had gone on to occupy the Oval Office. Although Secretary Rice explained that she had neither the desire nor the intention to run for office, Mr. Russert proceeded to ask her – eleven different times – about the possibility of throwing her hat into the ring. Secretary Rice repeatedly stated that she had no interest in seeking the nomination, ultimately asserting: "I don't want to run for president of the United States. I have no intention of doing so. I don't think I will be president of the United States ever. Is that good enough?" But Mr. Russert continued to push, wondering about her political ambition beyond 2008. The conversation concluded with Secretary Rice stating definitively, "I will not run."

In July 2009, another politically experienced woman also chose not to pursue high-level office. Rhode Island Lieutenant Governor Elizabeth Roberts surprised voters and the media when she announced that she would not contest the open seat for governor.[1] Following months of lobbying by hopeful supporters, likely endorsements from prominent women's organizations, and several hundred thousand dollars in her

[1] Elizabeth Roberts for Rhode Island, "Lieutenant Governor Elizabeth Roberts Announces Re-Election Campaign," Press Release, July 1, 2009.

campaign coffers that would have been available for a gubernatorial bid, she opted to seek reelection as lieutenant governor. Roberts would have faced a crowded and competitive Democratic primary for the seat; Attorney General Patrick Lynch and General Treasurer Frank Caprio also planned to run.[2] With more than a year to go until Election Day and no clear favorite to garner the nomination, however, 2010 provided an excellent opportunity for each of these candidates to climb the political ladder. Yet Lieutenant Governor Roberts stepped aside, clearing the way for an eventual male Democratic nominee who surpassed her neither in electoral experience nor in political accomplishments.

Together, these examples embody the two central points we strive to make in this chapter. Foremost, widespread gender bias no longer prevents women from emerging as viable, prospective candidates, even at the presidential level. Both Condoleezza Rice and Elizabeth Roberts were considered just as credible and formidable as the men against whom they would compete. When he pushed Secretary Rice to consider running for office, never did Tim Russert call attention to the fact that she could be the first woman to use her position as secretary of state as a launching pad to the presidency. Similarly, at no point did Elizabeth Roberts's sex detract from her appeal to supporters or lessen the threat she posed to potential competitors. Indeed, would-be opponents "showered Roberts with praise" on learning of her decision not to run.[3] Although women have traditionally been excluded from positions of political power, the normalcy with which these women's potential candidacies were discussed demonstrates considerable progress regarding women's reception into electoral politics.

Second, but perhaps more important, the decision to run for office might differ for women and men. Condoleezza Rice rebuked Tim Russert so ardently that she closed the door on any potential campaign at any point in the future. It is difficult to envision a man so resolutely dismissing even the smallest possibility of a political career, especially given the number of times Tim Russert inquired. Elizabeth Roberts behaved somewhat similarly, closing the door on a gubernatorial bid very early in the election cycle. The decision to run for office, or not to run, is complicated and strategic. In the case of Condoleezza Rice, many pundits might

---

[2] Ted Nesi, "Roberts Rules Out Bid for Governor," *Providence Business News*, July 1, 2009, http://www.pbn.com/detail/43320.html.

[3] Steve Peoples, "Lieutenant Governor Roberts Bows Out of Governor's Race," *Providence Journal*, July 2, 2009, B1.

conclude that her seeming lack of political ambition reflected her belief that it was inappropriate to express interest in running for office while serving as secretary of state. In Elizabeth Roberts's case, a clearly calculated strategy about her political future is less evident. Because of term limits, she will be forced out of the lieutenant governor's office in 2014, assuming she is reelected in 2010. If she decides to run for governor at that time, then she will face an incumbent, if not in the primary, then certainly in the general election. These examples suggest that even well-known, highly credentialed political women may be more hesitant than men to launch a candidacy.

This chapter sets the stage to examine the gender dynamics of the candidate emergence process and, subsequently, to gauge prospects for women's representation in U.S. political institutions. We begin by evaluating the conventional explanations for women's underrepresentation, concluding that they fail to consider the role gender plays in the process by which individuals emerge as candidates for public office. To understand the reasons so few women occupy positions of political power, we argue that we must turn to political ambition. We develop a two-stage candidate emergence process that accounts for patterns of traditional gender socialization. The chapter concludes with a description of the Citizen Political Ambition Panel Study, the research design and sample we employ to uncover and explain gender differences in the decision to run for office.

## Women and Elective Office: The Numbers

When we turn on the television, read the newspaper, listen to the radio, or browse the Internet, it is difficult not to see women in U.S. politics. Nancy Pelosi, a Democrat from California, is the Speaker of the House of Representatives. Former U.S. Senator and Secretary of State Hillary Clinton received 18 million votes in her 2008 bid for the presidency and is now the face of U.S. foreign policy around the globe. And former Alaska governor Sarah Palin was the first Republican woman ever nominated to be vice president.

But these famous faces obscure, at least in part, the dearth of women who hold elective office in the United States. Despite society's growing acceptance of women seeking high-level office, the fact remains that few women do so. The United States' political institutions continue to comprise primarily men. This statement holds whether we assess the inclusion of women in politics over time or in a cross-cultural context.

TABLE 2.1. *World Rankings of Women in National Legislatures*

| World Rank by Country | Percentage of Women |
|---|---|
| 1. Rwanda | 56.3% |
| 2. Sweden | 47.0 |
| 3. South Africa | 43.5 |
| 4. Cuba | 43.2 |
| 5. Iceland | 42.9 |
| 6. Finland | 41.5 |
| 7. Netherlands | 41.3 |
| 8. Argentina | 40.0 |
| 9. Denmark | 38.0 |
| 10. Angola | 37.3 |
| 11. Costa Rica | 36.8 |
| 12. Spain | 36.3 |
| 13. Norway | 36.1 |
| 14. Belgium | 35.3 |
| 15. Mozambique | 34.8 |
| 16. New Zealand | 33.6 |
| 17. Nepal | 33.2 |
| 18. Germany | 32.2 |
| 19. Andorra | 32.1 |
| 20. Belarus | 31.8 |
| 21. Uganda | 30.7 |
| 22. Burundi | 30.5 |
| 23. Tanzania | 30.4 |
| 24. Guyana | 30.0 |
| 25. Timor-Leste | 29.2 |
| 85. United States | 16.8 |
| World Average | 18.6 |

*Notes:* Entries represent the percentage of women serving in national legislatures. In bicameral systems, the percentage is for the lower house. *Source:* Inter-Parliamentary Union (2009).

Let us begin with the latter. When the 111th Congress convened in January 2009, 83 percent of its members were men (Center for American Women and Politics [CAWP] 2009a). As illustrated in Table 2.1, this places the United States eighty-fifth worldwide in the number of women serving in the national legislature. Certainly, cultural and political components factor into the total number of women who hold seats in any nation's legislature. But Table 2.1 demonstrates that the nations surpassing the United States vary with respect to their political system, electoral rules, geography, region, and culture. Even if we focus only on democratic states, as defined by the Freedom House ranking system, then the United States places fifty-seventh in the world.

Large gender inequities are also evident at the state and local levels, where more than three-quarters of statewide elected officials and state legislators are men. Men occupy the governor's mansion in forty-four of the fifty states, and they run city hall in eighty-nine of the one hundred largest cities across the country (CAWP 2009a). Figure 2.1 presents the percentages of women holding positions in Congress, state legislatures, and statewide elective offices since 1979. When we compare the percentages of women who occupy these positions in 2009 to the percentages from thirty years ago, we see somewhat-dramatic gains for women's representation. A closer examination of the figure, however, indicates that, whereas the 1980s saw a gradual increase in the numbers of women holding elective office, and 1992 represented a rather remarkable surge in women's presence in politics, the past several election cycles mark a plateau in women's entry into the political sphere. In fact, following the 2008 elections, fewer women held statewide elective office than did after the 1994 elections. Further, even though the U.S. House of Representatives continues to experience incremental gains in female members, more women filed to run for Congress in 1992 than have ever since. Whether we consider recent election cycles or the United States' global ranking on women in politics, it is evident that our political institutions are a far cry from gender parity.

## Existing Explanations for Women's Underrepresentation

Scholars have devoted the past few decades to gaining a better understanding of why so few women occupy positions of political power in the United States. Initially, the scholarship attributed women's exclusion from the political sphere to discrimination and overt bias against women candidates. Over the course of the past thirty years, however, cultural attitudes toward women in politics have evolved, and an increasing number of women have sought and won election to public office. Scholars, therefore, began to focus on structural barriers, most notably the incumbency advantage, and "situational" factors, such as the proportion of women in the pipeline professions that precede political careers, to explain the low number of women officeholders. Discrimination, structural barriers, and women's presence in the candidate pipeline certainly contribute, in

FIGURE 2.1. Women Serving in Elective Positions, 1979–2009.

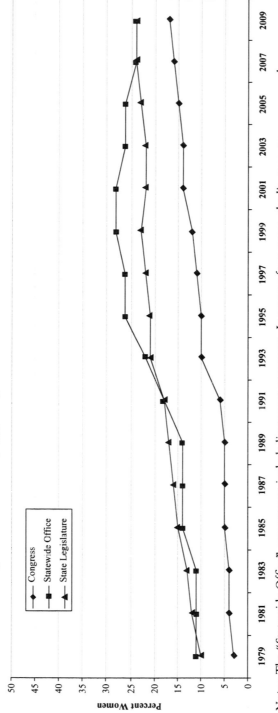

*Notes*: The "Statewide Office" percentages include lieutenant governors. In twenty-four states, the lieutenant governor and governor run on the same ticket. In these states, women occupy more than 50 percent of lieutenant governor positions. *Source*: CAWP (2009b).

varying degrees, to the gender disparities in our political institutions. But the power of these explanations, even combined, is limited; none tackles the fundamental question of whether women are as politically ambitious as men to emerge as candidates.

*Societal Rejection and Cultural Evolution:*
*The Discrimination Explanation*
Much of the earliest research in the women and elections subfield asserted that overt discrimination accounted for the gender disparities in office holding (Githens and Prestage 1977; Kirkpatrick 1974). Electoral gate-keepers all but prohibited women from running for office in the 1970s. Those women who did emerge as candidates often faced sexism and a hostile environment. Reflecting on the political arena for women in 1972, for example, U.S. Senator Barbara Boxer (1994, 73–4) recounts that being a woman was a "distinct, quantifiable disadvantage," at least when she ran for the Board of Supervisors in Marin County, California:

> [T]o be a woman in politics was almost a masochistic experience, a series of setbacks with not a lot of rewards. If I was strong in my expression of the issues, I was strident; if I expressed any emotion as I spoke about the environment or the problems of the mentally ill, I was soft; if I spoke about economics, I had to be perfect, and then I ran the risk of being "too much like a man."

It is easy to compile a list of similar experiences women candidates endured (see Witt, Paget, and Matthews 1994). In fact, so few women ran and won prior to the mid-1980s that meaningful data collection was difficult and empirical analyses were rare.

In the contemporary electoral environment, the degree to which the political system remains rife with gender bias is more difficult to determine. At the candidate level, individual accounts of women who face overt gender discrimination once they enter the public arena are increasingly uncommon (Woods 2000). Barbara Boxer (1994, 74), herself, notes that, when she ran for the U.S. Senate two decades later, "It was different. Being a woman running for public office in 1992 was a distinct advantage. The polls showed it." Former Congresswoman Nancy Johnson (R-CT) agrees: "Women aren't facing the daunting fundraising problems that I faced in 1982. Many of the men you were asking for money had never even made a serious decision with a woman. There has been a tremendous cultural change."[4] Indeed, in her first three months in the U.S. House of

---

[4] Terry Neal, "As More Women Run, Gains in Congress Predicted," *Washington Post*, October 1, 1998, A16.

Representatives in 2007, now U.S. Senator Kirsten Gillibrand (D-NY) raised more money than any other first-term lawmaker.[5]

The public's attitudes toward women in politics have certainly evolved. As illustrated in Figure 2.2, an overwhelming majority of Americans no longer believe that men are better suited emotionally for politics than are women. An even greater proportion of citizens express a willingness to support a qualified, female party nominee for the presidency. Trends in American public opinion indicate that, whereas majorities of Americans were unwilling to vote for a woman presidential nominee in the 1930s and 1940s, even if she were nominated by the respondent's political party and qualified for the job, levels of support increased throughout the following several decades. By the 1980s, more than 80 percent of survey respondents expressed willingness to vote for a woman presidential candidate. And by the late 1990s, more than 90 percent of those surveyed did so.

Skeptics might contend that such levels of support simply mean that it is no longer acceptable to express overt sexism, but behind closed doors, Americans remain reluctant to elect women candidates. Studies of actual election results do not support such an argument. When we turn to campaign fundraising receipts and vote totals, generally considered the two most important indicators of electoral success, we see that women fare just as well as, if not better than, their male counterparts.[6] A national study of voting patterns in elections across the country, for example, led one group of political scientists to state emphatically: "A candidate's sex does not affect his or her chances of winning an election. . . . Winning elections has nothing to do with the sex of the candidate" (Seltzer, Newman, and Leighton 1997, 79). Echoing this finding, Robert Darcy, Susan Welch, and Janet Clark (1994, 100) concluded that, because women receive their share of the nominations, successfully raise campaign money, and garner as many votes as do their male counterparts, "If more women run, more women will be elected." Kathleen Dolan (2004, 50) arrived at the same conclusion after analyzing a series of public opinion polls and election results: "Levels of bias are low enough to no longer provide significant

---

[5] Josh Kraushaar, "Freshman Lawmakers Raise Big Bucks," *Politico* 44, February 11, 2009, http://www.politico.com/news/stories/0209/18684.html (accessed December 19, 2009).

[6] Political scientists uncover no voter bias against women candidates for either the U.S. Senate (Smith and Fox 2001) or the U.S. House of Representatives (Lawless and Pearson 2008; Fox 2010; Cook 1998; Dolan 1998). Experiments that rely on hypothetical elections have produced mixed results. Some studies uncover bias against women candidates (Fox and Smith 1998; Huddy and Terkildsen 1993b), whereas others do not (Thompson and Steckenrider 1997). In terms of fundraising, at least at the congressional level, Richard Fox (2010) provides evidence of gender parity in campaign contributions.

FIGURE 2.2. Public Attitudes toward Women in Politics, 1937–2007.

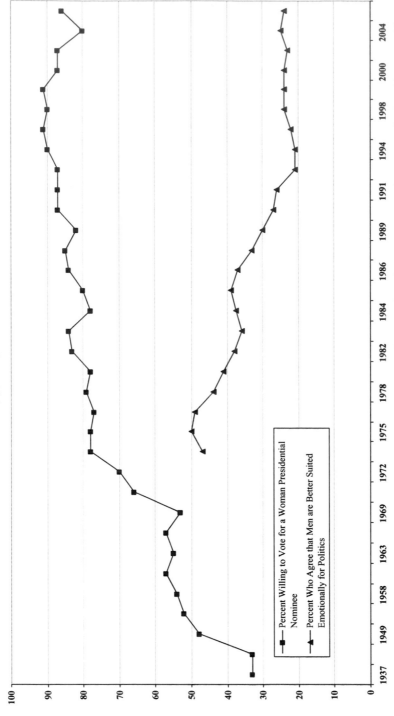

*Notes:* Data depict citizens' responses to the following questions: "If your political party nominated a woman for president, would you be willing to vote for her if she were qualified for the job?" and "Tell me if you agree or disagree with this statement: Most men are better suited emotionally for politics than are most women." *Sources:* The data for the question on willingness to vote for a woman president are drawn from multiple sources, including polls: Gallup (1937–71, 1984, and 2003); the National Opinion Research Council (1972–98); CBS (1999); the *Wall Street Journal* (2000); Roper (2005); and *Newsweek* (2006). The "men better suited emotionally" data are from the National Opinion Research Council's General Social Survey and begin in 1972.

impediments to women's chances of election." The notion that discrimination accounts for the low number of women in politics, therefore, has fallen out of favor with political scientists.

Yet the role of gender and discrimination in the electoral process is more complex than scholarship that focuses on aggregate vote totals might have us believe. Under the right circumstances, women can compete evenly against men, but despite the cultural evolution that has taken place, women's entry into the political arena is not always embraced. We need not look beyond the 2008 presidential race for evidence. When two men chanted "Iron my shirt!" at a Hillary Clinton campaign rally in New Hampshire days before the 2008 primary, the candidate responded, "Ah, the remnants of sexism – alive and well."[7] Campaign rallies were not the only venue in which sexism seemed to rear its head. Consider *Hardball* host Chris Matthews's use of the words *stripteaser* and *witchy* to describe Clinton.[8] MSNBC's Tucker Carlson's assessment of the marketing of a Hillary Clinton nutcracker serves as another example: "That is so perfect. I have often said, when she comes on television, I involuntarily cross my legs."[9] A list of similar comments – by pundits, pollsters, reporters, and voters – is virtually endless.[10]

Hillary Clinton's circumstances may be somewhat unique in that she sought the presidency, but several studies demonstrate that gender continues to affect campaigns and elections more generally. Women in Congress, for example, still refer to the male culture of the House of Representatives (Margolies-Mezvinsky 1994). Female congressional candidates face more primary competition than do their male counterparts (Lawless and Pearson 2008), and they must raise more money to perform as well as men do at the polls (Fiber and Fox 2005). In addition, geographic differences facilitate women's election in some congressional districts, but lessen their chances of success in others (Palmer and Simon 2008). In-depth examinations of campaigns also reveal the manner in which gender remains relevant in the electoral process. Gender stereotypes play a role in how

---

[7] "Quotes of the Day," *Time*, January 8, 2008, http://www.time.com/time/quotes/0,26174,1701281,00.html (accessed December 19, 2009).

[8] *The Chris Matthews Show*, transcript, MSNBC, November 18, 2007.

[9] *Tucker*, transcript, MSNBC, July 16, 2007.

[10] For an assessment of the extent to which sexist commentary pervaded the media's coverage of Hillary Clinton and other female candidates, see Lawless 2009; Duerst-Lahti 2008; Falk 2008. For detailed examples and analysis of the manner in which sexism affected news coverage in the 2008 election cycle, see Women's Media Center, "Sexism Sells, but We're Not Buying It," May 23, 2008, http://www.womensmediacenter.com/sexism_sells.html (accessed December 19, 2009).

the media cover candidates (Fowler and Lawless 2009; Rausch, Rozell and Wilson 1999; Fox 1997; Kahn 1996). Party recruiters invoke stereotypes when identifying eligible candidates for political contests (Sanbonmatsu 2006; Niven 1998). And voters rely on stereotypical conceptions of women and men's traits, issue expertise, and policy positions when casting ballots (Lawless 2004b; Koch 2000; McDermott 1997, 1998).

As women have achieved parity on some dimensions, then, other barriers remain deeply embedded in the institutions that shape political competition. A closer look at Figure 2.2 reveals that nearly one in every four Americans still agrees that "[m]ost men are better suited emotionally for politics than are most women." As recently as 2008, pollsters uncovered that 51 percent of Americans believed that the country was not "ready to elect a woman to high office."[11] Further, 40 percent of women did not think Hillary Clinton was treated fairly in her presidential campaign.[12]

Discrimination in the electoral process has clearly grown subtler over time. Overt discrimination no longer prevents women's aggregate-level electoral success, and episodes of clear bias against women candidates are far less pervasive than they were even two decades ago. At the individual level, however, gender expectations and stereotypes persist and can affect the evaluations and experiences of women candidates and officeholders.

### Institutional Inertia: The Incumbency Explanation

In light of the growing contradiction between a political system that elects few women and a body of research that identifies the electoral environment as increasingly unbiased against women candidates, political scientists have turned to institutional explanations for women's underrepresentation. Perhaps most notably, they point to the incumbency advantage (Palmer and Simon 2008; Nixon and Darcy 1996; Darcy, Welch, and Clark 1994). Not only do incumbents seek reelection in more than 75 percent of state legislative and congressional elections, but their reelection rates are also consistently greater than 90 percent (Duerst-Lahti 1998, 19). The 2008 congressional election cycle saw even fewer open seats than usual; only thirty-one incumbents (7 percent of the total House of Representatives' membership) chose not to seek reelection. More than

[11] Pew Research Center, "Men or Women? Who's the Better Leader?" *Social and Demographic Trends*, August 25, 2008.
[12] Lifetime Networks, "New Lifetime Every Woman Counts Poll Sheds Light on Women's Reactions to Historic Presidential Election, Their Agenda for New Leaders and the Future of Female Candidates," http://www.smartbrief.com/news/aaaa/industryPR-detail.jsp? id=41B8FE28-A000-4F39-A0F2-3B9B8A23A6E3 (accessed July 15, 2009).

90 percent of congressional incumbents also sought reelection in 2004 and 2006. As Keith Gaddie and Charles Bullock (2000, 1) conclude, "Open seats, not the defeat of incumbents, are the portal through which most legislators enter Congress." Under these circumstances, increasing the number of electoral opportunities for previously excluded groups, such as women, can be a glacial process.

Institutional inertia undoubtedly explains part of women's slow ascension into politics, particularly at the federal level, but its explanatory power appears to be somewhat limited. After all, the conventional proposal to overcome the incumbency advantage is term limits. If members of Congress were barred from serving more than three terms, then only 39 percent of the incumbents throughout the 1990s could have stood for reelection. Even with a less stringent twelve-year limit, 28 percent of incumbents who chose to seek reelection would have had to give up their seats (Theriault 2005). Term limits at the federal level are unlikely because the Supreme Court has ruled that states do not have the power to alter the conditions necessary to serve in the U.S. Congress.[13] At the state legislative level, however, term limits have increased the number of open seats in the fifteen states that currently mandate them.[14]

The implementation of these term limits allows for an assessment of the degree to which incumbency alone serves as a barrier to women's representation. In 1998 and 2000, the number of incumbent women forced to vacate their state legislative positions because of term limits exceeded the number of women elected to seats that opened as a result of them (Jenkins and Carroll 2003). More broadly, Thad Kousser (2005) demonstrates that states that implemented term limits experienced no changes in the percentage of female legislators. As political scientist Gary Moncrief concludes, "The evidence has shown that [term limits] have had absolutely no positive effect at all. The logic was impeccable, the empirical evidence not at all."[15] Clearly, although incumbency and the lack of open seats certainly pose barriers to women's inclusion in politics,

---

[13] The 1992 5–4 U.S. Supreme Court decision in *United States v. Thornton* ruled that the power granted to each chamber of Congress to judge the "Qualifications of its own Members," art. 1, sec. 5, cl. 1, does not include the power to alter or add to the qualifications set forth in the Constitution's text.

[14] Twenty-one states have passed legislative term limits at some point, but since the late 1990s, six states have repealed them on the grounds that they are unconstitutional (National Conference of State Legislatures 2009b).

[15] Peter Slevin, "After Adopting Term Limits, States Lose Female Legislators," *Washington Post*, April 22, 2007, A4.

terms limits and increased electoral opportunities may present less of a workable solution than previously thought.

### The Candidate Eligibility Pool: The Pipeline Explanation

Women's historical exclusion from the professions that tend to lead to political careers also accounts for the gender disparities in office holding. Our analysis of the professional occupations of members in the 111th Congress reveals that law, business, education, and politics are the leading four professions that precede congressional careers.[16] The same is true at the state legislative level (CAWP 2001). Despite the fact that most candidates, regardless of sex, yield from these pipeline professions, far more men than women constitute them. As Janet Clark (1994, 106) explains, "Women are not found in the professions from which politicians inordinately are chosen – the law and other broker-type businesses. Therefore, they do not achieve the higher socioeconomic status that forms the eligibility pool for elective office."

The basic implication of the pipeline explanation is that as more and more women come to occupy the careers that are most likely to lead to political candidacies, more and more women will acquire the objective qualifications and economic autonomy necessary to pursue elective office. Accordingly, we can assume that an increasing number of women will run for office, contest open seats, and face no discrimination at the polls. This explanation has become widely accepted. In a leading American government textbook, Morris Fiorina and Paul Peterson (2002, 340–1) state that the underrepresentation of women "will naturally lessen as women's career patterns become more like those of men."[17]

Full integration of women into all of the pipeline professions, however, may take decades. Turning first to the field of law, the National Association for Law Placement (2009) finds that women account for only 19 percent of the partners in the nation's major law firms (as indicated in Figure 2.3, women occupy a significantly greater proportion of associates

---

[16] We drew this information from the *Almanac of American Politics* (Barone and Cohen 2008) and from the websites of members of the 111th Congress (see also Moncrief, Squire, and Jewell 2001; Dolan and Ford 1997).

[17] Although many political scientists whose research focuses on women's underrepresentation might not arrive at such an adamant conclusion, they do agree that women's increasing proportion in the candidate pipeline will work to promote greater gender balance in the United States' political institutions (Duerst-Lahti 1998; Thomas 1998; Conway, Ahern, and Steuernagel 1997; Darcy, Welch, and Clark 1994).

FIGURE 2.3. Women's Presence in the Pipeline Professions, 1972–2009.

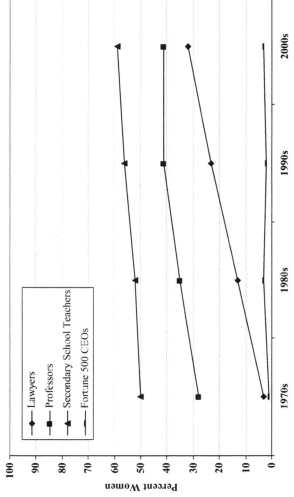

*Sources:* The percentages of women lawyers were drawn from Curran (1995), Curran and Carson (1994), and the American Bar Association (2008). The percentages of women professors and secondary school teachers were drawn from the *Statistical Abstracts from the United States* (2008). Catalyst (2009) provided the data on the number of women chief executive officers of Fortune 500 companies.

and senior attorneys). Although a growing number of women have been earning law degrees and moving into the legal profession, progress is slow. A decade ago, 13 percent of the partners in major law firms were women.

In the business world, about 51 percent of the 42 million employees working in managerial and professional specialty occupations are women, up from 35 percent in 1992. But a closer inspection of the business world indicates that men overwhelmingly dominate the upper ranks, and that women's increasing entrance into these positions is nearly stagnant. Only two companies (DuPont and Kraft Foods) included in the Dow Jones Industrial Average have female chief executive officers; and only fifteen Fortune 500 companies have female CEOs. Merely 16 percent of the Fortune 500's eleven thousand corporate officers are women. Seventy-five of these companies do not have any women serving as corporate officers. Men continue to comprise 94 percent of the most highly compensated officers in these companies. If we move beyond the Fortune 500, women constitute only 16 percent of the corporate officers at the nation's five hundred largest public companies.[18] Moreover, data from the U.S. Equal Employment Opportunity Commission reveal that men constituted roughly two-thirds of the officials and managers in the securities industry in 2006. According to the Securities Industry Association, men occupy four out of five executive management positions and represent more than 70 percent of investment bankers, traders, and brokers (Roth 2006).

Gender segregation is also quite evident in higher education, especially when climbing the career ladder. Since 2003, women have constituted slightly more than half of all doctoral recipients, up from 12 percent in 1966 (Falkenheim and Feigener 2008). But the percentage of women among tenured faculty is not appreciably higher than it was in the mid-1970s (Banerji 2006; Mason and Goulden 2002). That is, the gender gap in tenured faculty has remained constant, despite women's increasing presence in the tenure-track faculty pool.

There is no question that, as women increase their proportions in the pipeline professions that precede political careers, there will be an increase in the number of women candidates. The data on career patterns suggest, however, that these increases may be very incremental.

---

[18] These data were gathered by Catalyst, a New York City–based nonprofit research organization.

## The Missing Piece: Developing a Theory of Gender and Political Ambition

The conventional assessment that emerges from the current explanations for gender disparities in elective office is that, overall, we are on a steady course toward equity in women's representation. To some degree, discriminatory attitudes toward women in politics still exist. And overcoming institutional inertia might be more complex than researchers tend to suggest. Nevertheless, the horizon looks bright. When women run for office, they fare at least as well as men. As women's presence in the candidate eligibility pool approaches men's, we should see the number of women elected officials approach the number of men as well. Completely missing from this prognosis, however, is an understanding of the gender dynamics underlying the process by which individuals move from the eligibility pool into elective office. Prospects for gender parity in our electoral system cannot be evaluated without an in-depth assessment of the manner in which gender interacts with and affects levels of political ambition.

In developing a theory of political ambition, most scholars employ a rational choice paradigm and examine the decision to enter specific political contests. The rational choice framework conceptualizes political ambition as primarily a strategic response to a political opportunity structure. Aspiring candidates tend to be more likely to seek office when they face favorable political and structural circumstances. More specifically, the number of open seats, term limits, levels of legislative professionalization, partisan composition of the constituency, and party congruence with constituents are among the factors individuals consider when seeking any elective position or deciding whether to run for higher office.[19] With the exception of general gauges of political interest, financial security, and political experience, candidate characteristics, including sex, are treated as relatively exogenous. In other words, the "seats available and the hierarchy of positions for advancement give shape and definition to the political career" (Prinz 1993, 27).

---

[19] A substantial body of work that addresses political ambition falls within this rational choice paradigm. For the most recent scholarship pertaining to candidate emergence, see Maestas et al. 2006; Stone and Maisel 2003; Goodliffe 2001; Moncrief, Squire, and Jewell 2001; Kazee 1994. For earlier assessments of political ambition, see Rohde 1979; Eulau and Prewitt 1973; Black 1972; Schlesinger 1966.

Focusing on the political and structural circumstances involved in running for a particular office has enabled scholars to generate broad theoretical claims regarding expressive ambition – that is, whether individuals will choose to enter specific political contests and, once they hold office, whether legislators will maintain their current position (static ambition), run for higher office (progressive ambition), or choose to retire rather than seek reelection (discrete ambition). Existing theories of political ambition, however, are very limited in the extent to which they shed light on the gender dynamics of the candidate emergence process.

The first limitation of the extant rational choice conception of political ambition is that it tends to take ambition as given. The paradigm assumes that, when faced with a favorable political opportunity structure (e.g., a retiring incumbent, party congruence with the district), an eligible candidate will opt to enter a race. But a distinct, yet vitally important phase of the development of political ambition occurs well before the actual decision to enter a specific race ever transpires. If the notion of a candidacy has never even crossed an individual's mind, then he or she never actually faces a political opportunity structure. To understand fully the decision dynamics involved in moving from eligible potential candidate to actual officeholder, it is necessary to step back and assess the evolution of political ambition.

This earlier stage of the candidate emergence process is particularly important for developing a theory of gender and political ambition. The inclination to consider a candidacy is far less proximate to a particular race than is the decision to enter a political contest. In the initial step of the candidate emergence process, interest in seeking elective office is likely motivated not by the political opportunity structure, but by attitudinal dispositions and personal experiences. More than sixty years ago, Harold Lasswell (1948, 20) observed that the "conception of a 'political type' is that some personalities are power seekers, searching out the power institutions of the society . . . and devoting themselves to the capture and use of government." Patterns of traditional gender socialization – as manifested through traditional family role orientations, a masculinized ethos, and the gendered psyche – provide ample reason to suspect that women and men's attitudinal dispositions and personal experiences differ such that they are not equally likely to consider a candidacy and ultimately face the political opportunity structure.

The second, but related, limitation of the current rational choice approach to political ambition is that it does not indulge the notion that the candidate emergence process might differ for women and men, both when considering a candidacy and when facing the decision to enter an actual political contest. In the classic model of political ambition, Gordon Black (1972) proposed that individuals who consider running for a specific office carefully weigh the costs and benefits of entering the electoral arena. Consistent with this approach, we expect both women and men to operate as strategic politicians; eligible candidates will incorporate their experiences and perceptions into their political decision making. But because of patterns of traditional gender socialization, women and men might accord different probabilities to the costs and benefits associated with considering a candidacy and ultimately throwing their hats into the ring. The pervasive influence of traditional gender socialization clearly might affect the cost-benefit calculus eligible candidates employ, but it has been largely disregarded.

Our notion of political ambition involves a two-stage conception of the initial decision to run for office. The first stage involves *considering a candidacy*. In some cases, the idea arrives early in life. Former President Bill Clinton (2004, 63), for instance, wrote in his memoir: "Sometime in my sixteenth year I decided I wanted to be in public life as an elected official.... I knew I could be great in public service." For many, though, the idea of running for office takes hold more slowly. Anne Stein, an attorney we interviewed for this study, serves as an example of someone with a more muted evolution of political ambition. When Ms. Stein moved to Delaware in the early 1980s, she became active in the Democratic Party and began to volunteer for a local Democratic committee. Although she had always been interested in politics, Ms. Stein never thought of herself as a candidate. She explained, "It had never occurred to me to run for anything. It wasn't something that had even been in the back of my mind." Her work with the committee, however, spurred her political ambition: "We were always trying to come up with people to run for different positions. I started to think that maybe that's something I might do at some point down the road."

Only after the notion of a candidacy occurs to an eligible candidate does he or she reach the second stage of the process: *deciding to enter the first race*. For Bill Clinton, the decision came at the age of twenty-seven, when he sought a seat in the U.S. House of Representatives. In the aftermath of Watergate, and amid skyrocketing oil prices and gasoline rations, Arkansas Democrats appeared well positioned to make gains in the 1974 congressional elections. But as Clinton (2004, 210) noted, "It became clear that no one in our area who could run a strong race was willing to do it." So, he began to think about entering the race himself: "I was young, single, and willing to work all hours of the day and night. And even if I didn't win, if I made a good showing I didn't think it would hurt me in any future campaigns I might undertake." Although he lost his congressional bid, two years later, Clinton was elected attorney general of the state of Arkansas. And two years after that, he won the governorship. For Anne Stein, the second stage of the process meant running for the board of assessors. She described the circumstances that propelled her first actual candidacy: "In the late 1980s, we realized that we didn't have anyone to run for the board. The committee asked me to do it. The more I thought about it, the more I realized that the timing and the position were right for me. So, I decided to run." Ms. Stein won the race and continued to serve in an elective capacity for many years, first becoming the secretary and then the chair of the board.

The literature on political ambition has largely ignored the role gender plays in the evolution of a political candidacy. Our two-stage candidate emergence process serves as a vehicle through which to investigate gender, political ambition, and women's underrepresentation. Our conception of traditional gender socialization serves as the mechanism that accounts for the gender gap in political ambition and candidate emergence. In allowing sex to interact with the process by which qualified individuals become actual candidates, we challenge the very precarious assumption that women and men are equally likely to emerge from the eligibility pool, run for office, and win their races.

## The Citizen Political Ambition Panel Study

Despite the importance of exploring how people come to run for office, an empirical study is very difficult to execute. Many undocumented considerations enter the decision to run, thereby creating a number of methodological and sample design issues for us to confront. Foremost, when an eligible candidate decides not to enter a race, the decision is often unknown, thereby making it hard for researchers to assemble a reasonable sample. In addition, many individuals who ultimately run for office may never have considered themselves eligible candidates prior to being recruited to run. It is difficult to construct a sample that accounts for local and state party organizations' widely varying recruitment efforts. Political concerns can also impede research attempts to identify eligible candidates. Sandy Maisel and Walter Stone (1998) explain that some members of Congress attempted to persuade the National Science Foundation not to fund a study of eligible House of Representatives candidates because the members feared that the study might spur qualified challengers to enter races they would not have otherwise considered entering. These methodological obstacles have generally meant that information pertaining to political ambition and the decision to run for office yielded from samples of actual candidates and officeholders.[20]

The Citizen Political Ambition Panel Study provides the first research design aimed specifically at exploring gender differences in the manner in which women and men emerge as candidates for the first public office they seek. Our approach involves compiling a random, national sample of citizens who occupy the four professions and backgrounds that tend to yield the highest proportion of political candidates: law, business, education, and politics. We disproportionately stratified by sex, so the sample includes roughly equal numbers of women and men. This conception of the eligibility pool serves as a stringent test case through which to explore gender differences in political ambition. Female lawyers and business leaders have already entered and succeeded in male-dominated fields, which suggests that the women in the sample may have overcome the forces of traditional gender socialization to a greater extent than the overall population of eligible women candidates.

In carrying out the study, we conducted a two-wave survey. In 2001, we administered by mail an elaborate survey to a national sample of 6,800 members of this candidate eligibility pool (Appendix A offers a detailed description of the sampling design). The survey asked respondents about their sociodemographic backgrounds, familial arrangements, political activism, political outlook, political experience, and willingness to run for office. We heard from 3,765 respondents (1,969 men and 1,796 women). After taking into account undeliverable surveys, this represents a 60 percent response rate, which is higher than that of similar elite sample mail surveys.[21] We supplemented the survey data with evidence gathered from two hundred in-depth interviews with our survey respondents

---

[20] Linda Fowler (1993) provides an elaborate discussion of the theoretical, contextual, and empirical obstacles involved in uncovering the disincentives to seek public office (see also Rohde 1979).

[21] Walter Stone and Sandy Maisel's (2003) response rate for their survey of eligible candidates for Congress was 43 percent. In our pilot study, we achieved a 49 percent rate of response among members of the candidate eligibility pool in New York (Fox, Lawless, and Feeley 2001).

(for a full copy of the survey and the interview questionnaire, see Appendices B and D).

In early 2008, we completed the second wave of the panel study. We designed a new survey that delved more deeply into political ambition, political proximity and exposure to politics, political recruitment, and eligible candidates' perceptions of themselves and the political arena (see Appendix C). The timing of the second survey carries the additional benefit of allowing us to examine gender differences in political ambition over the course of seven years that saw dramatic changes in the political landscape. Through extensive Internet searches and phone calls, we obtained current address information for 2,976 members (82 percent) of the original sample of respondents who completed the questionnaire in 2001. After employing standard mail survey protocol, we heard from 2,060 women and men, 2,036 of whom completed the questionnaire. This represents a 75 percent response rate for the second wave of the study.

Table 2.2, which presents a description of the 2001 eligibility pool, reveals that no remarkable sociodemographic or professional differences distinguish the men from the women. The subsamples are comparable in terms of race, educational background, and household income. We recognize that work status and the prerequisites for success in each profession might vary geographically. The data presented in Table 2.2, however, demonstrate no significant geographic variation between the samples of women and men. It is important to note two statistically significant gender differences, though. Women are more likely to be Democrats, whereas men are more likely to be Republicans and Independents. Further, women in the sample are, on average, three years younger than men, a probable result of women's relatively recent entry into the fields of law and business. Our empirical analyses will be sensitive to these differences and attempt not only to explore their origins, but also to control for them.

The respondents who completed the 2008 survey are a representative subsample of the original eligibility pool. Controlling for sex, race, and profession, individuals who expressed some degree of political ambition in 2001 were no more likely than respondents who had never considered a candidacy to complete the 2008 survey. Moreover, no significant demographic or professional factors distinguish the 2001 and 2008 samples. The first column in Table 2.3 summarizes the profile of potential candidates who completed the survey in 2001. The second and third columns in Table 2.3 present demographics at two points in time for the subset of respondents who completed the 2008 survey. In terms of sex, race, level of education, household income, and age, the respondents who completed

TABLE 2.2. *Demographic and Political Profile of the Candidate Eligibility Pool (in 2001)*

| | Overall Sample | | Attorneys | | Business People | | Educators | | Activists | |
|---|---|---|---|---|---|---|---|---|---|---|
| | Women | Men | Women | Men | Women | Men | Women | Men | Women | Men |
| **Party Affiliation** | | | | | | | | | | |
| Democrat | 55%** | 37% | 53% | 42% | 29% | 15% | 58% | 48% | 65% | 40% |
| Republican | 23** | 35 | 23 | 36 | 52 | 58 | 21 | 18 | 14 | 22 |
| Independent | 18** | 24 | 18 | 21 | 17 | 24 | 19 | 29 | 18 | 32 |
| Other | 3 | 4 | 2 | 2 | 2 | 3 | 3 | 5 | 4 | 7 |
| **Race** | | | | | | | | | | |
| White | 84 | 82 | 81 | 83 | 87 | 82 | 83 | 81 | 87 | 84 |
| Black | 10 | 9 | 13 | 10 | 6 | 5 | 9 | 8 | 10 | 14 |
| Latino/Hispanic | 4 | 6 | 4 | 5 | 5 | 12 | 6 | 7 | 1 | 1 |
| Other | 2 | 3 | 2 | 2 | 2 | 1 | 2 | 4 | 2 | 1 |
| **Level of Education** | | | | | | | | | | |
| No college degree | 8 | 7 | 0 | 0 | 30 | 19 | 0 | 0 | 13 | 13 |
| Bachelor's degree | 21 | 20 | 0 | 0 | 45 | 50 | 12 | 10 | 41 | 34 |
| Graduate degree | 71 | 73 | 100 | 100 | 25 | 31 | 88 | 90 | 46 | 53 |
| **Household Income** | | | | | | | | | | |
| Less than $50,000 | 11** | 6 | 3 | 2 | 7 | 2 | 13 | 6 | 22 | 16 |
| $50,001–$75,000 | 12 | 12 | 6 | 3 | 7 | 4 | 15 | 21 | 21 | 23 |
| $75,001–$100,000 | 19 | 17 | 13 | 10 | 15 | 12 | 21 | 24 | 25 | 24 |
| $100,001–$200,000 | 33 | 35 | 33 | 35 | 32 | 34 | 41 | 40 | 24 | 29 |
| More than $200,000 | 25** | 29 | 45 | 50 | 38 | 48 | 10 | 9 | 24 | 8 |
| **Mean Age (Years)** | 47* | 50 | 41 | 47 | 48 | 51 | 49 | 50 | 51 | 51 |
| **N** | 1,704 | 1,910 | 549 | 594 | 278 | 388 | 444 | 501 | 433 | 427 |

*Notes:* Number of cases for each question varies slightly, as some respondents chose not to answer some demographics questions. Levels of significance in difference of means and chi-square tests comparing women and men: ** $p < .01$; * $p < .05$.

TABLE 2.3. *A Comparison of First- and Second-Wave Respondents*

|  | Wave 1 Respondents (in 2001) | Wave 2 Respondents (in 2001) | Wave 2 Respondents (in 2008) |
|---|---|---|---|
| **Sex** | | | |
| Men | 53% | 54% | 54% |
| Women | 47 | 46 | 46 |
| **Party Affiliation** | | | |
| Democrat | 46 | 49 | 60 |
| Republican | 30 | 28 | 32 |
| Independent | 21 | 21 | 8 |
| **Political Ideology** | | | |
| Liberal | 28 | 32 | 36 |
| Moderate | 52 | 50 | 44 |
| Conservative | 20 | 18 | 20 |
| **Race** | | | |
| White | 83 | 84 | 84 |
| Black | 10 | 9 | 9 |
| Latino/Hispanic | 5 | 5 | 5 |
| Other | 3 | 2 | 2 |
| **Highest Level of Education** | | | |
| No college degree | 7 | 6 | 6 |
| Bachelor's degree | 21 | 17 | 17 |
| Graduate degree | 72 | 78 | 78 |
| **Household Income** | | | |
| Less than $50,000 | 9 | 10 | 4 |
| $50,001–$75,000 | 12 | 12 | 8 |
| $75,001–$100,000 | 18 | 17 | 13 |
| $100,001–$200,000 | 34 | 34 | 34 |
| More than $200,000 | 27 | 29 | 40 |
| **Mean Age (Years)** | 48 | 48 | 54 |
| **N** | 3,568 | 2,036 | 2,036 |

*Notes:* In 2001, we used a three-point scale to measure party identification; in 2008, we used a seven-point scale. Included in our 2008 partisan categories are "Independent Leaners," who constitute 17 percent of "Democrats" and 11 percent of "Republicans."

the second survey are a representative subset of the original respondents. They were slightly more liberal and Democratic in 2001 than was the overall sample, but these differences are minor.[22]

[22] The data presented in column 3, however, highlight that the profile of the eligibility pool has changed, at least somewhat, between the two waves of the study. Household incomes, overall, have increased. In addition, a significant portion of respondents has

In presenting the central findings from the Citizen Political Ambition Panel Study, we present results from both waves of the survey. When the findings are consistent from both waves of the study, we rely on the original data and sample. We incorporate data from the 2008 survey to introduce new analysis or expand our discussion of the manner in which traditional gender socialization affects political ambition. In Chapters 3 and 4, for example, we include new data on eligible candidates' political proximity, the persistent gender gap in political ambition, the role of early family socialization, and changes in family structures. Chapters 5 and 6 feature the new data most prominently, where results from the 2008 survey allow us to shed substantial new light on the roots and manifestations of the masculinized ethos and the gendered psyche. The second-wave data include detailed new findings about political recruitment, the role of women's organizations, eligible candidates' self-assessments of their qualifications to enter politics, and gender differences in perceptions of the electoral environment.

Our eligibility pool approach and sample allow us to offer a nuanced examination of the manner in which women and men initially decide to run for all levels and types of political office, either now or in the future. And our approach is particularly suited to the question of the initial decision to run. The small group of scholars who examine eligible candidates' political ambition tend to employ the reputational approach (Stone and Maisel 2003; Kazee 1994). They compile a pool of eligible candidates by seeking out current officeholders and political informants, many of whom are party leaders, convention delegates, county chairs, elected officials, and political and community activists. Researchers ask the informants to name prospective, viable candidates, typically for election to the U.S. House of Representatives. The prospects are then contacted and surveyed, as are many current officeholders who are positioned to run for higher office. Although the reputational approach allows scholars to shed light on ambition to seek high-level office, as well as to explore the specific dynamics that might spur a candidacy for a particular seat,

increased their identification with the Democratic Party. Included in our partisan categories in 2008, however, are "Independent Leaners," who constitute 17 percent of "Democrats" and 11 percent of "Republicans." Considering that political ideology has remained fairly constant, it is likely that the shift in party identification also reflects disillusionment with the Republican Party's face and name, as opposed to its ideological underpinnings, perhaps spurring a disproportionate share of Independents to align with Democrats.

it succumbs to several limitations when we turn to the initial decision to seek a political position. In most states, politics is a career ladder. Studies that focus on the decision to seek high-level office, therefore, are likely to identify as eligible candidates individuals for whom the initial decision to run has long since passed. Further, contacting only elected officials and informants for the names of eligible candidates restricts the sample to individuals who are currently deemed ready to run. Women and men who may be well positioned to consider a candidacy later in life are overlooked. Informants' personal biases can also influence the eligible candidates they name (Maisel and Stone 1998). This is particularly relevant when we turn to gender and political ambition, as bias can result in too few women being identified, thereby prohibiting statistical comparisons among women in the pool.

Although the Citizen Political Ambition Study represents a methodological breakthrough, we acknowledge two specific limitations involved in employing the eligibility pool approach. Our method means that we must forgo a nuanced analysis of the structural and contextual variables that might exert an impact on the decision to enter the electoral arena. If we focused on a single race or election, then the number of potential candidates would be extremely small. We assembled a broad sample at the expense of analyzing the political opportunity and structural aspects of the decision calculus in any particular race or set of races. The absence of a specific office focus does mean, however, that we are limited in the extent to which we can assess the effects that constituency demographics, incumbency, and other political opportunities exert on the inclination to consider a candidacy. Second, our approach relies on eligible candidates' perceptions of the political environment and their future candidacies, as opposed to more objective indicators of their electoral viability. Thus, our results might reflect a distorted version of reality. Because we are interested in the consideration process that members of the eligibility pool undergo, self-perceptions are perhaps as relevant as are objective assessments of the eligible candidates' likelihood of winning. After all, individuals often distort the probability of winning an election, but engage in behavior based on these distortions.

In short, what our approach sacrifices in precision and leverage in predicting who will enter a specific race at a specific time it makes up for in the broad-based nature of the sample. Because the strength of our research design is its ability to address considering a candidacy, Chapters 4, 5, and 6 focus on this inclination. In Chapter 7, we turn to the decision to enter an actual race and the role gender plays in that phase of the candidate emergence process. No other study allows for as thorough an assessment of the critically important intersection between gender and political ambition in accounting for women's underrepresentation.

# 3

# The Gender Gap in Political Ambition

If I'm angry about something that the government has done, I write letters and I sign petitions. I'm very interested in politics. I read the paper and I listen to National Public Radio. It would just never occur to me to be part of the fray. Running for office is something I'd just never think to do.

— Melissa Stevens-Jones, 51, Attorney, New Mexico

I follow many political issues – health care, the environment, school choice, tax reform. I read the newspaper, listen to talk radio, and watch cable news. The more and more I see, the more and more I know that I have to get in there. I can't imagine not running for office in the future.

— Larry Ginsberg, 53, Attorney, Florida

Politics is a thankless job. It takes your soul. Entering it has never even crossed my mind. If I ever wanted to do something new professionally, politics wouldn't be it. Politics would be at the bottom of the list.

— Lila Meyers, 47, Business Owner, Massachusetts

Sure, I've considered running. I'm not interested in it right now, but who knows? Maybe in ten years I'll want a career change. Maybe I'll want to be a mayor . . . or an astronaut.

— Charles Bartelson, 44, Business Owner, Missouri

With roughly five hundred thousand elected positions in the United States, democracy cannot function as intended if competent, politically interested citizens do not exhibit a sincere, sustained interest in running for office and a willingness to present a battle of ideas to the voters. Though high-level positions, such as seats in the U.S. Congress, are quite professionalized, most elective offices are situated at the local and state levels. Designed to be filled by citizen-politicians, many of these positions pay only a token salary and meet on a limited basis. Forty states, for example, have part-time legislatures in which members must be available to serve only for a few months each year (National Conference of State Legislatures 2009a). The overwhelming majority of school boards and city councils also operate on a part-time basis. Thus, the very manner in which most elective positions are structured is geared to allow politically interested individuals to step forward and serve as representatives of the people.

Indeed, a central criterion in evaluating the health of democracy in the United States is the degree to which citizens are willing to engage the political system and run for public office. As Joseph Schlesinger (1966, 2) remarked in his seminal work on political ambition, "A political system unable to kindle ambitions for office is as much in danger of breaking down as one unable to restrain ambitions." More recently, Thomas Mann and Bruce Cain (2005, 1) highlighted the need for contested elections: "The essence of any democratic regime is the competitive election of officeholders. It is only by making candidates compete for their seats that politicians can be held accountable by the public."[1]

The central question before us is whether women and men are equally ambitious to occupy these positions. This chapter employs the two-stage conception of candidate emergence we presented in Chapter 2 as a framework through which to examine whether and how gender interacts with the decision to run for office. Our empirical assessment reveals that, despite similarities in levels of political participation, proximity, and interest, eligible women candidates are less politically ambitious than men. Women are not only less likely than men to consider running for office, but they are also less likely than men to enter actual political contests. These results emerge in both the 2001 and 2008 survey data. Ultimately, this chapter establishes the critical finding of this book: the presence of a pronounced and enduring gender gap in political ambition.

---

[1] Relatively limited electoral competition, however, dominates the U.S. political system. Since 1958, for example, 37 percent of congressional incumbents have faced no primary challenger whatsoever (Lawless and Pearson 2008). More than one-third of seats in all of the state legislatures across the country went uncontested throughout the 1990s (Squire 2000). And although the lack of systematic election data at the local level makes it difficult to provide an exact rate of electoral competition, the number of uncontested seats on city councils and school boards is likely much higher (see Schleicher 2007). Without an understanding of the factors that trigger interest in running for office, we cannot fully gauge prospects for political accountability or women's entrance into the political system.

Very Much the Same: Gender, Political Participation, Proximity,
and Interest

Running for public office represents the ultimate act of political participation; it signals an individual's willingness to put himself or herself before
the voters and vie to become a member of an elected body. Citizens with
relatively high levels of political activism, interest, and proximity to the
political arena, therefore, are most likely to emerge as candidates. Thus,
it is important to determine whether women and men in the candidate
eligibility pool are equally likely to engage the political system and gain
firsthand exposure to politics.

Let us turn first to levels of political participation. Figure 3.1 presents
the percentages of women and men who participated in various political
activities over the course of the last year. Not only are the respondents
very politically active, but women and men are also roughly equally likely
to engage in all types of political participation. These comparable rates
of participation between women and men in the candidate eligibility pool
are largely consistent with patterns of political participation at the mass
level. In every presidential election since 1980, and in all congressional
elections since 1986, women have voted in equal or greater proportions
than men (Center for American Women and Politics 2008). Women also
sign petitions, attend public meetings and rallies, and write to elected government officials at rates similar to those of men (Conway, Steuernagel,
and Ahern 2004).[2]

The 2008 survey data allow us to move beyond typical measures of
political participation and examine more nuanced gauges of exposure
to politics and the electoral arena. More specifically, we included in the
second-wave survey a series of questions pertaining to respondents' direct
contact with and observation of elected officials. The new findings are
similar to the participation results (see Table 3.1). On three of the four
measures of political proximity, we uncover no gender differences. More
than half of the women and men in the pool of potential candidates
interact with elected officials professionally or socially.

Despite the general similarities between women and men's levels of
political activism and proximity, two noteworthy gender differences merit
acknowledgment. Statistically, women are less likely than men to have

---

[2] For examples of some of the earlier studies of gender and political participation that
found men to be more likely than women to participate in politics, see Campbell et al.
1960; Lane 1959.

FIGURE 3.1. Eligible Candidates' Levels of Political Participation (in the past year).

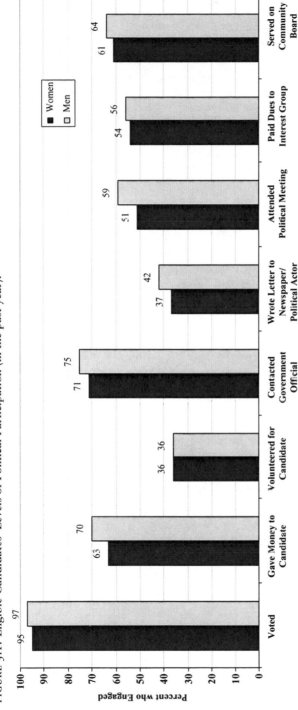

*Notes:* Results are based on the 2001 survey data. Bars indicate the percentage of respondents who engaged in each activity over the course of the past year. For voting, respondents were asked whether they voted in the most recent presidential election. Levels of political activity might be somewhat inflated, as they are based on respondents' self-reports, but there is no reason to expect levels of inflation to correlate with respondent sex. Sample sizes: for women, N = 1676; for men, N = 1885.

TABLE 3.1. *Eligible Candidates' Proximity to Politics*

|  | Women | Men |
|---|---|---|
| Attended state legislative committee meeting or floor session | 53% | 51% |
| Interacted with elected officials as part of job | 64* | 69 |
| Interacted with elected officials socially | 74 | 75 |
| Has an elected official as a family member or friend | 51 | 52 |
| N | 922 | 1,106 |

*Notes:* Results are based on the 2008 survey data. Percentages reflect the proportion of eligible candidates who have had each particular political experience. Significance levels of chi-square test comparing women and men: * $p < .05$.

contributed money to a campaign. Again, this finding is consistent with political behavior in the general population. In 2008, for example, women comprised 44 percent of Barack Obama's donor base and 28 percent of John McCain's.[3] Men are also statistically more likely than women to attend political meetings or interact with elected officials as part of their job, though the substantive differences are quite small. Although the gender gap in these participatory acts is not striking, these differences could certainly carry implications for running for office. Both checkbook activism and networking with other politically minded citizens might confer to eligible candidates the name recognition and familiarity that attracts the recruitment often needed to spur on candidacies.

The slight advantage men appear to have in political participation and proximity is offset by women's slightly higher levels of political interest. Forty-three percent of women in the candidate eligibility pool follow national politics and current events "closely" or "very closely," compared to 33 percent of men (difference significant at $p < .01$). We uncover an 8 percentage-point gender gap in following local politics "closely" or "very closely" (49 percent of women versus 41 percent of men; difference significant at $p < .01$).

Nancy Burns, Kay Lehman Schlozman, and Sidney Verba (2001, 259) conclude that gender differences in levels of political activity in the general population are the result of disparities in the factors that facilitate participation, not of sex itself:

[3] OpenSecrets.org provides detailed donor demographic information for the 2008 presidential election, as well as election data from 1976 to 2008. These statistics can be accessed at http://www.opensecrets.org/pres08/donordemCID_compare.php?cycle=2008 (accessed July 15, 2009).

Increments to the reserves of participatory factors – whether more education, income, or the civic skills and requests for activity derived from involvements on the job, in organizations, or in church – foster activity for women and men in essentially the same way. What counts is the size of those reserves.[4]

The data presented in Figure 3.1 and Table 3.1 provide compelling evidence that the members of our sample – male and female – have all accrued substantial "reserves." If heightened levels of political activity, proximity, and interest situate members of the eligibility pool to emerge as actual candidates, then the women in the sample are as well positioned as the men.

## Very Much Different: Gender and Political Ambition

Despite the similar political experiences and levels of activism among the women and men in the candidate eligibility pool, we uncover widespread gender differences in political ambition. We depict our two-stage conception of the candidate emergence process in Figure 3.2. The left-most box contains the roughly equal samples of women and men who constitute our pool of eligible candidates. The figure's final box includes only those respondents who sought office and won their races. We can assess the entire candidate emergence process because more than three hundred members of the sample had actually run for office by the time we conducted the 2001 survey. An additional fifty-four respondents launched candidacies between the two waves of the study.

As we would expect from the literature on gender and elections (see Chapter 2), there is no statistically significant gender difference in the likelihood of winning political contests. Table 3.2 illustrates that women are more likely than men to run for local-level offices, whereas men are more likely to seek state-level positions. But women and men fare equally well, regardless of the level of office they seek: 63 percent of the women and 59 percent of the men who ran for office at the time of the first wave of the study launched successful campaigns. When we supplement these

---

[4] Recent studies of political skill acquisition through church participation, however, find that men are more likely than women to translate the civic skills they acquire into political participation (Djupe, Sokhey, and Gilbert 2007; see also Djupe and Gilbert 2006). For a discussion of the manner in which increased educational and occupational opportunities have afforded women the characteristics that correlate positively with the propensity to engage the political system, see Verba, Schlozman, and Brady 1995; Teixeira 1992; Conway 1991; Dolbeare and Stone 1990; Bergmann 1986; Baxter and Lansing 1983.

TABLE 3.2. *Offices Sought and Won by Eligible Candidates*

|                          | Women    | Men   |
|--------------------------|----------|-------|
| **Level of Office Sought** |          |       |
| Local                    | 84%**    | 77%   |
| State                    | 14**     | 19    |
| Federal                  | 4        | 3     |
| **Level of Office Won**  |          |       |
| Local                    | 68       | 67    |
| State                    | 47       | 38    |
| Federal                  | 0        | 1     |
| N                        | 109      | 211   |

*Notes:* Results are based on the 2001 survey data. N represents the number of respondents who ran for office. The "Level of Office Won" percentages reflect the proportion of candidates who won the race for each level of office sought. Significance levels of chi-square test comparing women and men: ** $p < .01$.

data with election outcomes from the additional fifty-four respondents who ran for office between 2001 and 2008, the results are nearly identical; 63 percent of the women and 60 percent of the men who ran for office won their races. Although there are no gender differences at the end stage of the electoral process, the second and third boxes in Figure 3.2 highlight the gender dynamics of the candidate emergence process and the substantial role gender plays in the initial decision to run for office.

### Stage 1: Considering a Candidacy

As we outlined in Chapter 2, the first stage of the candidate emergence process (see Figure 3.2, second box from the left) is considering running for any political office. More than half of the respondents (51 percent) stated that the idea of running for an elective position had at least "crossed their mind." Turning to the respondents who considered a candidacy, however, a substantial and statistically significant gender difference emerges: 59 percent of men, compared to 43 percent of women, considered running for office. The gender gap in considering a candidacy in 2008 is essentially unchanged. When we include in the analysis the 163 respondents whose first considerations of running for office occurred between the two waves of the study, we find that the gender gap in political ambition is 17 percentage points. That is, overall 47 percent of women, compared to 64 percent of men, reported that the idea of running for office had at least "crossed their mind." Although the proportion of

FIGURE 3.2. The Gender Gap in Candidate Emergence from the Eligibility Pool.

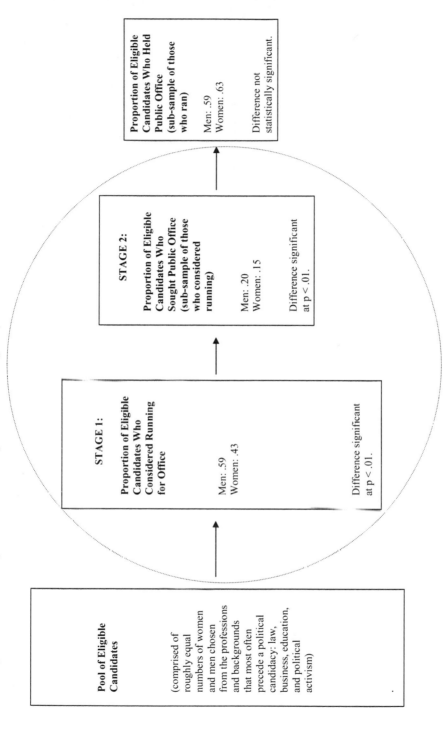

**Pool of Eligible Candidates**

(comprised of roughly equal numbers of women and men chosen from the professions and backgrounds that most often precede a political candidacy: law, business, education, and political activism)

**STAGE 1:**

**Proportion of Eligible Candidates Who Considered Running for Office**

Men: .59
Women: .43

Difference significant at p < .01.

**STAGE 2:**

**Proportion of Eligible Candidates Who Sought Public Office (sub-sample of those who considered running)**

Men: .20
Women: .15

Difference significant at p < .01.

**Proportion of Eligible Candidates Who Held Public Office (sub-sample of those who ran)**

Men: .59
Women: .63

Difference not statistically significant.

*Notes:* Results are based on 2001 survey data.

TABLE 3.3. *Eligible Candidates' Interest in Running for Office, by Profession*

| | Question: Have you ever thought about running for office? | | | | | | | | | |
|---|---|---|---|---|---|---|---|---|---|---|
| | Total Sample | | Lawyers | | Business Leaders/ Executives | | Educators | | Political Activists | |
| | Women | Men | Women | Men | Women | Men | Women | Men | Women | Men |
| Yes, I have seriously considered it. | 10% | 19% | 10% | 23% | 5% | 11% | 5% | 10% | 19% | 31% |
| Yes, it has crossed my mind. | 33 | 40 | 38 | 44 | 21 | 30 | 24 | 40 | 44 | 47 |
| No, I have never thought about it. | 57 | 41 | 53 | 34 | 74 | 59 | 72 | 50 | 36 | 23 |
| N | 1,653 | 1,870 | 542 | 585 | 273 | 382 | 435 | 490 | 402 | 412 |

*Notes:* Results are based on the 2001 survey data. Gender differences are significant at p < .01 within each profession.

TABLE 3.4. *The Baseline Model of Candidate Emergence from the Eligibility Pool (Logistic Regression Coefficients, Standard Errors, and Change in Probabilities)*

| | Considered Running for Elective Office | | Ran for Elective Office | |
| --- | --- | --- | --- | --- |
| | Coefficient (Standard Error) | Maximum Change in Probability (Percentage Points) | Coefficient (Standard) Error) | Maximum Change in Probability (Percentage Points) |
| Sex (female) | −.63** (.08) | 15.6 | −.34* (.15) | 2.7 |
| Education | .16** (.04) | 19.9 | −.08 (.26) | – |
| Income | −.06* (.03) | 7.6 | −.04 (.06) | – |
| Race (White) | .04 (.11) | – | −.03 (.18) | – |
| Democrat | −.02 (.10) | – | .12 (.18) | – |
| Republican | −.05 (.11) | – | .26 (.19) | – |
| Political Knowledge | .09* (.05) | 6.5 | .18 (.12) | – |
| Political Interest | .16** (.03) | 23.3 | .19** (.06) | 10.2 |
| Political Efficacy | .01 (.04) | – | −.05 (.07) | – |
| Political Participation | .31* (.02) | 60.0 | .30** (.05) | 22.1 |
| Constant | −3.08** (.34) | | −4.50** (.67) | |
| Pseudo-R² | .24 | | .14 | |
| Percentage Correctly Predicted | 68.2 | | 82.4 | |
| N | 3,251 | | 1,667 | |

*Notes:* Results are based on the 2001 survey data. Maximum changes in probabilities are based on the logistic regression results. These probabilities were calculated by setting all continuous independent variables not under consideration to their means and dummy variables not under consideration to their modes. The change in probability reflects the independent effect a statistically significant variable exerts as we vary its value from its minimum to maximum (i.e., the change in probability for Sex [female] reflects the fact that a woman is 15.6 percentage points less likely than a man, all else equal, to consider running for office). Significance levels: ** $p < .01$; * $p < .05$.

respondents who considered running differs by profession, with lawyers and political activists most likely to have considered a candidacy (see Table 3.3), the gender differential is statistically significant at $p < .01$ within each subgroup.

Sex remains a significant predictor of considering a candidacy even after controlling for many traditional correlates of political behavior. The left-hand column in Table 3.4 presents the logistic regression coefficients of a series of sociodemographic and political variables that might affect candidate emergence from the eligibility pool (see Appendix E for a complete description of all variables included in the multivariate analyses throughout this book). This regression equation, which serves as the baseline model of political ambition on which we build throughout the remainder of this book, also withstands fixed effects for the various professions from which the respondents are drawn.[5] As expected, when levels of education, political interest, political knowledge, and political participation increase, so does the inclination to consider a candidacy. But regardless of these factors, women are less likely than men to consider running for office.[6] Moreover, the gender gap in political ambition persists across racial lines.[7]

The second column in Table 3.4 reveals the substantive effect of each statistically significant independent variable. Each maximum change in probability represents the independent effect exerted by a statistically significant variable as we vary its value from its minimum to its maximum, holding all other variables at their sample means and modes. Women are 15.6 percentage points less likely than men, all else equal, to consider running for office.

Our measure of whether a respondent ever considered a candidacy captures even the slightest inclination of running for office. The four quotations that opened this chapter, however, suggest that men might be more cavalier than women when retrospectively assessing whether they ever thought about pursuing an elective position. Even when we turn to the concrete steps that are often required to mount a political campaign, though, we uncover gender gaps of at least the same magnitude. We asked the members of our eligibility pool sample whether they ever investigated how to place their name on the ballot or ever discussed running with potential donors, party or community leaders, family members, or

---

[5] Each of the models and empirical results we discuss in this chapter and throughout the remainder of the book withstands fixed effects for professional subgroups. In almost all cases, levels of statistical significance and the magnitude of the regression coefficients remain unchanged when we include in the models dummy variables for each profession.

[6] Regression analyses with interaction terms between the significant background variables and the sex of the respondent indicate that these traditional correlates of political ambition do not exert differential impacts on women and men. None of the interaction terms achieves conventional levels of statistical significance. Further, when interaction terms are included, the principal effects' coefficients, magnitudes, and levels of significance remain unchanged.

[7] The gender gap in political ambition remains significant when we replace the "White" dummy variable with a series of dummy variables for each racial group (African American, Latino or Latina, Asian). Interacting these race dummy variables with sex does not yield statistically significant results. For a discussion of race and political ambition within this sample of the candidate eligibility pool, see Fox and Lawless 2005.

TABLE 3.5. *Eligible Candidates' Levels of Engagement in Activities That Often Precede a Political Candidacy*

| Question: Have you ever . . . | Women | Men |
|---|---|---|
| Discussed running with friends and family? | 22%** | 33% |
| Discussed running with community leaders? | 9** | 15 |
| Investigated how to place your name on the ballot? | 6** | 13 |
| Discussed running with party leaders? | 6** | 12 |
| Solicited or discussed financial contributions with potential supporters? | 3** | 7 |
| N | 1,653 | 1,870 |

*Notes:* Results are based on the 2001 survey data. Significance levels of chi-square test comparing women and men: ** p < .01.

friends. Comparisons between women and men's answers to all of these questions highlight stark gender differences. Table 3.5 reveals that, across professions, men are at least 50 percent more likely than women to have engaged in each of these fundamental campaign steps (gender differences significant at p < .01).[8] The magnitude of the gender gap on several of the concrete steps did close somewhat between the two waves of the study. On every measure, however, men remain more than 25 percent more likely than women to have taken the step; and the gender differences across all measures remains statistically significant.[9] At both points in time, therefore, and across a variety of measures, what started out as a gender-balanced eligibility pool winnows to one that is dominated by men.

### Stage 2: Deciding to Enter the First Race

When we move to the second stage of the candidate emergence process depicted in Figure 3.2 (third box from the left), and examine those members of the sample who actually ran for elective office, gender differences again emerge. Twenty percent of the men, compared to 15 percent of the women, who considered running for office actually chose to seek an elective position. Put somewhat differently, 12 percent of the men from the initial pool of eligible candidates actually threw their hats into the ring

[8] The gender gap at the aggregate level is approximately the same size as the gap within each profession. Because of these similarities, unless otherwise noted, we pool the data and consider the entire sample of the eligibility pool. In later chapters, when substantively important, we explore more thoroughly some of the professional differences.

[9] For a more detailed account of the 2008 survey results pertaining to gender differences in the concrete steps that precede a candidacy, see Lawless and Fox (2008).

and sought elective positions, whereas only 7 percent of the women did so (difference significant at p < .01). Here, too, the results are similar when we include the fifty-four new candidates who emerged between the two waves of the study. Taking into account the total number of women and men who ran for office, 22 percent of the men who considered running, compared to 17 percent of the women, actually emerged as candidates.

Although the baseline correlates of political ambition are not as significant at this stage of the candidate emergence process, the gender gap withstands statistical controls for the aforementioned demographic and political variables (Table 3.4, column 3). The gender gap also persists even after controlling for statewide structural variables, such as measures of political culture, the size and openness of the political opportunity structure, levels of legislative professionalization, and respondents' party congruence with elected officials in the state (regression results not shown). We offer a more nuanced examination and discussion of such structural variables in Chapter 7. For our purposes here, it is important simply to recognize that, in the baseline model, sex is one of only three statistically significant predictors of entering an actual political contest, and women in the eligibility pool are at a disadvantage.

### The Persistent Winnowing Effect
Women and men in the candidate eligibility pool may be similarly situated in terms of their professional success and levels of political participation, proximity, and interest, but women exhibit significantly lower levels of political ambition to enter electoral politics than do their male counterparts. Given relatively equal proportions of credentialed women and men, and regardless of the fact that women are just as likely as men to win elections, men are nearly twice as likely as women to hold elected office: 7 percent of the men, compared to less than 4 percent of the women, from the initial pool of eligible candidates were elected to office (difference significant at p < .01).

Despite the dramatic events that occurred between the two waves of the panel – the waging of two major wars, hyperpartisan gridlock in Washington, the Hurricane Katrina disaster, the highly unpopular presidency of George W. Bush, Nancy Pelosi's selection as Speaker of the House of Representatives, and Hillary Clinton's campaign for president – the gender gap in political ambition remained strikingly static. Moreover, there were no gender differences in aggregate-level gains or losses in ambition across the two waves of the study. Women and men were equally likely to report shifts in interest in running for office, and the same factors drive the shifts for both women and men.[10]

## The Gender Gap in Elective Office Preferences

If we want to establish a more complete understanding of political ambition, then we must also assess whether women and men in the candidate eligibility pool are equally open to seeking high-level positions. In many cases, politics is a career ladder; politicians often move from local to state to national office. More than 70 percent of the members of the U.S. Congress, for instance, held office prior to running for the U.S. House or Senate (Malbin, Ornstein, and Mann 2008). Yet among actual officeholders, evidence suggests that women are less likely than men to climb the political career ladder (Fulton et al. 2006; Lawless and Theriault 2005). In fact, school boards, which are the offices with the highest ratio of women officeholders (estimated at about 40 percent), are not typically utilized by politicians who harbor ambition to launch political careers at higher levels of office (Deckman 2007; see also Hess 2002; Bullock et al. 1999). The gender disparity in progressive ambition could be a result of differences in the reasons women and men enter politics in the first place. Timothy Bledsoe and Mary Herring's (1990, 221) study of city council members concludes that men are more likely than women to be "self-motivated – guided by political ambition."[11] By contrast, women tend to be more motivated by community issues (Fox 1997; Astin and Leland 1991).

To determine where eligible candidates focus their office-specific interests, we asked the members of the sample to state the first office they would seek, should they enter a political contest. We then presented them with a list of several local, state, and federal positions and asked whether

[10] The fluctuations in ambition that we found across the two waves of the panel tend not to result from changes in the traditional gauges of political participation. Rather, shifts in levels of external and internal political efficacy account for much of the variation in levels of political ambition over time. Changes in patterns of political recruitment, as well as in personal and professional circumstances, also contribute to the likelihood that potential candidates will gain or lose interest in seeking elective office. We uncovered no gender differences on any of these predictors, though. For a more thorough discussion of changes in political ambition over time and the factors that predict increases and decreases in eligible candidates' interest in running for office, see Fox and Lawless 2009.

[11] For similar findings pertaining to gender differences in the motivating forces behind political ambition, see Carroll 1994; Costantini 1990; Sapiro 1982.

they would ever consider running for any of those posts. The data reveal that women are less likely than men to consider running for high-level elective offices.

Let us begin with an analysis of the first office for which respondents would consider running. Many eligible candidates seem well aware of career-ladder politics. Most respondents who are willing to consider running for office at some point in the future would get involved at the bottom rung of the ladder. Seventy-six percent of the women and 60 percent of the men select a local office – school board, city council, or mayor – as the first office for which they might run (gender difference significant at p < .01). The gender gap in interest reverses itself with increases in the stature of the level of office. Men are significantly more likely than women to identify a state office (25 percent of men compared to 18 percent of women) or federal office (15 percent of men compared to only 6 percent of women) as their first choice (gender differences significant at p < .01). The gender gap in ambition for high-level office is greater when we consider that more women than men are unwilling to enter any electoral contest. Thirty-one percent of women, but only 23 percent of men, stated, unequivocally, that they had ruled out any consideration of a future run for office.

The magnitude of the gender gap in interest in high-level office is even greater when we turn to the positions respondents might ever be interested in seeking. Table 3.6 presents the percentages of eligible candidates who would entertain a candidacy for nine elective offices. Whereas men are about as likely as women to consider running at the local level, women are significantly more likely than men to dismiss the possibility of ever running for a state or federal position. In fact, if we consider high-level office to include federal positions, as well as statewide offices (e.g., governor, attorney general), then men are 59 percent more likely than women to express interest (22 percent of women compared to 35 percent of men; gender difference significant at p < .01).[12]

Even though they have risen to the top ranks within often male-dominated professions, and despite the fact that they yield from the management and leadership positions that tend to position candidates for the highest public offices, women express far less ambition than men to enter the upper echelons of the political arena. This evidence suggests

[12] Members of the educator and businesspeople subsamples are less likely than members of the attorney and political activist subsamples to consider running for high-level office. The gender gap within each profession, however, is at least 11 percentage points.

TABLE 3.6. *Gender Differences in Eligible Candidates' Elective Office Preferences*

| Question: If you were going to run for office – either now or in the future – what position(s) would you ever be interested in seeking? | | |
| --- | --- | --- |
| | Women | Men |
| **Local Office** | | |
| School board | 41%* | 37% |
| Town, city, county council | 36 | 37 |
| Mayor | 11** | 17 |
| **State Office** | | |
| State legislator | 27** | 36 |
| Statewide office (e.g., attorney general) | 11 | 10 |
| Governor | 6* | 13 |
| **Federal Office** | | |
| House of Representatives | 15** | 28 |
| Senate | 12** | 21 |
| President | 3* | 5 |
| N | 1,653 | 1,870 |

*Notes:* Results are based on the 2001 survey data. Entries indicate the percentage of respondents who said they would consider running for the specified position. Percentages do not add up to 100 percent because respondents often expressed interest in more than one position. Significance levels of chi-square test comparing women and men: ** p < .01; * p < .05.

that the context of gender dynamics in the United States and historical patterns of career segregation continue to influence the political offices that women and men consider seeking.[13]

## Conclusion

Our results provide the first evidence from a national sample that eligible female candidates are significantly less likely than their male counterparts to emerge as actual candidates. The gender gap in political ambition that we identified in the first edition of this book remains largely unchanged. Indeed, the 2008 survey results reveal that, despite gender-neutral outcomes on Election Day, women continue to be significantly less likely than men to reach that stage of the candidate emergence process. Women are also less likely than men to consider running for high-level positions.

[13] Richard Fox and Zoe Oxley (2003) find an interaction between candidate sex and office type in state executive elections. Women are less likely to run for offices that are inconsistent with their stereotypical strengths.

The conventional indicators of political ambition, such as political participation, proximity, and interest, as well as basic sociodemographic traits,
do not account for the gender differences in the likelihood of considering
a candidacy or entering an actual race.

These findings suggest that the leading theoretical explanations for
women's continued exclusion from politics are incomplete because they
do not take into account the selection process by which eligible candidates become actual candidates. It is at the candidate emergence phase
of the electoral process that critical gender differences exist. Thus, even
though women who run for office are just as likely as men to emerge vic-
torious, the substantial winnowing process in candidate emergence yields
a smaller ratio of women than men. The next three chapters highlight the
specific ways in which patterns of traditional gender socialization manifest themselves and contribute to the gender gap in political ambition.

# 4

# Barefoot, Pregnant, and Holding a Law Degree

## Family Dynamics and Running for Office

On July 3, 2009, Alaska Governor Sarah Palin announced her resignation. Although she acknowledged a litany of reasons for her decision – ranging from legal bills associated with charges of ethics violations to nonstop media coverage of her every move – she told the group of supporters gathered outside her home in Wasilla, Alaska, that her decision ultimately came down to family concerns:

> This decision comes after much consideration, and finally polling the most important people in my life – my children, where the count was unanimous ... well, in response to asking: "Want me to make a positive difference and fight for all our children's future from outside the Governor's office?" It was four "yeses" and one "hell yeah!" [1]

Two days later, and amid widespread speculation that Governor Palin's decision actually had little to do with her family, but rather, was the result of either an impending scandal or more financially lucrative opportunities, Vice President Joe Biden commented on the resignation. In an exchange on *This Week with George Stephanopoulos*, the vice president said he took Palin "at her word":

STEPHANOPOULOS: Were you surprised by her decision to step down?

BIDEN: Well, look, you and I know – and I shouldn't say that because that implicates you in my answer, so. But those who have been deeply involved in politics know at the end of the day it is really and truly a personal deal.

---

[1] Office of Alaska Governor Sarah Palin, "Palin Announces No Second Term, No Lame Duck Session Either," July 3, 2009, http://www.gov.state.ak.us/exec-column.php (accessed July 10, 2009).

And personal family decisions have real impact on people's decisions. I love reading these history books and biographies of people, the reason they made the choice to run or not run was because the state of the economy.

It maybe had a lot to do with what the state of their life was, and the state of their family, et cetera. So I'm not going to second guess her.[2]

Sarah Palin was neither the first, nor will she be the last, politician to invoke family when explaining a political career decision. In an interview with New Jersey's *Star-Ledger*, for example, U.S. House member Mike Ferguson (R-NJ) stated that his choice not to seek a fifth term in 2008 was a "family decision." Referring to his children – who were ages three, four, seven, and nine – Ferguson said, "This is about the four little sleeping faces who are almost never awake when I come home. They need their Dad around."[3]

Elected officials at the local level also often rely on family circumstances to justify their decisions to exit the political sphere. Dallas Mayor Laura Miller decided to leave city hall in 2007 because the reality of the political process meant "throwing the towel in on [her] family." She explained, "I'm desperate to be with my kids.... My kids have always been in politics. They've always been in the limelight. This is about my quality of life, and theirs."[4] Ken Camp, a staff member in the Washington lieutenant governor's office, opted not to seek an open city council seat in Tumwater, Washington, despite widespread encouragement. In the end, he cited family reasons for not entering the race: "With my wife pregnant and due to give birth to our third child ... I don't believe I'd be able to dedicate my full attention to the campaign."[5]

Although there are certainly conditions under which we might be dubious of the family explanation offered by outgoing elected officials, concerns about family responsibilities clearly play an important role in politicians' desires to remain in the political arena or seek higher office. And although we do not want to trivialize the fact that family concerns affect both women and men, women who enter politics tend to face closer scrutiny and are forced to reconcile their familial and professional roles in a way that men are not. On former Congresswoman Pat Schroeder's

---

[2] *This Week with George Stephanopoulos* transcript, July 5, 2009.
[3] Susan K. Livio and Josh Margolin, "Representative Ferguson Won't Seek Reelection," *Star-Ledger (NJ)*, November 19, 2007.
[4] Emily Ramshaw, "Miller: My Work Is Done: Kids Need Her, So Mayor's Race Is Out," *Dallas Morning News*, July 7, 2006.
[5] Ken Camp, "Tumwater City Council," Press Release, February 25, 2009, http://kencamp. net/?p=304 (accessed July 12, 2009).

(D-CO) first day in the House of Representatives, for instance, Congresswoman Bella Abzug (D-NY) commented, "I hear you have little kids. You won't be able to do this job" (Schroeder 1999, 35). Implicit in this statement is the assumption that, in addition to being a member of Congress, Representative Schroeder would naturally be expected to remain the primary caretaker of her children. More than thirty years later, these sentiments still ring true on Capitol Hill. A 2007 *Washington Post* article chronicled the trials and tribulations of the ten congresswomen with children younger than the age of thirteen. The article characterizes these female House members as residing on "a shaky high wire, balancing motherhood with politicking, lawmaking, fundraising, and the constant shuttle between Washington and their home states."[6] Many of these women recounted the judgment and scrutiny they regularly withstand for the parenting and professional balance they choose to strike. Examples of male politicians having to offer a public defense and justification of their parenting skills or family life are far less common. In fact, in an open letter to his daughters, President Barack Obama recognized the time he spent apart from his children and how much he missed them during his two years on the campaign trail. Rather than apologize for his absence, however, he explained that his life "wouldn't count for much" unless he ran for president and tried to ensure that all children have opportunities for happiness and success.[7]

In this chapter, we provide evidence of the manner in which traditional family role orientations continue to hinder women's emergence in the political sphere. We conceptualize the role of family rather broadly. We begin by considering how eligible candidates' early political socialization relates to their levels of political ambition as adults. The bulk of the chapter then examines the gender dynamics in respondents' current households and the relationship between family arrangements and political ambition. We take advantage of the seven years between the two waves of the panel to shed new light on the manner in which fundamental changes in family structures – such as marital status and parental responsibilities – affect interest in running for office and on how these changes vary across gender lines. Ultimately, we find that, even in 2008, traditional family roles and responsibilities make considering a candidacy

---

[6] Lyndsey Layton, "Mom's in the House, with Kids at Home: For Congresswomen with Young Children, a Tough Balance," *Washington Post*, July 19, 2007, A01.

[7] President Barack Obama, "What I Want for You and Every Child in America," *Parade Magazine*, January 18, 2009.

a much more complex and distant endeavor for women than men. These findings hold among the youngest generation in the candidate eligibility pool.

### Raised to Be a Candidate?

History is rife with politicians from different generations of the same family. Thomas D'Alesandro, the father of U.S. Speaker of the House Nancy Pelosi (D-CA), was a Maryland congressman for eight years and the mayor of Baltimore for more than a decade. United States Senator Mary Landrieu (D-LA) is the daughter of Moon Landrieu, former New Orleans mayor and secretary of housing and urban development. U.S. Senator Susan Collins's (R-ME) mother and father each served as the mayor of Caribou, Maine. U.S. Senator Mark Begich's (D-AK) father served in the U.S. House of Representatives. And U.S. Senator Bob Casey's (D-PA) father was governor of Pennsylvania. In the 111th Congress alone, Senators Evan Bayh (D-IN), Bob Bennett (R-UT), Chris Dodd (D-CT), Lisa Murkowski (R-AK), Mark Pryor (D-AR), and Mark Udall (D-CO) are the children of former U.S. senators. Perhaps the most recent high-level example of political family ties is the 2000 presidential election, which pitted Al Gore, the son of a former U.S. senator, against George W. Bush, the son of a former president.

Although it may be somewhat uncommon to inherit the political ambition and opportunities of these elected officials, more modest levels of political interest are often passed on within the family unit (Flanigan and Zingale 2002). Consider the case of Kay Hagan, who was elected to the U.S. Senate from North Carolina in 2008. The niece of "Walkin' Lawton" Chiles – a former governor and U.S. senator from Florida – Hagan recounts a childhood of affixing bumper stickers onto supporters' cars, ultimately working her way up to serving as an intern.[8] Raised with a sense of civic duty and the notion that elective office is a way to fulfill that obligation, she became active in North Carolina politics, ran Jim Hunt's successful 1996 gubernatorial campaign in Guilford County, and ran for the state senate herself two years later. In another example, former Massachusetts State Senator Carol Amick recalls that when her daughter, Jennie, was three and a half years old, she used to pretend she

---

[8] Senator Kay R. Hagan Biography, http://hagan.senate.gov/?p=biography (accessed July 15, 2009).

was a politician: "She ha[d] a little case that she call[ed] her briefcase and [went] off to give speeches."[9]

We uncovered a similar pattern in many of the interviews we conducted with eligible candidates. Jim Heller, a high school teacher from Texas, has been politically active since high school, in large part because of his parents' political behavior. He recalled, "Seven out of every ten conversations at the dinner table were about politics. That really left an imprint." Shana Mills, a social sciences professor who frequently attends demonstrations and rallies promoting social justice, also attributed her political interest and activism to her very political family: "Cesar Chavez and Martin Luther King were a big part of my life at home. Their pictures were on the walls. They were my role models." More generally, political scientists Paul Allen Beck and M. Kent Jennings (1982, 98) find that highly politicized parents often create a family environment "charged with positive civic orientations . . . thus endowing their children with the motivation prerequisites for later [political] participation." Recent studies suggest that adolescents who discuss politics and current events with their parents also develop higher levels of political knowledge and demonstrate a greater propensity to vote, attend community meetings, and engage the political system through signing petitions, participating in boycotts, or contributing money (McIntosh, Hart, and Youniss 2007; Andolina et al. 2003).[10]

Involvement in political associations, campaigns, community service, and school elections also affects levels of political interest and activism (Hart et al. 2007; Fox, Lawless, and Feeley 2001; Verba, Schlozman, and Brady 1995). Further, greater exposure to civics education in high school can result in long-term gains in political efficacy and interest, both of

[9] Keith Hendersen, "Senator Carol Amick Balancing Family and Political Life," *Christian Science Monitor*, November 4, 1986, 29.
[10] Alva Myrdal (1941, 1968) offered some of the earliest attempts to urge social scientists to consider the role of family when explaining individual-level behavior. The family unit as a tool of analysis in American political science scholarship has since been employed as a mechanism through which to understand political socialization (Hess et al. 2006; Owen and Dennis 1988; Jennings and Markus 1984; Jennings and Niemi 1981; Almond and Verba 1963) and political participation and issue preferences (Burns, Schlozman, and Verba 2001; Renshon 1975; Niemi 1974). More recently, scholars have also begun to explore the extent to which political attitudes and behaviors are the result not only of environmental and socialized factors, but also of genetic factors passed on from one generation to the next (Alford, Funk, and Hibbing 2005, 2008; Beckwith and Morris 2008).

TABLE 4.1. *Eligible Candidates' Early Political Socialization Patterns*

|                                                    | Women   | Men   |
| -------------------------------------------------- | ------- | ----- |
| Parents spoke to them about politics               | 72%*    | 69%   |
| Mother spoke to them about politics more often     | 17      | 15    |
| Father spoke to them about politics more often     | 32**    | 38    |
| Parents suggested that they run for office         | 35**    | 43    |
| Ran for office as a student                        | 56      | 55    |
| N                                                  | 1,657   | 1,877 |

*Notes:* Results are based on the 2001 survey data. Number of cases varies slightly, as some respondents omitted answers to some questions. Significance levels of chi-square test comparing women and men: ** $p < .01$; * $p < .05$.

which heighten levels of political activism (Pasek et al. 2008). Congresswoman Jane Harman (D-CA), for instance, was introduced to politics when her high school boyfriend enlisted her to work on a local congressional campaign.[11] Following that initial exposure, she never left the political arena. Representative Harman served first as a legislative assistant to Senator John Tunney (D-CA), then as chief counsel and staff director to the Senate Judiciary Subcommittee on Constitutional Rights, deputy White House secretary to Jimmy Carter, and special counsel to the U.S. Defense Department. She currently represents California's thirty-sixth congressional district in the U.S. House of Representatives.

The early political socialization process can clearly instill in many individuals the belief that they have the power to take part in the democratic process. Thus, it is important to determine whether women and men in the candidate eligibility pool were exposed to similar patterns of political socialization. We can begin to answer this question by examining how often respondents recall having discussed politics with their parents, whether they ever received encouragement to run for office from their parents, and whether either of their parents ever ran for office. Table 4.1 reveals that respondents were raised in quite political households. Approximately 70 percent grew up in households where political discussions regularly occurred.[12] More than half of the women and men

[11] Dana Wilkie, "Harman, Prototypical Politicians of the 90s, Juggles Family, Career," Copley News Service, April 9, 1998.

[12] In the general population, 51 percent of women and 54 percent of men state that they discussed politics at least occasionally in their childhood homes. To compare the candidate eligibility pool to the general population, we replicated many questions we asked the eligible candidates and administered, through Knowledge Networks, a stand-alone survey to a random sample of U.S. citizens. From August 23–September 11, 2002,

ran for office as high school and college students. About one-third of the respondents received parental enticements to seek political office at some point in the future. And 16 percent of the women and 13 percent of the men came from families in which a parent actually sought public office.

Although the majority of eligible candidates were raised in relatively politicized homes, we do uncover some notable gender differences. Women were 15 percent less likely than men to have their parents encourage them to run for office. They were nearly 20 percent less likely to have their fathers speak with them about politics.[13] Women were also twice as likely as men to have mothers who ran for office (4 percent of women compared to 2 percent of men). The proportion of respondents whose mothers ran for office is small, but this finding suggests that political women might have played a role in encouraging their daughters to strive for success in traditionally male domains.[14]

Although these differences may not seem dramatic, they reflect patterns of traditional gender socialization that promote men's greater suitability to enter the political sphere. In the 2008 survey, we asked respondents who had considered running for office whether they could remember when the idea of a candidacy first occurred to them. Although we should be careful in analyzing the results, as they rely on retrospective assessments of political ambition, clear gender differences emerged. Fifteen percent of men, compared to only 9 percent of women, reported that they first considered running for office before they graduated from high school (difference significant at $p < .05$).

Many of the eligible candidates we interviewed noted that the politicized households in which they were raised triggered thoughts of candidacies once they entered adulthood. Jill Steinberg, a lawyer from Florida, serves as a good example. When asked about her initial interest in pursuing public office, she referred to her childhood: "I remember as a kid that

Knowledge Networks surveyed 2,859 adults. The general population data we reference here and throughout the remainder of this book are based on responses from the 1,104 women and 1,015 men who completed the survey (for a 74 percent response rate). For a complete description of the sample and sampling procedures, see http://www.knowledgenetworks.com; see also Lawless 2004b.

[13] The gender gap in the general population is of a similar size, although the proportion of individuals whose parents spoke to them about politics is much smaller (Knowledge Networks 2002). We discuss generational differences in patterns of political socialization later in this chapter.

[14] Richard L. Fox and Robert A. Schuhmann (2001) find role model effects within a sample of city managers. Women who occupied positions in city management were more likely than men to have had women mentors, even among family members.

I talked to my parents about becoming the first female Supreme Court judge. When Sandra Day O'Connor got the appointment, I remember thinking, 'Darn, I wanted that.'" Susan Minor, a political activist from Pennsylvania, also linked her interest in politics to her political childhood:

> My parents died when I was a teenager and I moved into my grandparents' house. My grandparents, unlike my parents, were very liberal and exposed me to an entirely different political philosophy than I had ever been exposed to before. I realized then that I might want to be in politics. From that point on, I've been very politically active.

Tom Harborside, a chief executive officer in Virginia, grew up in a very political household and ran for the student council in high school. These experiences triggered his thoughts of running for office as an adult. After he ran for class president, Mr. Harborside thought, "Maybe someday I'll run for president of the United States."

The regression results presented in Table 4.2 confirm the pattern we uncovered in our interviews: political discussions and exposure to politics in childhood significantly increase the propensity to consider running for office as an adult. We modeled whether a respondent ever considered running for office, supplementing our controls for the baseline correlates of political ambition (as discussed in Chapter 3) with indicators of a politicized upbringing. Sex remains a significant predictor of considering a candidacy, with women less likely than men to have considered running. But a politicized upbringing nearly doubles both women and men's likelihood of considering a run for office. A woman whose parents never suggested that she run for office and never talked about politics in the home has only a 0.36 probability of considering a candidacy. Frequent political discussions and regular parental encouragement to run for office in childhood increase a woman's likelihood of considering a candidacy to 0.68. If either parent ever ran for office, then a woman's probability of thinking about launching her own run for office in adulthood further increases to 0.76.[15] As the data presented in Table 4.1 make clear, however, women were less likely than men to grow up in such highly politicized homes.

[15] Unless otherwise noted, all predicted probabilities generated from logistic regression equations are based on setting the continuous variables to their means and dummy variables to their modes. The impact of a politicized upbringing on the likelihood of considering a run for office does not differ between women and men; interaction terms between the sex of the respondent and any of the politicized upbringing variables do not achieve statistical significance.

TABLE 4.2. *The Impact of a Politicized Upbringing on Considering a Candidacy (Logistic Regression Coefficients, Standard Errors, and Change in Probabilities)*

| | Coefficient (Standard Error) | Maximum Change in Probability (Percentage Points) |
|---|---|---|
| **Baseline Indicators** | | |
| Sex (female) | −.74 (.09)** | 18.1 |
| Age | −.03 (.00)** | 13.8 |
| Education | .12 (.04)** | 14.7 |
| Income | −.05 (.04) | − |
| Race (White) | .11 (.11) | − |
| Democrat | .04 (.10) | − |
| Republican | −.06 (.11) | − |
| Political interest | .20 (.03)** | 28.1 |
| Political participation | .32 (.02)** | 61.1 |
| Political knowledge | .14 (.05)** | 10.2 |
| Political efficacy | .01 (.04) | − |
| **Politicized Upbringing Indicators** | | |
| "Political" household | .22 (.04)** | 27.4 |
| Parent ran for office | .37 (.12)** | 8.1 |
| Ran for office as a student | .44 (.08)** | 10.5 |
| Constant | −3.19 (.44)** | |
| Pseudo-R$^2$ | .30 | |
| Percentage Correctly Predicted | 71.0 | |
| N | 3,157 | |

*Notes:* Results are based on the 2001 survey data. Maximum changes in probabilities are based on the logistic regression results. These probabilities were calculated by setting all continuous independent variables not under consideration to their means and dummy variables not under consideration to their modes. The change in probability reflects the independent effect a statistically significant variable exerts as we vary its value from its minimum to maximum (e.g., the change in probability for Sex [female] reflects the fact that a woman is 18.1 percentage points less likely than a man, all else equal, to consider running for office). For age, we varied the values from one standard deviation above to one standard deviation below the mean. Significance levels: $^{**}p < .01$; $^{*}p < .05$.

## Eligible Candidates' Family Structures and Roles

A great deal of women's political participation and activism throughout U.S. history can be linked to their family roles. As early as the women's suffrage revival in 1890, women relied on their distinct "private sphere" roles, as mothers and caretakers of the home, to justify their entry into politics. Susan B. Anthony and advocates of women's suffrage argued that women were the solution to the rampant government corruption and party machines and bosses that dominated late-nineteenth-century American politics. More specifically, women possessed the characteristics needed to take the corruption out of politics: benevolence, morality, self-lessness, and industry (DuBois 1987). Further, women's exclusion from public life meant that their partisan loyalties were not firm; they were less likely than men to be vulnerable to party bosses. In other words, women's service to their families and communities could also serve the public interest. The suffrage movement's affiliation with the temperance movement conformed to the notion that women and men occupy separate domains. Women bore witness to the trouble that liquor wrought in the private sphere and, accordingly, were well suited to encourage its prohibition.[16]

By the 1960s, the rallying cry for women's full equality and political integration focused on dismantling the gendered conceptual framework of private (in the home) and public (in politics and industry) spheres.[17] Political activists, such as Betty Friedan, and feminist theorists, such as Carole Pateman and Susan Moller Okin, argued that the dichotomy itself was false.[18] As Estelle Freedman (2002, 327) summarizes, "The Western social contract, in which men became citizens, rested upon an unstated sexual contract, in which women served the interests of men." The notion of the autonomous male, free to engage the public world, failed to recognize that men were not independent. Rather, their public sphere entry and success relied on women's familial care. Advocates of women's rights, therefore, began to argue that the private realm of women's lives must be made part of the public discourse. In effect, these efforts aimed to break down the dichotomy and integrate private sphere issues, like child care and domestic abuse, into public sphere policy debates.

---

[16] For a detailed history of women's political involvement in U.S. history, see Evans 1997. For a discussion of the manner in which women's adherence to their private sphere roles served as an impetus for their participation in the temperance, moral reform, antislavery, and women's rights movements, see Alexander 1988; Ginzberg 1986.

[17] Ethel Klein (1984) brings to our attention the fact that many married women worked outside of the home in the late 1940s and 1950s. This trend, however, was not accompanied by much reflection about the direction society should take regarding women's proper place.

[18] Betty Friedan's book *The Feminine Mystique* burst onto the scene in 1963 and provided the popular impetus for questioning the division of household labor. Carole Pateman (1988) and Susan Moller Okin (1989) provided pathbreaking theoretical conceptualizations of the relationship between traditional family roles and the patriarchal institutions of the family and the household.

The extent to which traditional family structures and roles continue to affect women's inclusion in public life is not entirely evident. Many of the barriers to women's advancement in formerly male fields are drastically changing, as identified in Chapter 2. Correspondingly, the conception of a rigid set of sex roles has dissipated with the increasing number of two-career families (Coltrane 2000). Yet surveys of two-income households continue to find that women spend twice as many hours as men working on household tasks, such as cleaning and laundry. Married women also continue to perform significantly more of the cooking and child care than do their spouses, even when they are the primary breadwinners in a family.[19]

When women do enter the public sphere, they often face what scholar Kathleen Hall Jamieson calls the "double bind." She explains that "the history of western culture is riddled with evidence of traps for women that have forcefully curtailed their options" (Jamieson 1995, 4). Women who venture out of the "proper sphere" often find themselves in a catch-22: if they achieve professional success, then they have likely neglected their "womanly" duties; if they fail professionally, then they were wrong to attempt entering the public domain in the first place. Liane Sorenson, the president of the Women's Legislative Network of the National Conference of State Legislatures and a member of the Delaware State Senate, summarized the implications of the double bind: "If a male lawmaker leaves a meeting to watch his son play soccer, everyone says he's a wonderful father. But if a woman does it, you'll hear she's not managing her responsibilities."[20] The essence of the bind is that professional women are constantly judged not only by how they manage their careers, but also by how well they perform the duties of a wife and mother. To be successful public citizens, women must also be successful private citizens. Thus, it is not surprising that political scientist Sue Thomas (2002) finds that female state legislators continue to be primarily responsible for housework and child care even after they are elected to public office.

Navigating these dual roles has proved difficult for many women who choose to enter public life, including those who have been quite successful. Congresswoman Ileana Ros-Lehtinen (R-FL), for instance, is the ranking

[19] For evidence of the gendered division of household labor and child-care responsibilities over the course of the past twenty years, see McGlen et al. 2005; Burns, Schlozman, and Verba 2001; Galinsky and Bond 1996; Apter 1993; Blumstein and Schwartz 1991; Hochschild 1989.

[20] Sonji Jacobs, "Politicians Who Are Moms Must Juggle Priorities," *Atlanta Journal-Constitution*, May 16, 2004, 1D.

member of the House Foreign Affairs Committee. But acquiring seniority and her leadership position in Congress involved significant trade-offs, both personal and professional:

> It's difficult to balance it all. We are fed that myth that you can have it all, as a "Wonder Woman." . . . I found that you can't be the best mom and the best congressperson. You try to strike a balance. But you can't do 100 percent. . . . You keep the balls in the air, and you hope for the best. There is great guilt and angst as to what is the proper way.[21]

Congresswoman Debbie Wasserman-Schultz (D-FL) commiserates, explaining the difficulty of working in Washington while her husband stays with their three children in Florida: "It feels like someone's ripping my heart out. . . . No matter how good your spouse is, kids want their mom when they're sick."[22] A survey of corporate women found that the majority are also not satisfied with their ability to handle the balancing act. Because of difficulty fulfilling both their professional and their familial roles, more than 60 percent opted out of their high-level careers, either to take off several years to raise a family or to pursue nonprofit or foundation work, which is more "family friendly."[23] The media often reinforce the notion that leaving a high-level career is the appropriate way for women to deal with their dual roles. Laura Schlessinger, who hosts the fourth most popular talk radio program in the United States, urges her more than 7 million listeners each week, most of whom are women, to quit their jobs and stay at home with their children.[24]

---

[21]  Richard E. Cohen, "Member Moms," *National Journal*, April 6, 2007.
[22]  Lyndsey Layton, "Mom's in the House, with Kids at Home: For Congresswomen with Young Children, a Tough Balance," *Washington Post*, July 19, 2007, A01.
[23]  Lisa McKenzie, "Are Women Opting Out of Corporate Careers?" *PR Web Wire Service*, http://www.emediawire.com/releases/2004/6/prweb130800.htm (August 13, 2004).
[24]  "The 100 Most Important Talk Show Hosts in America," *Talkers Magazine*, July/August 2009. Laura Schlessinger's (2009) book, *In Praise of Stay-at-Home Moms*, for example, encourages women to leave the workforce not only because it benefits their children, but also because it strengthens women's marriages. Talk radio's antifeminist sentiment transcends Laura Schlessinger. According to a 2001 analysis by the Women's International News Gathering Service, "Concerned Women for America's" twenty-seven minute syndicated radio program airs on ninety-seven stations across the country six days a week. Phyllis Schlafly's three-minute commentaries are syndicated on more than four hundred radio stations daily. Rush Limbaugh airs live three hours a day on more than 575 AM radio stations. And Focus on the Family offers eighteen different regular radio programs (varying from two minutes to two hours in length) that air on approximately five hundred stations and are present in every state. All of these programs and radio pundits avidly reinforce the desirability of traditional family roles with women as the primary caretakers of the home and the children. For more, see *Talkers Magazine Online*'s "Talk Radio Research Project, Part II," http://www.talkers.com/talkaud.html.

TABLE 4.3. *Eligible Candidates' Current Family Structures and Responsibilities*

|  | Women | Men |
|---|---|---|
| **Marital Status** | | |
| Single | 15%** | 8% |
| Married or living with partner | 70** | 86 |
| Separated or divorced | 12** | 6 |
| **Parental Status** | | |
| Have children | 66** | 84 |
| Children living at home | 38** | 49 |
| Children under age 6 living at home | 14 | 15 |
| **Household Responsibilities** | | |
| Responsible for majority of household tasks | 48** | 4 |
| Equal division of labor | 40** | 33 |
| Spouse/partner responsible for majority of household tasks | 11** | 61 |
| **Child-Care Responsibilities** | | |
| Responsible for majority of child care | 42** | 4 |
| Equal division of child care | 25** | 26 |
| Spouse/partner responsible for majority of child care | 6** | 46 |
| N | 1,659 | 1,875 |

*Notes:* Results are based on the 2001 survey data. Household responsibilities figures are based on the subsample of respondents who are married or living with a partner. Child-care arrangements figures are based on the subsample of respondents who have children (e.g., numbers do not total 100 percent because 26 percent of women and 24 percent of men had grown children, live-in help, or day-care providers). Significance levels of chi-square test comparing women and men: ** p < .01.

The double bind clearly transcends into the candidate eligibility pool and serves as a dilemma that women who are well positioned to run for public office today must reconcile. The top portion of Table 4.3 reveals that women with professional careers continue to be significantly more likely than men not to have traditional family arrangements. Women are about twice as likely as men to be single; they are also almost twice as likely to be separated or divorced. Further, women are nearly 20 percent less likely than men to have children.[25] There are no gender differences in these components of family structures within the general population (Knowledge Networks 2002).

Eligible women candidates' family structures might reflect that being a wife or mother can serve as an impediment to professional achievement,

[25] With data from the 1970s, Susan J. Carroll and Wendy Strimling (1983) and Marcia Manning Lee (1976) uncover similar gender differences in candidates and legislators' family structures. The past three decades, therefore, have seen little change in the sociodemographic attributes of well-situated eligible candidates.

a goal that women in the sample already attained. Lori Corrigan, who has practiced law in New York for more than twenty years, recognized this pattern among women associates in her firm: "The child thing is still a big issue for women and probably always will be. We have just lost three dynamite young [women] associates because they had to take time out to have children. Men never, in my experience, have left for child-care duties." Ms. Corrigan, a very successful litigator, went on to note that she and her husband decided that if she wanted to be a "go-getter as a lawyer," then they just could not have children: "It was a painful decision, but we decided that my career was more important." Julia Finch, an attorney with broad experience in her community, echoed this sentiment: "Of the top five women attorneys in my city, only two are married, and only one has a child. That can't be a coincidence." Put somewhat differently by Wilma Morales, the vice president of marketing for a large company based in Chicago:

> Women are less willing to compromise on family and are thus willing to sacrifice professionally. Men are not forced to choose. If you choose to cut back at work to take care of kids, you are looked down upon, but especially if you're men. Women are expected to take care of the kids, men aren't.

The gendered demands and expectations of these professions may make women in the candidate eligibility pool less likely than men to enter into traditional family arrangements (see also Alejano-Steele 1997).

Those women who are married and who do have children, however, tend to exhibit traditional gender-role orientations. We asked respondents whether they or their partners were responsible for the majority of household tasks and child care. The bottom half of Table 4.3 reveals a gendered division of labor. In families where both adults are working (generally in high-level careers), women are twelve times more likely than men to bear responsibility for the majority of household tasks and about ten times more likely to be the primary child-care provider. These differences in family responsibilities are not merely a matter of gendered perceptions. Both sexes fully recognize this organization of labor. More than 60 percent of men acknowledge that their spouses are responsible for a majority of household tasks, whereas fewer than 5 percent of women make the same claim. Regardless of the advances women have made in entering the workforce and achieving professional success, both women and men identify the prevalence of traditional household roles and responsibilities.

Although both the men and the women with whom we spoke agree that traditional gender roles define their households, they offer different explanations for the division of labor. Don Garcia, a business owner from the Midwest, epitomized the thoughts of many of the men interviewed for this study when he stated simply: "Women prefer to take care of the family." Stephen Gilmour, a lawyer from Washington, concurred, adding that "women have stronger bonds with young children and feel the pull to be at home. We love our kids but it is not the same." Many men contend that women choose to take on the majority of the household and child-care responsibilities not only because they excel at these tasks, but also because, as several men noted, it feels "natural" for them.

A number of the women also referenced women's different "natures" and the strong pull to be a "stay-at-home mom." A typical sentiment was expressed by Beth Peltz, a state director for a national public interest group:

> There's a nurturing quality that women have and they have a natural incli-nation to take over household and childcare tasks. My husband always helps and participates, but I'm very fortunate. There's just a division and this is the way it is. Women have survived this long doing two jobs. They can keep doing it. That's not to say it's fair. But it is life.

Genevieve Moran cited an example of a woman she perceived as willing to relinquish her public role to her male partner. The San Francisco attorney recounted:

> A female associate in my firm just gave notice – she wants to take a three- to four-year leave of absence to take care of her children.... The interesting thing is that her husband is a self-employed plumber who hasn't worked in about three years. The kids were in day care even though he was home all day. And even more surprising is that the shift is coming about because he wants to get his business going again.

But the pervasive subtext of the comments by women respondents sug-gests that, in most cases, the traditional roles that women take on are so ingrained that the behaviors are programmed. Taking on a greater pro-portion of the household work and child-care duties, in essence, becomes part of the gendered psyche. As Sarah Gibson, a lawyer from Ohio, com-mented, "Women still aren't raised to assume responsibility. Women are supposed to get married and are socialized into being second-class citizens who give all their power to the men in their lives. It's sickening, and we don't realize it happens still, but it does." In a moment of self-reflection,

Teri Morse, a professor of English, bemoaned the fact that she succumbs to the same pattern:

> You know, we don't even realize that we're doing it. For instance, my son, who is a college senior, is bringing a bunch of his friends home for the weekend to go to a concert. He tells me not to worry about cooking. What have I done? I've spent the last four days baking cookies and cakes, buying food, cooking everything imaginable in preparation for their visit. He tells me that the house is already clean and, besides, they live in a disgusting fraternity house. Still, I've swept and polished every floor, vacuumed every carpet and cleaned every cabinet. We take this upon ourselves because it's what our mothers did. And they did it because their mothers did it, too.

The results presented in Table 4.3, coupled with the qualitative responses from the respondents, culminate to reveal that traditional family structures and roles are still entrenched, even among highly educated professional citizens. Many women may have overcome some of the barriers associated with patterns of traditional gender socialization by virtue of attaining the utmost levels of professional success in often male-dominated fields. But many of these women have not married, have not had children, or have been forced to reconcile their careers with their family responsibilities, something their male counterparts have generally not been required to do.

### Wife, Mother, and Candidate?
### Family Roles as Impediments to Political Ambition

Research finds that married people are more likely to participate politically (e.g., Wolfinger and Wolfinger 2008; Verba, Schlozman, and Brady 1995). But studies also indicate that, at least for women, the same traditional family structures that spur political participation might actually detract from the likelihood of pursuing and maintaining a political career. Political scientists Margaret Conway, Gertrude Steuernagel, and David Ahern (2004) identify the sociocultural expectation that women are the primary caretakers of children as a leading reason for the exclusion of women from elite level politics (see also Carroll 1989).

Many women who have served as elected officials have the same impression. As former Congresswoman Pat Schroeder (1999, 35) observes, women first elected to Congress in the 1970s followed two career tracks:

> [Congressional service] was either a capstone at the end of a career for those with grown children, or it *was* the career for unmarried or childless

women. You could have a career or a family, or maybe a career *after* your family was grown. But rearing a family while in Congress was unheard of.

Three decades later, young children continue to impede women office-holders' political careers. Georgia State Representative Stephanie Stuckey Benfield, for example, entered politics in 1998, several years before she was married or a parent. Now a seasoned politician, she recently engaged in a door-to-door reelection campaign while pushing her twenty-two-month-old son in a stroller. She explains, however, that she would never have "taken on such a tremendous task as running for office the first time with a husband and a young child."[26] Indeed, Susan Molinari (R-NY) was a rising star in the Republican Party when she announced her decision to leave the U.S. House of Representatives in 1996. She accepted a position as an anchor of a CBS news program so that she could spend more time with her daughter, Ruby.[27] When she was first elected in 1990, Ms. Molinari had no children. Summarized by Congresswoman Jane Harman, "The schedule is the pits. There is absolutely no way to be a full-time parent and serve in Congress."[28]

The gendered division of labor we uncovered among our sample of the candidate eligibility pool is important not only because it demonstrates that women and men who are similarly situated professionally are not similarly situated at home, but also because those disparities might hinder women's freedom to consider running for office. Virginia Sapiro (1982), in a study of national party delegates, found that the presence of children still at home made women less likely than men to express interest in seeking office. Among eligible candidates in New York, we found that traditional family structures somewhat decreased women's likelihood of running for office as well (Fox and Lawless 2003).[29]

Multivariate analysis provides a starting point for assessing the degree to which traditional family structures and roles account for the gender gap in political ambition. Table 4.4 replicates our baseline model of considering a candidacy (see Table 3.4), but also includes gauges of family

[26] Ibid.
[27] "Molinari to Resign from Congress for CBS," *AllPolitics*, May 28, 1997.
[28] Dana Wilkie, "Harman, Prototypical Politicians of the 90s, Juggles Family, Career." *Copley News Service*, April 9, 1998.
[29] Conversely, Barbara Burt-Way and Rita Mae Kelly (1992), in a study of Arizona legislators, found that the presence of children in the home did not exert a differential impact on women and men's interest in pursuing higher office. Of course, in their study, all of the respondents already held elective office and, therefore, already had reconciled political ambition with their child-care arrangements.

TABLE 4.4. *The Impact of Family Structures and Responsibilities on
Considering a Candidacy (Logistic Regression Coefficients and
Standard Errors)*

|  | Coefficient (Standard Error) |
| --- | --- |
| Sex (female) | −.74** (.10) |
| Married | .12 (.14) |
| Children | −.08 (.13) |
| Children under age 6 living at home | .06 (.14) |
| Responsible for majority of household tasks | −.03 (.09) |
| Responsible for majority of child care | .09 (.15) |
| Constant | −2.05** (.39) |
| Pseudo-R$^2$ | −.27 |
| Percentage Correctly Predicted | 69.3 |
| N | 3,082 |

*Notes:* Results are based on the 2001 survey data. The regression equation controls for
the baseline correlates of political ambition, as well as age. Significance levels: ** $p < .01$.

structures and responsibilities. The regression results indicate that family
dynamics are not statistically significant predictors of considering a run
for office. This result holds when we interact the sex of the respondent
with the family structure and role variables.

From a statistical standpoint, the fact that women's disproportionate
levels of household and familial responsibilities do not dramatically affect
whether they have ever considered running for office is not altogether
surprising. Our empirical measures and survey questions may not be sufficiently subtle to capture the full effects of family dynamics. The women
we surveyed are all educated citizens who operate professionally in the
public sphere. It is plausible to posit that women were as likely as men
to have considered running for office in the early stages of their careers,
well before they assumed many household and childcare responsibilities.

Moreover, the data indicate that women with young children are less
likely to volunteer for candidates, attend political meetings, and serve on
boards. The negative correlation between parental status and political
participation, therefore, may obscure the independent effect that household and family responsibilities exert on political ambition. In other
words, because our baseline model takes into account political participation, it may also speak to the freedom – or lack thereof – with which
women with young children can pursue a political career.[30]

---

[30] Another possible explanation for the seemingly counterintuitive finding that traditional
family roles do not predict political ambition is that women and men may have different
interpretations of what it means to consider a candidacy.

Alternatively, we should consider the possibility that the presence of children and greater household burdens, in and of themselves, do not diminish eligible women candidates' thoughts of running for office. The second-wave survey data allow us to examine this proposition empirically and delve more deeply into the extent to which family roles and responsibilities affect women and men's political ambition. On both surveys, we included a question about prospective interest in running for office, so as to gauge respondents' attitudes about the likelihood of running at some point in the future (Chapter 7 includes a detailed discussion of these data). Thus, we can compare eligible candidates' responses across the two waves of the study, taking into account whether the women and men experienced shifts in marital and parental status.

Turning first to changes in marital status, women are more inclined than men to lose ambition to run for office after they get married. Of the sixty-four women and seventy-four men who entered marriages or civil unions between 2001 and 2008, 41 percent of women, compared to 32 percent of men, expressed less interest in running for office than they had in 2001. Sixteen percent of women, compared to 23 percent of men, reported heightened levels of interest in running for office (gender differences significant at p < .01).

For the most part, however, changes in family structures, and the concomitant shifts in family roles and responsibilities, do not systematically shift respondents' levels of political ambition. Of the 191 respondents who had or adopted a child between the two waves of the study, for example, 15 percent of women and 15 percent of men gained interest in running for office. Fifteen percent of women and 17 percent of men with new children lost ambition over the seven-year interval. And 70 percent of women and 69 percent of men reported no change in interest in running for office. Similar patterns emerge when we turn to other changes in parental status. For the 163 respondents who had a child younger than the age of six living at home in 2001 but no longer did in 2008, for instance, women and men were equally likely to gain and lose political ambition. The same is true for the respondents whose children moved out of the house between the two waves of the study. These findings suggest that, once family structures and roles exist, changes to traditional family dynamics do not instantly (or necessarily) unburden women or provide them with more freedom to think about pursuing elective office.

The results presented in Table 4.4 reveal the complexity and limitations of employing quantitative measures to gauge the effects traditional family role orientations exert on political ambition. After all, even if family structures and arrangements do not preclude women from thinking about a full range of lifetime career options and possibilities, the circumstances under which such thoughts cross eligible candidates' minds might differ for women and men. As one gender politics scholar so aptly characterized political ambition in the contemporary environment, "Women may now think about running for office, but they probably think about it while they are making the bed."[31]

Indeed, the qualitative evidence from the interviews we conducted sheds substantial light on the manner in which family structures and responsibilities affect candidate emergence. Of the one hundred women we interviewed, sixty-five stated that children made seeking office a much more difficult endeavor for women than for men. In the one hundred interviews with men, only three respondents raised the issue of children serving as an impediment to running for office. And one of the three was Keith Dillman, a businessman from Pennsylvania who had already run for elective office and served on the city council. At that point, he realized he wanted to spend more time with his children. For the most part, men do not express concerns about reconciling their careers or family roles with the decision to run for office.

For many women who "consider" running for office, their family roles and responsibilities make the process very different from that of their male counterparts. Loretta Jenkins, who is both a mother and a business owner, questioned how many barriers women could be expected to face: "Women tend to be responsible not only for the family but also increasingly as the primary breadwinner. Taking on yet another role of being in the political arena, while breaking down the cultural norm at the same time is even more difficult. How much can you possibly ask?" Tracy Ball, the director of a state environmental organization, wondered:

> How can women really expect to be able to do it all? I don't understand this. I am so tired after spending a day in the office then coming home to take care of whining, sniffling kids and having to cook dinner. I can't even imagine going to a town council meeting or a PTA meeting, never mind running a campaign for state senate.

Several of the women with whom we spoke elaborated specifically on the different weight that women and men place on children when considering entering the electoral arena. Michelle Arnold, a political science professor from Iowa, believes that "women consider running, but can't get involved until their children are older. Men aren't husbands and

---

[31] We thank Georgia Duerst-Lahti for this comment.

fathers before they are career people. Women are wives and mothers first, elected officials, lawyers, professors, whatever, second." Barbara Kim, a New York executive, noted that families are more important to women than they are to men:

> Women are busier than men, especially professional women, because once we get home from work, we have a whole second shift to do. The house-work, taking care of the children. And we're more attached to our families, so the time we do have, we want to spend with our spouses and chil-dren.... For men, there are fewer outside of the job responsibilities and family time is just not as important.

Massachusetts attorney Denise Zauderer offered a similar assessment:

> A lot of women want to have it all, but we're realistic to know that we can't have it all at once. There's a season for everything. You establish your career, then your family, then you try to merge the two. Then, when family stuff is out of the way, you can get involved in your community, which is where politics fits in. The mommy and career mix don't allow for much energy beyond that. So, you either wait until you retire, or until your children are grown.

In fact, several women in the sample described a similar path for political involvement. Dominique Beaulieu assessed her political future this way:

> When I was single, I often worked on campaigns, and was much more politically active. With young kids, this whole side of me has been put on hold. I'd like to resume working in politics when the kids are older. Right now, I can only handle being a lawyer and a mother.

Jan Henderson, a public school administrator in Kansas, mentioned a long-term plan to run for the state legislature, but she noted, "I am a mom, so I have to wait until my girls are grown. They range in age from six to sixteen." Ms. Henderson then elaborated on how she planned to pursue her political ambition:

> I can retire when I'm fifty-three, which is still young enough and energetic enough to launch a sort of second career, which could be politics.... And the timing coincides nicely with the ages of my children. I mean, they'll be old enough where they won't need me at home as much and they could probably deal with me campaigning.

Lilly Bates, a lawyer from the Midwest, explained that her plan to run for office is contingent on her ability to retire early:

> [Running for office] is something I would seriously consider if I am able to retire in my late fifties and pursue politics as almost a second career. I am

forty-one, a partner in my own law firm, and have three small children –
ages four, five, and six. There is no way I could run now. School board or
city council might seem like a good idea in fifteen or twenty years, though.

In many of these examples, family roles and responsibilities do not preclude women from considering a candidacy. But these politically ambitious women mention the possibility of entering politics as an option only
after their child-care duties abate. Substantially delaying their entrance
into the political arena makes it less likely that they will be able to climb
very high on the political career ladder.

Eligible candidates' personal and family environments reinforce
women's dual roles and hinder their entry into the public sphere. As illustrated in Figure 4.1, women are less likely than men to exist in an environment that encourages entry into the political arena. Women in all four
eligibility pool professions are less likely than men to receive encouragement to run for office from a spouse or partner, family member, or friend.

The effect of a supportive personal environment cannot be overstated.
If we add to the baseline model that predicts who considers running
for office a measure of whether the respondent ever received personal
encouragement or a suggestion to run, then the probability of considering
a candidacy increases by approximately 45 percentage points. For many
women and men we interviewed, this type of personal support would
serve as a prerequisite to considering entering politics. Mona Gregory,
a college professor from Louisiana, attributed her ongoing interest in
seeking elective office to support from her inner circle: "I wouldn't be able
to do anything like run without the backing of my husband and friends."
Tom Beard, an attorney from Oregon, noted that the only reason he has
ever considered running for office is because his spouse always pushes
him to "run for something." Alabama businessman Edwin Thompson,
who actually ran for office, also identified the importance of personal
sources of encouragement:

> When I first ran for the school board my kids were in junior high. I knew
> a lot of people on the school board; many of them brought their kids
> swimming at the same country club. That's ultimately how I was persuaded
> to run. It wasn't about parties or money, but about friends. About knowing
> that they thought it was a good idea for me to run, knowing that they'd
> support me through the process.

Women's lower likelihood of receiving the suggestion to run for office
from a personal source, therefore, significantly depresses their political
ambition and exacerbates the gender gap in considering a candidacy.
The lack of support from family members and friends corroborates many

FIGURE 4.1. Support for a Political Candidacy from a Spouse or Partner, Family Member, or Friend.

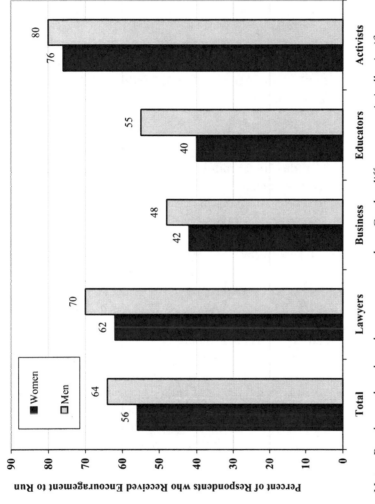

*Notes:* Results are based on the 2001 survey data. Gender differences statistically significant at p < .01 for the total sample, lawyers, and educators. Sample sizes: for women, N = 1,632; for men, N = 1,846.

women's own notions that a political candidacy is just not possible given their professional and personal obligations.

### Are Times Changing? Generational Differences in Political Ambition

Individuals who were socialized in political households and who do not have to reconcile family life and public life have a less complex calculus to face when considering whether to enter politics. Women are disadvantaged on both of these fronts. All of our analysis about traditional family structures and roles, however, considers the entire pool of eligible candidates. With the dramatic cultural shifts and evolving attitudes toward women in politics, we would certainly expect some generational differences.

When we focus on the division of household labor, older respondents are more likely to come from traditional households and to perpetuate these patterns in their own homes. Whereas 82 percent of women and 83 percent of men in the 40–59 and over-60 cohorts grew up in households where the father was the primary breadwinner and the mother was the primary caretaker of the home, only 73 percent of respondents in the under-40 cohort report such a pattern.[32] We see a similar generational change in current divisions of household labor. Forty-one percent of women in the over-60 cohort state that they are responsible for the majority of the household tasks, compared to 35 percent of women in the 40–59 cohort and 31 percent of women in the under-40 age cohort. Younger generations were raised in a society and in households that held greater expectations for gender equality.

Although it is certainly important to note that, among younger generations, there is a move, albeit a slow one, toward a more egalitarian distribution of household labor and child-care responsibilities, it is also necessary to temper this finding. A recent national survey of twenty-five- to thirty-five-year-olds found that three-quarters of both women and men sought a loving family as their top priority. But 60 percent of men said that their jobs were more important than household and child-care responsibilities; women contended that work and home responsibilities were equally important.[33]

---

[32] We experimented with a number of different age divisions. The results hold regardless of the manner in which we divide age cohorts.

[33] Ann McFeatters, "Powerful Women in Washington Ask: Can We Have It All?" *Post-Gazette National Bureau*, May 5, 2002.

Turning to more specific political socialization via the family unit, we also see generational changes. The gender gap in households where parents spoke to their children about politics withers away entirely among members of the under-40 cohort; 72 percent of women and 71 percent of men in this youngest age group reported having discussed politics in their households when they were children. The younger the respondent, the more likely it was that he or she received parental encouragement to run for office as well. In terms of parental encouragement to run for office, though, a gender gap across generations advantages men by approximately 7 percentage points. Fifty-two percent of men in the under-40 cohort, compared to 45 percent of women, received parental encouragement to run for office (difference significant at p < .01).[34]

These changes over time lead to the expectation that women and men of the younger generations will express more comparable levels of political ambition than women and men of the older generations. Although we expect a smaller gender gap in ambition within younger generations, baseline levels of ambition should be higher among older respondents. The older an individual is, the more likely it is that, over the course of his or her lifetime, running for office crossed his or her mind. The results presented in Table 4.5 lend no support to our gender gap expectation. Older women and men are more likely than younger women and men ever to have considered running for office, but the largest gender gap in political ambition is among the youngest age group. Men in the under-40 cohort are more than 40 percent more likely than women in the under-40 cohort ever to have considered running for office. Among the under-40 age cohort, men are also roughly three times more likely than women to say they have "seriously" thought about launching a political career and five times more likely than women to have discussed running for office with party leaders.[35]

Not only does the under-40 age cohort exhibit the largest gender gap in political ambition, but the gender gap in political ambition also actually

---

[34] These generational differences might also reflect a selection effect. Individuals who are sufficiently successful and visible in their careers at a relatively young age to fall into our candidate eligibility pool may have had parents who encouraged them not only to consider politics, but also to achieve other professional goals.

[35] Women's attitudes toward running for office may evolve across the life cycle. If we had been able to survey women and men in the over-60 cohort when they were in the under-40 cohort, then perhaps we would have found a substantially greater gender gap than the one we uncovered in the current under-40 age cohort. Such findings, however, would not detract from the dramatic ambition gap between young women and men.

TABLE 4.5. *Eligible Candidates' Interest in Running for Office, across Generations*

|  | Percentage Who Have Considered Running for Any Political Office | |
|---|---|---|
|  | Women | Men |
| Under age 40 | 45%** | 64% |
| Ages 40–59 | 40** | 58 |
| Ages 60 and over | 49* | 60 |
| N | 1,605 | 1,838 |

*Notes:* Results are based on the 2001 survey data. Significance levels of chi-square test comparing women and men: ** p < .01; * p < .05.

grew among this cohort between the two waves of the study. Turning once again to the prospective interest in running for office question that appeared on both the 2001 and 2008 surveys, the data indicate that 29 percent of women compared to 18 percent of men who were in the under-40 cohort at the time of the first survey reported lower levels of interest in running for office in 2008 than they did in 2001 (significant at p < .01). Women in the two older age cohorts were no more likely than their male counterparts to report decreases in political ambition across the two waves of the study.

Prospects for women's representation are further dampened by the results of a national survey of college students. As recently as 2003, a significant gender gap in political ambition existed among eighteen- to twenty-four-year-olds. Male and female undergraduates are roughly equally likely to participate politically, but women are 40 percent less likely than men to imagine running for office in the future (see Table 4.6).[36]

Consistent with these results, the evidence we uncovered throughout the course of our interviews reflects that women of all generations identify the burdens that confront women who are well positioned to pursue political careers. Comments by three women from three generations illustrate this point nicely. Thirty-four-year-old Connecticut lawyer Cheryl Perry offered a succinct assessment of the dilemma women face: "Political office seems like it's a twenty-four-seven job. That just isn't possible for a working mom." Her remarks sound very similar to those of Margie Wallace, a fifty-five-year-old high school principal from Georgia: "There are many more duties and responsibilities placed on women in society

---

[36] We thank David King for making these data available.

TABLE 4.6. *College Students' Political Activism and Attitudes toward Running for Office*

|  | Women | Men |
|---|---|---|
| **Prior Levels of Political Activism and Participation** | | |
| Registered to vote | 67%* | 71% |
| Volunteered on a political campaign | 12 | 12 |
| Attended a political rally or demonstration | 24* | 29 |
| Signed a petition or boycotted a product | 32 | 32 |
| **Future Interest in Entering the Political Arena** | | |
| Considers running for office a possible career path | 16** | 27 |
| N | 650 | 552 |

*Notes:* Number of cases varies slightly as some respondents omitted answers to some questions. Significance levels of chi-square test comparing women and men: ** p < .01; * p < .05. Data based on David King's national survey of college undergraduates, conducted September 3–12, 2003.

and women are constantly stretched. I would like to think that this is evolving now that most families are two income households, but I don't think that it is really." Helen Nelson, a seventy-year-old retired business-woman from Florida, offered a comparable assessment: "Not much has changed regarding perceptions of the 'woman's place.' People still think that a woman should be in the home raising a family." Many women we interviewed, across generations, mentioned cultural evolution, only to conclude that society had not fully transformed its gender role expectations. The irony of these assessments is that many of the women making these statements have broken down the barriers they identify as obstacles.

## Conclusion

The degree to which traditional upbringings and family roles depress women's likelihood of considering running for office is complicated. Politicized upbringings positively influence political ambition, so women are somewhat disadvantaged because they are less likely than men to have received encouragement to run for office or to have engaged in political discussions with their parents. The effects of current family structures and roles on political ambition are subtler. Somewhat surprisingly, our empirical measures of family structures and responsibilities do not predict political ambition. Yet strong qualitative evidence suggests that women's roles as the primary caretakers of the children and the household complicate their likelihood of considering a run for public office. Further, empirical evidence indicates that women are less likely than men to receive the suggestion to run from those who know them the best – their spouses and partners, family members, and friends – perhaps a result of their being perceived as too busy, extended, or involved on the home front.

What clearly emerges from this analysis is the fact that women, across all generations, face a more complex set of choices. It is irrefutable that, unlike men, women continue to confront the difficulty of reconciling their careers and their families. The consequences of this double bind – even in 2008 – remain a force in the lives of many professional women, often leaving them unsatisfied. Maggie Carter, a lawyer with broad experience working in the public and private sectors, remarked, "I don't know any professional women who are happy with the choices that they have made.... Women are constantly pulled in different directions." Our findings suggest that we remain in a period where women must continue to disentangle work and family life. As a result, for many women in the pool of eligible candidates, entering the electoral arena would simply be a third job, which is quite unappealing because they already have two.

# 5

# Gender, Party, and Political Recruitment

Following the 1989 abduction of her eleven-year-old son, Patty Wetterling created the Jacob Wetterling Foundation, a national organization that focuses on missing children, child abduction, and sex abuse. Through her work at the foundation, Ms. Wetterling successfully advocated for the national AMBER alert system and was instrumental in passing federal legislation that required states to implement registries of individuals who commit crimes against children.[1] Given Ms. Wetterling's policy background and reputation for working well with people on both sides of the political aisle, Democrats heavily recruited her to run for Congress when their presumed candidate withdrew from the 2004 race in Minnesota's sixth congressional district. Until she was approached by party officials to run for the seat, Ms. Wetterling commented that she had never "really seriously considered [running]" at all.[2] The Democrats' recruitment efforts propelled her into the race.[3]

Recruitment by the Democratic Party also paved the way for Tammy Duckworth's decision to run for Congress in 2006. The previous year, U.S. Senator Dick Durbin (D-IL) invited wounded Illinois veterans to

---

[1] Tom Schenck, "Wetterling Foundation Ponders Its Future in a Political World," *Minnesota Public Radio*, March 10, 2006.

[2] Greg Gordon, "Wetterling Sets Her Sights on House Seat; Experts Say She Is a Long Shot against Incumbent Kennedy," *Star Tribune (MN)*, April 27, 2004, 1A.

[3] Ms. Wetterling lost her 2004 race against incumbent Mark Kennedy by an 8 percent margin (she garnered 46 percent of the vote; Kennedy received 54 percent). After coming up short in her 2004 bid, Ms. Wetterling was recruited and ran again in 2006, this time facing Michelle Bachmann in an open-seat contest. The outcome for Wetterling was the same (Bachmann won the general election by an 8 point margin).

the State of the Union address. Ms. Duckworth, who had recently lost both legs in combat in Iraq, attended as one of the honored guests. A few months later, when she earned a promotion to major, she once again found herself face-to-face with Senator Durbin; Duckworth's new responsibilities involved advocating on behalf of military families and testifying before Congress about military health care. Amid the increasingly unpopular Iraq war, and in an attempt to refute the notion that Democrats were "soft" on national security, the party sought to convince veterans to enter U.S. House races in traditionally Republican districts (Bendavid 2007). So, Senator Durbin targeted Ms. Duckworth, who had never before considered a career in elective office. Within two months, Duckworth found herself on the campaign trail, often accompanied by Democratic heavy hitters, such as Rahm Emanuel and Barack Obama.[4]

Party recruitment is often important even for women with political backgrounds and who operate in political circles. Brought up in a political home, U.S. House Speaker Nancy Pelosi (D-CA), for instance, became a Democratic activist at an early age. She worked for California Governor Jerry Brown's 1976 presidential campaign and served as the party chairwoman for northern California. Remarkably, Ms. Pelosi did not consider entering the political arena as a candidate, herself, until Congresswoman Sala Burton, who was dying of cancer, urged Ms. Pelosi to run. She ran for Burton's House seat in 1988 and has represented the San Francisco Bay Area ever since.[5]

As the stories of Patty Wetterling, Tammy Duckworth, and Nancy Pelosi demonstrate, encouragement by party officials and political elites is critical in the candidate emergence process. Moreover – as suggested by the Democratic Party affiliation of each of the women we mentioned – there is a widening party gap in the number of women who seek and hold elective office. This chapter focuses on the intersection of gender, party, and political recruitment among eligible candidates. First, we examine eligible candidates' partisanship and political ideology. Women are more likely than men to hold liberal policy preferences and affiliate as Democrats. Party affiliation, however, does not predict eligible candidates' levels of political ambition. Women of all political parties are

---

4  Peter Slevin, "After War Injury, an Iraq Vet Takes on Politics," *Washington Post*, February 19, 2006, A01. Duckworth won a competitive Democratic primary against Christine Cegelis by a 4 percent margin, but lost the general election to Peter Roskam by 2 percentage points.

5  Dana Wilkie, "From Political Roots to Political Leader, Pelosi Is the Real Thing," *Copley News Service*, November 13, 2002.

less likely than ~~men to consider running~~ for office. Second, we turn to the role political parties play in encouraging eligible candidates to seek public office. Regardless of party affiliation, women are significantly less likely than men to report receiving encouragement to run for office from party leaders, elected officials, and political activists. A series of new questions from the 2008 survey allows us to document women's lesser likelihood to be recruited often and by a wide range of political actors. Further, the new analysis reveals an important party gap; the recruitment disadvantage is particularly pronounced for Republican women, most of whom do not benefit from the recent emergence of progressive women's organizations that bring Democratic women into the electoral process. Despite the party differences, the overall gender gap in recruitment provides evidence of a masculinized ethos that shrouds party organizations and hinders the selection of women candidates.

### Eligible Candidates' Political Attitudes and Partisanship

Substantially more women officeholders identify as Democrats than as Republicans. In the 111th Congress, 77 percent of women serving in the House of Representatives and 76 percent of women in the Senate are Democrats. Seventy percent of all women serving in state senates are Democrats, as are 71 percent of women serving in the states' lower chambers.[6] Democratic women outnumber Republican women in roughly 90 percent of state legislatures.[7] By contrast, at both the federal and state levels, the majority of male legislators are Republicans.

The disproportionate partisan breakdown of women elected officials may be due, in part, to the disproportionate breakdown of the women who comprise the candidate eligibility pool. Regardless of their professional similarities, women are more likely than men to self-designate as liberal and to identify with a progressive policy agenda. The comparisons presented in Table 5.1 reveal that, on a broad host of fiscal and social policy issues – taxes, abortion, health care, and crime – women are

---

[6] The numbers of women occupying most statewide offices, such as governor and attorney general, reveal a similar partisan divide; of the seventy-three women who hold statewide elective positions, fifty affiliate with the Democratic Party (Center for American Women and Politics 2009b).

[7] The four state legislatures with more women Republicans than Democrats are Alaska, North Dakota, Oklahoma, and Pennsylvania. Nebraska is excluded from consideration because of its nonpartisan state legislative races.

TABLE 5.1. *Eligible Candidates' Political Ideology*

|  | Women | Men |
|---|---|---|
| **Self-Identified Political Ideology** | | |
| Liberal | 34%** | 23% |
| Moderate | 53 | 51 |
| Conservative | 13** | 26 |
| **Policy Preferences** | | |
| Taxes are too high. | 48** | 55 |
| More gun control laws should be passed. | 74** | 58 |
| Abortion should always be legal in first trimester. | 73** | 55 |
| The U.S. should move toward universal health care. | 60** | 51 |
| Congress should enact hate crime legislation. | 65** | 51 |
| Mean number of "liberal" policy preferences (out of 5) | 3.2** | 2.6 |
| N | 1,642 | 1,843 |

*Notes:* Results are based on the 2001 survey data. For policy preferences, cell entries represent the percentage of respondents who "agreed" or "strongly agreed." Number of cases varies slightly, as some respondents omitted answers to some questions. Significance levels of chi-square test and difference of means test comparing women and men: ** $p < .01$.

significantly more likely than men to express progressive attitudes.[8] Women are also approximately two and a half times more likely than men to self-identify as "feminists" (53 percent of women compared to 21 percent of men; difference significant at $p < .01$).[9]

Eligible women candidates are not only more liberal and feminist than men; they are also more likely than men to prioritize "women's issues" as motivating forces behind their political engagement. Women's issues include education, health care, the environment, consumer protection, and helping the poor. "Men's issues" include military or police crises, the

[8] The same general pattern is true in the general population. For recent analyses of the intersection of gender, voting behavior, political ideology, and attitudes about contemporary policy issues, see Norrander and Wilcox 2008; Simon and Hoyt 2008; Whitaker 2008; Jennings 2006.

[9] Many supporters of feminism and the women's movement contend that far fewer citizens identify with the "feminist" label than do with its ideals because the mainstream press characterizes feminists as humorless, aggressive, man hating, and unattractive (Roy, Weibust, and Miller 2007; Hymowitz 2002; Douglas 1994; Faludi 1991). Indeed, many more eligible candidates contend that feminism has improved social and political life in the United States than self-identify as feminists, although women are still 36 percent more likely than men to hold such a belief. Further, Maryann Barakso and Brian Schaffner (2006) demonstrate that television and print media tend to portray (inaccurately) the women's movement and feminism as embodying a narrow agenda – one focused primarily on reproductive rights – that carries little widespread appeal.

TABLE 5.2. *Eligible Candidates' Issue Priorities*

| Consider Issue "Very Important" When Deciding Whether to Participate Politically | | |
| --- | --- | --- |
| | Women | Men |
| **Women's Issues** | | |
| Abortion | 45%** | 23% |
| Education | 64** | 56 |
| Health care | 49** | 36 |
| Gay rights | 18** | 10 |
| Environment | 41** | 31 |
| **Men's Issues** | | |
| Economy | 40** | 47 |
| Foreign policy | 39 | 37 |
| Crime | 25 | 25 |
| Mean total number of issues deemed "very important" | 3.7* | 3.2 |
| N | 1,665 | 1,873 |

*Notes:* Results are based on the 2001 survey data. Number of cases varies slightly, as some respondents omitted answers to some questions. Significance levels of chi-square test comparing women and men. ** p < .01; * p < .05.

economy, business, agriculture, and crime control. Certainly, this categorization of women's issues and men's issues is somewhat superficial. But based on voter perceptions of candidate expertise, as well as studies pertaining to officeholders' legislative priorities, this classification is widely used throughout the gender politics literature.[10]

We asked respondents to identify the policy issues that drive their voting behavior and political participation. The data presented in Table 5.2 reveal that four of the top five issues motivating women's political engagement are women's issues. Further, women are significantly more likely than men to consider each of the five women's issues important when participating politically. We uncover no such pattern for men. The most important issue fueling political activism among men is education – a women's issue – but the economy and foreign policy, both of which are men's issues, place second and third. Health care and the environment

[10] For examples of empirical work that relies on classifications of men's and women's issues, see Fowler and Lawless 2009; Lawless 2004b; Swers 2002; Huddy and Terkildsen 1993a, 1993b; Leeper 1991; Rosenwasser and Dean 1989; Sapiro 1981–2.

TABLE 5.3. *Eligible Candidates' Predicted Probabilities of Considering a Candidacy, by Party*

|                   | Democrat | Republican | Independent |
|-------------------|----------|------------|-------------|
| Male respondent   | .59      | .58        | .59         |
| Female respondent | .43      | .42        | .44         |
| Gender Gap        | 16%**    | 16%**      | 15%**       |

*Notes:* Results are based on the 2001 survey data. Predicted probabilities are based on setting the variables included in Table 3.3 to their respective means. Dummy variables are held constant at their modes. Significance levels of the gender gap: ** $p < .01$.

round out men's lists of motivating issues.[11] Notably, men are less inclined than women to rate almost all issues as "very important" determinants of their political activity. This finding suggests that women may be more likely than men to view politics as an avenue through which to implement policy goals.

In light of their policy preferences, ideologies, and political priorities, it is not surprising that eligible women candidates overwhelmingly align with the Democratic Party. If we refer back to Table 2.2, which breaks down party affiliation by sex and profession, we see that, except in the case of business leaders and executives, a majority of women identify as Democrats. Even among business leaders, a profession in which the majority of women and men are Republicans, women are nearly twice as likely as men to be Democrats. Regardless of profession, men are more evenly divided across parties.

Subscription to the policy preferences and priorities consistent with the Democratic Party may shed light on why the majority of women office-holders are Democrats. That is, Democratic women constitute a greater proportion of the candidate eligibility pool than Republican women. But party identification, political ideology, and issue priorities themselves do not predict interest in running for office. Table 5.3 presents the predicted probabilities that result from the baseline logistic regression equation that models whether a respondent ever considered running for office (see Table 3.4). Men in the eligibility pool, regardless of party affiliation, are approximately one-third more likely than women to have thought about

---

[11] The data regarding issue priorities and positions come from the 2001 survey, which we conducted prior to the war in Iraq and the economic downturn that began in 2007. Our purpose in presenting these data is not to identify the most important issues of the day, but to demonstrate the gender gap in policy preferences and priorities. We expect that both men and women in the candidate eligibility pool would confer greater importance to the economy as a pressing issue if we asked the question today.

seeking public office. The gender gap is remarkably consistent across the three party identifications. Democratic women are no more likely than Republican or Independent women to consider running for office.[12] We find comparable results when we examine the gender gap across political ideology (liberal, moderate, conservative) and feminist identification. These gender differences hold within each professional subsample as well (results not shown).

It is important to recognize, however, that even though party affiliation in and of itself does not affect political ambition to seek office, party is still important in the candidate emergence process. Because the issues and policy agenda associated with the Democratic Party lead more women than men to identify as Democrats, more Democratic women than Republican women will meet and interact with electoral gatekeepers who recruit eligible candidates to run for office.

### Who Gets Asked to Run for Office?

Political parties are often critical in candidate recruitment and nomination, especially at the state legislative and congressional levels (Jewell and Morehouse 2001; Aldrich 2000). Party organizations' leaders, elected officials, and activists serve as formal electoral gatekeepers who groom eligible candidates to run for office. Although encouragement from the parties can be instrumental in propelling a candidacy for anyone, scholars have long known that electoral gatekeepers are strategic in their recruitment efforts (Maestas, Maisel, and Stone 2005) and that recruitment to public office is a selective process that reflects various dimensions of social stratification.[13]

More specifically, political parties have historically been enclaves of male dominance (Freeman 2000; Fowlkes, Perkins, and Tolleson Rinehart 1979). In the 1970s and early 1980s, political parties demonstrated a tendency to recruit women to relatively hopeless state legislative and congressional races (Bernstein 1986; Carroll 1985). It might not be entirely surprising, therefore, that early studies of women's election to office argued

---

[12] When we add interaction terms between sex and party identification, the results remain the same. The coefficients are in the expected directions (Female * Democrat is positive; Female * Republican is negative), but neither coefficient approaches statistical significance (p > .60 in both cases).

[13] Scholars have always identified socially stratified patterns of candidate recruitment not only for the highest elective offices (Matthews 1984; Aberbach, Putnam and Rockman 1981), but also for the state legislature (Seligman et al. 1974) and the city council (Prewitt 1970).

that gender bias and overt sexism in the recruitment process contributed to women's underrepresentation (Carroll 1994; Rule 1981; Welch 1978; Diamond 1977). Karen Brown, an attorney we surveyed and interviewed, recounted direct bias by party officials when she described her mother's experiences running for family court judge in New York in the late 1970s. Ms. Brown explained that when her mother chose to run for the position, she had "a well established law practice and had served as a junior judge for many years, too." The Democratic Party refused to endorse her the first two times she sought the position and she lost both races. Ms. Brown concluded that, in the early years, party operatives "basically thought that women couldn't win, so they didn't waste endorsements on people like my mother. When my mother ran the third time, they begrudgingly endorsed her because she was clearly going to finish first in the race."

More recently, studies of candidate recruitment paint a more complex picture. Gary Moncrief, Peverill Squire, and Malcolm Jewell (2001) and David Niven (2006) find that women officeholders and candidates are more likely than men to report that they were recruited by political gatekeepers. A recent study of state legislators' ambition to run for a seat in the U.S. House of Representatives also reveals that women and men are equally likely to be recruited to enter the electoral arena (Fulton et al. 2006).

But when we move from the experiences of candidates and officeholders to the party leaders and elected officials who tend to recruit candidates, we glean important evidence of both actual and perceived gender bias. Kira Sanbonmatsu (2006), in a six-state study of these electoral gatekeepers, uncovers little overt gender bias in the recruitment process of state legislative candidates; she does find, however, that gatekeepers' networks are still overwhelmingly male and that they identify and recruit candidates from these networks. Consequently, in states with strong political parties and systematic recruitment activities, women are disadvantaged. David Niven's (1998) four-state study of political recruitment reveals that a majority of local women officeholders believe that party leaders discourage women from running for office, both by openly belittling politically ambitious women and by channeling them into low-profile political roles (see also Niven 2006). His surveys of local party leaders in these states corroborated the officeholders' suspicions of bias; male party leaders prefer male candidates. Data from electoral gatekeepers, therefore, suggest that recruitment practices continue to embody a masculinized ethos that favors the selection of male candidates.

From the perspective of potential candidates, however, the extent to which gender affects the early candidate recruitment process remains a largely open question. The research that focuses on actual candidates and elected officials is limited in the extent to which it can speak to the impact of recruitment or the differential effect it might exert on women and men; all declared candidates and elected officials opted to enter the electoral arena, regardless of whether a political gatekeeper extended the invitation. Further, candidates' retrospective accounts of their recruitment experiences may be clouded by the support and encouragement they received when they entered the actual race. The research that relies on gatekeepers for information about recruitment cannot speak to the process as experienced by the women and men who are (or are not) recruited. Hence, to assess the degree to which gender affects patterns of political recruitment, we must turn to the experiences of the women and men who are well positioned to be tapped to run for office.

### The Gender Gap in Political Recruitment

In the first edition of this book, we identified a striking gender gap in political recruitment. Women, across party and profession, were less likely than men to receive encouragement to run for office. More detailed questions about women and men's recruitment experiences that we included in the 2008 survey allow us to offer a more nuanced empirical examination of the gender gap in recruitment and provide an opportunity to assess the extent to which the gap has changed over time.

To begin – and to confirm the findings from the first wave of the study – we asked respondents whether they ever received the suggestion to run for any political office from a party leader, elected official, or political activist (this includes nonelected individuals working for interest groups and community organizations). As illustrated in Figure 5.1, women remain less likely than men to receive the suggestion to run for office from each type of electoral gatekeeper. Certainly, not all political offices are alike, and patterns of recruitment might vary across level of office. But the overall gender gap is noteworthy, especially in light of the fact that the women and men in this sample of eligible candidates exist in the same tier of professional accomplishment and express comparable levels of political participation and political interest.

Because encouragement to run for elective office is perceived more seriously as the number of recruitment contacts increases, we also asked in the 2008 survey about the breadth and frequency with which the eligible

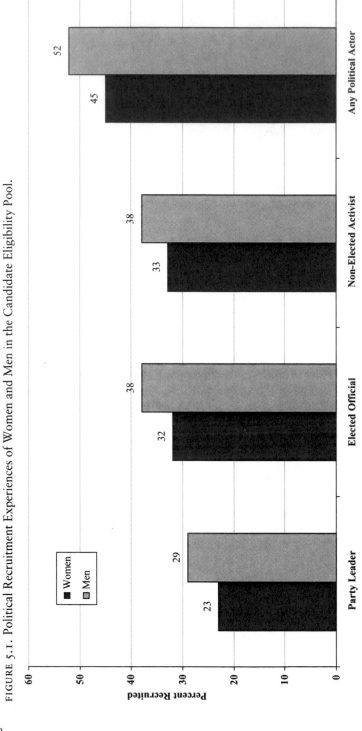

FIGURE 5.1. Political Recruitment Experiences of Women and Men in the Candidate Eligibility Pool.

*Notes:* Results are based on the 2008 survey data. Chi-square tests comparing differences between women and men are significant at $p < .05$ in each category. Sample sizes: for women, N = 916; for men, N = 1,102.

TABLE 5.4. *Gender and Recruitment by Political Gatekeepers (by profession and party)*

| | Women | Men |
|---|---|---|
| **Percentage of Respondents Who Have Ever Received the Suggestion to Run for Office by a Party Leader, Elected Official, or Political Activist** | | |
| **Professional Background** | | |
| Business leader | 29% | 35% |
| Lawyer | 44** | 54 |
| Political activist | 71 | 76 |
| Educator | 30** | 38 |
| **Political Party Affiliation** | | |
| Democrat | 48* | 54 |
| Republican | 40** | 53 |
| N | 916 | 1,102 |

*Notes:* Results are based on the 2008 survey data. Number of cases varies slightly, as some respondents omitted answers to some questions. Significance levels of chi-square test comparing women and men: ** p < .01; * p < .05.

candidates have been recruited. Figure 5.2 presents data on to two types of recruitment intensity: whether the respondent received encouragement to run by all three types of gatekeepers, and whether the respondent was recruited to run at least three times by any one gatekeeper. On both measures of recruitment intensity, we uncover substantive and statistically significant gender gaps.

The aggregate data paint a general picture of how women fare relative to their male counterparts in terms of political recruitment. But they obscure two larger gender differences across party identification and profession. Turning first to professional differences, women attorneys and educators are far less likely than men to be tapped to run for office by party leaders, elected officials, and political activists (see top of Table 5.4). Among business people, the gender gap in recruitment is comparable, though not statistically significant. The bivariate data suggest, therefore, that professional subcultures may play a role in positioning potential candidates for political recruitment.[14]

---

[14] This gender gap also persists when we focus on receiving the suggestion to run from a colleague. We might expect these patterns in the legal and business professions, which have historically been, and continue to be, male dominated. Education, however, is a much more neutral field. And political activists have already demonstrated to their peers a commitment to politics and public policy. Thus, we were somewhat surprised

FIGURE 5.2. Frequency and Breadth of Political Recruitment Received by Women and Men in the Candidate Eligibility Pool.

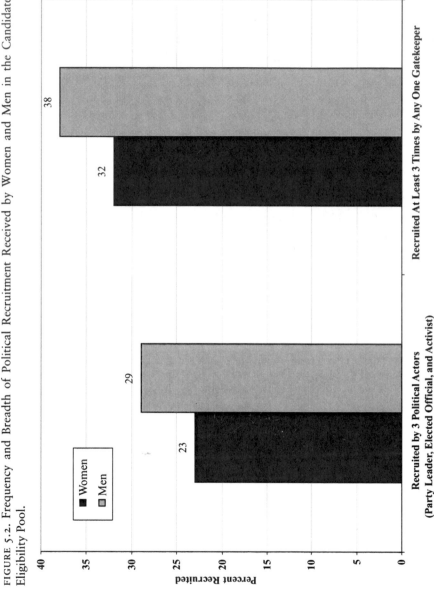

*Notes:* Results are based on the 2008 survey data. Chi-square tests comparing differences between women and men are significant at p < .05 in each category. Sample sizes: for women, N = 916; for men, N = 1,102.

When we turn to party affiliation, the bottom half of Table 5.4 reveals additional gender differences. Among Republicans, men are one-third more likely than women ever to have received the suggestion to run for office from a gatekeeper; among Democrats, the gender gap is still substantively important, but only about half that size.[15] These party differences are consistent with the party gap among elected officials. The second party-related finding to emerge from the data pertains to the change in patterns of recruitment over time. Among respondents who identify as Democrats, the gender gap in political recruitment decreased from 10 percentage points in 2001 to 6 percentage points in 2008. Conversely, the gender gap in political recruitment among Republican respondents increased from 8 percentage points in 2001 to 13 percentage points in 2008.

But the party gap in women's political recruitment appears to be the result of neither divergent strategies by the parties, nor more concerted or systematic recruitment activities by Democratic leaders and elected officials. Democratic and Republican women are equally unlikely to have received encouragement to run for office from elected officials (32 percent). And Democratic women (23 percent) are about as unlikely as Republican women (25 percent) to report recruitment from party leaders. The smaller recruitment gap among Democrats, therefore, can be attributed to the party gap in recruitment from political activists. Thirty-six percent of Democratic women, compared to 24 percent of Republican women, have been recruited to run for office by a political activist in the community (gender difference significant at p < .05).

Men's more frequent direct contact with party officials also came across in our interviews. Many men (twenty-three out of one hundred) provided accounts of recruitment efforts directed at them. Richard Mercer, for instance, is a fifty-four-year-old California businessman who heads a local chapter of the National Rifle Association. Though he has yet to run for any elective office, party officials and officeholders have formally approached him to run on numerous occasions. Several years

to find that only in the area of business were women no less likely than men to receive encouragement to run for office from their colleagues.

[15] Among Independents, we uncover no gender gap in recruitment from political actors; 40 percent of women and 39 percent of men received the suggestion to run for office from a party leader, elected official, or political activist. Independents, however, are less likely to receive support for a candidacy from any of the gatekeepers, regardless of sex. This is not surprising, as Independents are less likely to participate in the party activities and partisan networks through which candidates tend to emerge.

ago, the county Republican chair asked Mr. Mercer to run for the state senate. More recently, a city council member suggested that he run for a position on the council. Gary St. Clair regularly receives similar entreaties in Indianapolis, where he is a well-known lawyer. He has been asked on more than one occasion to run for governor, with some party leaders ensuring support if he enters the race. Dennis Burton, a Kansas lawyer who has been asked to run for office "dozens of times," also described his myriad recruitment experiences: "I have been asked to run mainly by friends and business associates. Oh, and party leaders, of course. I was including those as my friends." Mark Barnswell, a Texas businessman, remarked that he is asked to run for local level office "all the time. . . . I know most of the members of the city council. . . . I play golf with the mayor and he is always telling me to run." Other respondents referenced repeated and consistent encouragement to run for office from electoral gatekeepers:

> I have been approached by community leaders in the last three elections. (David Edwards, Teacher, Wisconsin)
>
> Politicians and party officials have suggested – lots of times – that I run for state office or for Congress. (Steven Chang, Political Activist, California)
>
> Other political activists and Democratic Party officials have approached me repeatedly. (Jonathan Morris, Political Activist, Nebraska)
>
> I would say I have been asked [to run] by all sorts of people – at least twenty times. (Russell Gordon, Businessman, New York)
>
> They [party leaders] ask every election. (Alan Grey, Political Activist, Indiana)
>
> Oh, I would say I have been asked on fifty different occasions. (Aaron Gardner, College Administrator, Oregon)

The men who have been recruited to run for office might make excellent candidates. What is noteworthy is not that they received the suggestion to run, but that the accomplished and politically engaged women we interviewed were only half as likely as men to have received such a suggestion. Lara Berman (Idaho), Bonnie Barrett (Utah), Rhonda Badger (Missouri), and Victoria Gorman (New Jersey) are all successful attorneys in their forties. All follow politics closely, both at the local and the national level. And all belong to political interest groups and contribute to political campaigns. Yet not one of these women has ever received the suggestion to run for office. These lawyers' experiences are quite typical; when asked whether party officials or political activists ever suggested a candidacy, politically active women from a variety of professions responded similarly:

No; no one has ever suggested it. (Natalie Keaton, Teacher, North Carolina)

Nope. I've never been recruited. (Claudia Foley, Businesswoman, California)

Absolutely not; I've never been encouraged to run. (Francine Beacher, College Administrator, Pennsylvania)

No, I've never been thought of as a candidate. (Elaine Kimball, Attorney, Michigan)

I don't really know that many party people, although the ones I do know have never asked me to run. (Marcie Jacobs, Political Activist, Massachusetts)

Certainly, these quotations highlight gender differences that might not be as stark in the overall sample. Our multivariate analysis does lend empirical support to the interview evidence and selected quotes, though. Table 5.5 presents a logistic regression equation predicting whether a respondent received the suggestion to run from an electoral gatekeeper. The model, which relies on the 2008 survey data, serves as a more authoritative assessment of gender and political recruitment than that from the first edition of the book. Here, we have the opportunity to include the measures of political proximity we introduced in Chapter 3 and gain a better grasp of the extent to which the sex of the respondent predicts political recruitment.

The gender gap in recruitment is dramatic. Even after controlling for basic demographics, party identification, and the types of political participation and proximity that facilitate direct contact with political actors who might suggest a candidacy, women are still 16 percentage points less likely than men to have a political actor suggest that they run for office. The typical woman has a 0.60 predicted probability of being recruited to run for office, compared to the 0.76 likelihood of her typical male counterpart. Politically active women who occupy the same professional spheres as politically active men are not equally sought by electoral gatekeepers.

### The Role of Women's Organizations

Democratic and Republican party leaders and elected officials are equally unlikely to recruit women to run for office. The gender differences in political recruitment across parties, therefore, may be the result of the work of women's organizations, both nonpartisan and those affiliated with a particular political party or its positions and priorities. Over the

TABLE 5.5. *Who Gets Recruited? (Logistic Regression Coefficients, Standard Errors, and Change in Probabilities)*

| | Received Suggestion to Run from an Electoral Gatekeeper | |
| --- | --- | --- |
| | Coefficient (Standard Error) | Maximum Change in Probability (Percentage Points) |
| **Sociodemographic Factors** | | |
| Sex (female) | $-.76^{**}(.14)$ | 16.2 |
| Age | .00  (.01) | – |
| Income | $-.01$  (.06) | 2.0 |
| Education | $-.21^{**}(.07)$ | – |
| Race (White) | $-.35$  (.18) | – |
| **Political Factors** | | |
| Democrat | $.54^{*}$  (.23) | 13.3 |
| Republican | $.54$  (.27) | – |
| Percentage of women in the state legislature | $-1.10$  (1.13) | – |
| Moralistic political culture | .16  (.16) | – |
| **Proximity to the Political Environment** | | |
| Worked or volunteered on a campaign | $1.11^{**}(.15)$ | 26.8 |
| Attended a political meeting | $.84^{**}(.18)$ | 20.7 |
| Served on a nonprofit board | $.75^{**}(.15)$ | 18.5 |
| Attended political party meeting or event | $.58^{**}(.14)$ | 13.0 |
| Interacted with elected officials at work | $.93^{**}(.14)$ | 22.9 |
| Contact with women's organization(s) | $2.44^{**}(.24)$ | 34.5 |
| Constant | $1.72^{**}(.73)$ | |
| Pseudo-$R^2$ | .42 | |
| Percentage Correctly Predicted | 75.5 | |
| N | 1,584 | |

*Notes:* Results are based on the 2008 survey data. Maximum changes in probabilities are based on the logistic regression results. Probabilities were calculated by setting all continuous independent variables not under consideration to their means and dummy variables not under consideration to their modes. The change in probability reflects the independent effect a statistically significant variable exerts as we vary its value from its minimum to maximum (i.e., the change in probability for Sex [female] reflects the fact that a woman is 16.2 percentage points less likely than a man, all else equal, to receive the suggestion to run for office from an electoral gatekeeper). For age, we varied the values from one standard deviation above to one standard deviation below the mean. Significance levels: ** $p < .01$; * $p < .05$.

course of the past decade, a series of women's organizations have burst onto the political scene. They vary in mission and target group, but collectively, these organizations endeavor to move more women into the networks from which candidates emerge. The White House Project, for example, is a national, nonpartisan organization that, since 1998, has advanced women's leadership and attempted to fill the candidate pipeline. In 2007, the Women's Campaign Forum launched its She Should Run campaign, a nonpartisan, online effort to build the pipeline of Democratic and Republican pro-choice women and inject them into the networks that can promote eventual candidacies. Emerge America, founded in 2002, trains Democratic women across the country to develop networks of supporters so that they can successfully run for and win elective office. The EMILY's List Political Opportunity Program, which began in 2001, trains and supports pro-choice Democratic women to run for all levels of office. Many statewide and local women's organizations have also recently launched aggressive campaigns to bring more women into political circles and positions of power. Because the objective of many of these organizations is to promote progressive women's candidacies, they likely disproportionately propel Democratic women into the circles and networks from which candidates tend to emerge.

The panel data provide us with a unique opportunity to assess the extent to which women's organizations affect the candidate emergence process. Not only do the 2008 survey results shed light on how broadly women's organizations cast their net, but the panel component of the study also allows us to determine the degree to which women's contact with these organizations has closed the recruitment gap for Democrats.

The regression results in Table 5.5 demonstrate that women's organizations do, in fact, play an important role mitigating the gender gap in political recruitment. Contact with a women's organization serve as a statistically significant predictor of recruitment, and it offsets the recruitment disadvantage women face. All else equal, an eligible candidate who has contact with a women's organization is more than 34 percentage points more likely than an eligible candidate with no such contact to be recruited to run for office by an electoral gatekeeper. The effect, therefore, means that a woman who has contact with one of these organizations is more likely than the average man in the candidate eligibility pool to be recruited. Although men benefit from the support of women's organizations as much as women do, 27 percent of the women in the sample, compared to 4 percent of men, report contact with one of these organizations (difference significant at $p < .01$). Hence, women's groups facilitate women's candidate emergence.

The data also highlight that women's organizations disproportionately benefit Democratic women in the candidate eligibility pool. Consider the party differences in recruitment among "new recruits" – eligible candidates who were recruited to run for office for the first time during the interval between 2001 and 2008. Among Democrats, women represented 55 percent of the new recruits who were tapped to run for office by a political actor for the first time (107 women and 86 men were newly recruited between 2001 and 2008; difference significant at p < .01). Of these new Democratic recruits, forty-five women, compared to three men, reported contact with a women's organization. The power of women's organizations to increase Republican women's political recruitment is less clear. Women comprised only 29 percent of the first-time Republican recruits (twenty-three women, compared to fifty-seven men; difference significant at p < .01). Among the new Republican recruits, eight women and four men reported contact with women's organizations. Overall, these results suggest that women's organizations – particularly progressive groups – now play a significant role in the candidate emergence process and closing the gender gap in recruitment, especially among potential Democratic candidates.

### Political Recruitment and Considering a Candidacy

The fact that men continue to be the preferred candidates of many electoral gatekeepers is critical not only because it highlights that a masculinized ethos pervades the political environment eligible candidates face, but also because of recruitment's impact on candidate emergence. Eligible candidates who receive the suggestion to run for office are significantly more likely to consider a political candidacy.

For many individuals we interviewed, recruitment from political leaders served as the key ingredient in fomenting their consideration of a candidacy. Attorney Mark Powers, for example, considered running for the state legislature because Republican party leaders suggested that he do it: "That was really influential for me. You need to have the party's support in order to have a viable run for any office. That's so ingrained in me that running wouldn't have occurred to me without the suggestion from the party." Sean Coughlin, a political activist from Michigan, offered a similar reflection:

> Party leaders suggested that I run for Congress. That was the first time
> I really seriously thought about it. If you're active with the party, you're

positioned to be recruited. A nomination from the party – or encouragement to run – is a great base of support. Actually, without that support, you can't really even think about running.

Wendy Miller, an anti-abortion activist, also first thought about running for office after party officials raised the idea of a candidacy. She explained:

> When I realized that I'd have the town committee of the party behind me – they told me I would – I thought [running] might be something to consider. I also have friends who are political activists. They're well connected, so they know people willing to work on my behalf.

In some cases, encouragement from party organizations and electoral gatekeepers even spurred actual candidacies, as was the case for Dan Warton, who currently operates a business in West Virginia:

> I once ran for Democratic alderman back when I lived in Buffalo. It was a pretty low-key thing. Someone from the Democratic council asked me to run, I did, and then I got the most votes. Since then, I have thought about running for the state legislature. Colleagues and party officials have all asked me to run. I know a lot of politicians. I know all the state legislators, too. I have the right connections with the party, so it's something that might be possible.

Even respondents who never received encouragement to run for office from a party leader or elected official are cognizant of the legitimacy and viability that recruitment efforts confer. Women and men – across parties – intimated that such support would bolster their willingness to run for office. Alison Joyce, a high school principal in Rochester, New York, epitomized this sentiment when she explained that she cannot really think about running for office because she does not have support from a political party: "My interest in seeking office is never that serious because I haven't been affiliated [with a party]. I don't think I would have a chance of ever getting nominated." A college dean from a small liberal arts college in New England drew the same conclusion:

> I'm not politically naïve enough to think that the kind of support I've had [from colleagues and friends] to run for mayor means anything. I'm not politically connected. I have very little name recognition. Without party support, there's nothing to consider.

Susan Moriarty, an environmentalist who works in California, considers suggestions from colleagues and fellow activists as nothing but "flattery." But she did go on to note, "If someone from the Democratic Party approached me, and made me realize that I had a broader base of support, I would consider running." A lack of recruitment has also kept an Illinois high school principal from running, despite her political interest:

> Sadly, the only person who has ever told me I should run is my husband. He always tells me that I'd be a good candidate because I listen well and I'm smart and I consider different sides of an issue before making any decisions. . . . If I had more support, particularly the support of those from the party. . . . I [would] be more likely to run.

Several respondents even indicated that recruitment would serve as the only catalyst for a serious consideration of a candidacy:

> People have suggested that I run for office, but nothing that serious. It's not like I've had members of political parties lined up with volunteers to pass out fliers and get my name out there. That's what it'd take to get me to really consider running for any position. (Carrie Hodge, Political Activist, Maryland)

> If someone from a political party or the mayor said, "C'mon, we really need your help," I can't say that I wouldn't give it serious thought. (Stephen Gilmour, Attorney, Washington)

> If I had serious people, like party officials, urging me to run, I wouldn't be able to not think about doing it. (Jason Roberts, Principal, Pennsylvania)

> My graduate school adviser and a high school teacher of mine were always telling me I should run. But no one with real political connections ever mentioned it. If people with connections wanted me to run then I would probably be more likely to give it serious thought. (Sam Parker, Business-man, Washington, D.C.)

> I'd run if someone from one of the political parties said they wanted me to run. I'm very easily influenced. It's just that right now, there's not enough support. (Roberta Simmons, Political Activist, Ohio)

In total, twenty-seven of the hundred men and twenty-two of the hundred women with whom we spoke raised at some point during the interview the notion that party support would enhance their likelihood of considering a candidacy.

To demonstrate more broadly the substantive effects of political re-cruitment, we present two logistic regression equations in Table 5.6. The first equation models whether a respondent ever considered running for office (column 1); the second predicts whether the eligible candidate took any of the concrete steps that tend to precede a campaign (column 2). In addition to the main explanatory variable – whether the respondent ever received the suggestion to run from an electoral gatekeeper – we

TABLE 5.6. *The Impact of Political Recruitment on Considering a Candidacy (Logistic Regression Coefficients, Standard Errors, and Change in Probabilities)*

| | Considered Running for Elective Office | | Took at Least One Concrete Step | |
|---|---|---|---|---|
| | Coefficient (Standard Error) | Maximum Change in Probability (Percentage Points) | Coefficient (Standard Error) | Maximum Change in Probability (Percentage Points) |
| Sex (female) | −.86** (.17) | 18.2 | −.52* (.24) | 6.2 |
| Education | .02 (.07) | – | .03 (.07) | – |
| Income | −.07 (.05) | – | −.09 (.06) | – |
| Race (White) | .05 (.17) | – | .06 (.18) | – |
| Age | −.02** (.01) | 17.1 | −.01 (.01) | – |
| Democrat | −.26 (.22) | – | −.45 (.24) | – |
| Republican | −.16 (.23) | – | −.18 (.25) | – |
| Political knowledge | .06 (.07) | – | .04 (.09) | – |
| Political interest | .08** (.03) | 11.3 | .12** (.05) | 17.5 |
| Political efficacy | .02 (.06) | – | −.13* (.06) | 12.8 |
| Political participation | .18** (.04) | 38.1 | .17** (.04) | 35.6 |
| Recruited to run by an electoral gatekeeper | 1.29** (.64) | 30.7 | 1.66** (.19) | 35.0 |
| Recruited by an electoral gatekeeper * sex | .31 (.24) | 5.7 | .29 (.28) | 0.5 |
| Constant | .34 (.65) | | −1.73** (.70) | |
| Pseudo R² | .28 | | .30 | |
| Percentage Correctly Predicted | 70.4 | | 73.1 | |
| N | 1,538 | | 1,538 | |

*Notes:* Results are based on 2008 survey data. Maximum changes in probabilities are based on the logistic regression results. These probabilities were calculated by setting all continuous independent variables not under consideration to their means and dummy variables not under consideration to their modes. For age, we varied the values from one standard deviation above to one standard deviation below the mean. Because of the inclusion of the interaction term, the coefficient (and predicted probability) associated with the sex variable – in and of itself – does not accurately capture the gender gap in political ambition. We must assess the joint effect of the principal components and the interaction term. Significance levels: ** p < .01; * p < .05.

control for the baseline correlates of political ambition. And because studies of candidates and officeholders report no gender differences in political recruitment, it may be that recruitment is especially important for women's candidate emergence. Each equation, therefore, includes an interaction term between the sex of the eligible candidate and whether he or she was recruited to run for office.[16]

Because of the inclusion of the interaction term, the coefficient (and predicted probability) associated with the sex variable – in and of itself – does not accurately capture the gender gap in political ambition. When we generate predicted probabilities, however, we find that the support from electoral gatekeepers provides a large boost in eligible candidates' political ambition. Both men and women who received encouragement to run are significantly more likely than those who received no such support to think about running for office. Political recruitment increases a man's likelihood of considering a candidacy from 0.41 to 0.71. Women who have not been recruited by a gatekeeper have only a 0.22 likelihood of considering a run for office. Women who receive support have a 0.59 probability. The pattern is the same for ever having taken a concrete step that precedes a candidacy; sex remains a significant predictor of political ambition, but recruitment by a gatekeeper partially closes the gender gap.

The quantitative and qualitative evidence lend clear support to the claim that recruitment by electoral gatekeepers spurs eligible men and women candidates' interest in and willingness to run for office. Comments from women and men who have been recruited reflect the political viability conveyed by gatekeepers' suggestions to run; party support brings the promise of an organization that will work on behalf of a candidate. Statements from individuals who have yet to receive political support for a candidacy demonstrate that, without encouragement, a political candidacy feels far less feasible. External support is important to eligible candidates from all political parties and professional backgrounds, but women are significantly less likely than men to receive it.

## Conclusion

Despite their gains in professions that are likely to precede electoral politics, women of all backgrounds and party identifications remain less likely than men to be tapped to run for office. The results from our analysis, particularly the second-wave survey data, suggest that a masculinized ethos pervades the recruitment process. The gender gap in recruitment

[16] When we substitute measures of recruitment intensity for the overall measure of ever having been recruited to run for office by a gatekeeper, the same variables achieve statistical significance and the magnitude of recruitment's impact is greater for both women and men. The interaction term behaves consistently, regardless of the measure of political recruitment we include.

emerges regardless of whether the gatekeeper is a party leader, elected official, or political activist. Moreover, in terms of breadth and frequency of recruitment, women in the candidate eligibility pool are disadvantaged. The recruitment patterns experienced by the eligible candidates we surveyed reflect entrenched stereotypical conceptions of a candidate and suggest that party gatekeepers more actively seek men than women to run for office. Considering the heavy weight that eligible candidates place on recruitment and the degree to which support for a candidacy bolsters levels of political ambition, both major political parties will continue to field an overwhelming majority of male candidates unless they make conscious efforts to recruit more women.

Our results also suggest that prospects for increasing the number of women candidates are brighter for Democrats than Republicans. All else equal, the gender gaps in political recruitment and political ambition persist across political parties. But all else is not equal. Women in the candidate eligibility pool are more likely to be Democrats, which gives the party a larger base to tap. In addition, the new survey data reveal the extent to which women's organizations – which tend to focus on increasing the number of progressive women's candidacies – mitigate the severity of the gender gap in political recruitment among Democrats. Their effect is particularly powerful in light of the fact that more than one-quarter of the women in our sample report having been in contact with them. Hence, if current recruitment patterns persist, then the party gap in women's representation will continue to grow at all levels of office.

The results we presented in this chapter carry broad implications for women's presence in electoral politics. Because gender interacts with the recruitment process, women's increasing presence in the candidate eligibility pool does not inevitably result in their increasing presence as candidates. As long as women's representation remains tied predominantly to the success of one political party, women's substantive representation will be far more precarious than men's. Women's full integration into political life cannot occur without a greater partisan balance among women candidates and officeholders.

# 6

# "I'm Just Not Qualified"

## Gendered Self-Perceptions of Candidate Viability

In November 2002, despite what was regarded as a shaky first term, California Governor Gray Davis was reelected. But persistent rolling blackouts, skyrocketing electricity costs, and the onset of failing dotcoms quickly contributed to a weakened state economy and a drop in state tax revenues. Because California state law requires a balanced budget, Governor Davis proposed to cut funding for a host of state programs and initiatives. Although these cuts were unpopular, they paled in comparison to the negative reception the governor received when he suggested raising taxes to balance the budget.[1] Within months, prominent Republicans began funding a gubernatorial recall effort; and by July 2003, they had collected more than the 1 million signatures required to mandate a new election.[2] Per California law, the lieutenant governor scheduled the recall to occur within eighty days.

The gubernatorial recall election presented Californians with a unique political opportunity. To get on the ballot, prospective candidates needed to collect sixty-five signatures and pay a $3,500 filing fee; or they could gather ten thousand signatures and pay no fee. These rather lax filing requirements allowed almost any mildly industrious person to put his or her name forward as a candidate for governor. Indeed, an eclectic array of more than 600 individuals requested petitions from the California

---

[1] Laura Kurtzman, "Republicans Blame Governor for Energy Crisis, Weak Economy," *San Jose (CA) Mercury News*, July 27, 2003.

[2] Beth Fouhy, "California OKs Recall Vote for Davis: 1.3 Million Signatures Certified in Drive to Oust Governor," *Chicago-Sun Times*, July 24, 2003.

secretary of state's office; 135 followed through and met the criteria to appear on the special election ballot.[3]

Certainly, a number of the candidates – such as former child actor Gary Coleman, the comedian known as Gallagher, and porn star Mary Carey – ran for office in an attempt to garner publicity. But most candidates articulated a sincere justification for entering the electoral arena. Teacher Joe Guzzardi, for instance, ran because he felt politicians were not willing to discuss the "great and tangible economic harm of illegal immigration." San Francisco public defender Paul Mariano ran to protest the recall process; he even pledged to select Gray Davis as his chief of staff. Structural engineer Bill Vaughn sought to "call attention to earthquake safety." Other candidates entered the race because of concerns about taxes, education, antismoking laws, and prison spending, among other issues.[4] Of the 135 candidates, however, only 16 were women. And of the five top-tier candidates who ultimately participated in a candidate debate, Arianna Huffington (who later withdrew from the race) was the only woman.

The recall election provided individuals who possessed an entrepreneurial spirit, confidence about their political abilities, or just plain old chutzpah the opportunity to throw their hats into the ring. Why did so many fewer women than men consider doing so? This chapter assesses gender differences in eligible candidates' self-appraisals of their qualifications to run for office. Our analysis yields some of the most important findings of this book. Women are more likely than men to underestimate their qualifications to seek and win elective office. Moreover, women's self-doubts are more likely than men's to keep them from considering a candidacy. In exploring the contours of the gender gap in qualifications, we supplement our evidence from the first edition of the book with new

---

[3] The recall ballot required voters first to choose whether they wanted to replace Gray Davis. Then, regardless of whether they voted to keep or replace the incumbent governor, voters selected their preference for a new governor from a list of candidates. The winning candidate would assume the position of governor only if more than 50 percent of voters chose to replace Davis. On Election Day, 55 percent voted to replace Davis, and Republican Arnold Schwarzenegger garnered the most votes as his successor. For more on the procedural aspects of the California recall, see "Recall in California," a comprehensive overview of the process by the Institute of Governmental Studies at University of California, Berkeley, at http://igs.berkeley.edu/library/htRecall2003.html (accessed August 8, 2009).

[4] For more on the candidates, their positions, and the factors that led them to consider a candidacy, see "Field: So Many, So Little Space," *Hotline*, August 15, 2003.

survey data we collected from the second wave of the panel. The new data allow us to highlight important differences in women and men's perceptions of their political skills, personal traits, and the electoral environment in which they would compete. These self-perceptions perpetuate a gendered psyche, whose imprint leaves women far less comfortable than men with the idea of pursuing public office.

## The Gender Gap in Self-Perceived Qualifications and Its Impact on Political Ambition

Alexander Casey, an active member of the Sacramento County Taxpayers' League who regularly recruits candidates, recounted his unsuccessful attempts to encourage Judy Morton, a lawyer friend, to run for the state legislature:

> She is an All-American Athlete, Phi Beta Kappa, Rhodes Scholar Finalist, Harvard Law Grad, and [was an] adviser to President Bush. I met with her for dinner the other night and basically begged her to run for office. She told me she doesn't think she's qualified. Who the hell is qualified if she isn't? I don't get it.

Ms. Morton went on to tell Mr. Casey that she could "never imagine" entering politics as a candidate.

Women in this sample of the candidate eligibility pool are, objectively speaking, just as qualified as men to hold elective positions. They have achieved comparable levels of professional success in the fields that precede political candidacies. They are equally credentialed and educated. And there are no notable gender differences either in levels of political knowledge and interest or in political participation and campaign experience. If the California recall election or Alexander Casey's experiences serve as an indication of a more general trend, though, then despite their similar backgrounds, women will be more likely than men to dismiss their qualifications and doubt that they have what it takes to run for office.

Indeed, though not directly related to politics, investigators from a variety of disciplines provide evidence to suggest that women are less likely than men to contend that they possess the skills and traits necessary to enter electoral politics. Turning first to gender differences in skills-based measures, researchers find that, from an early age, women are far more likely than men to diminish and undervalue their skills and achievements. Studies of gender differences in academic abilities provide a clear example. By the time of adolescence, male students rate their mathematical abilities higher than female students do, despite no sex differences in objective indicators of competence (Wigfield, Eccles, and Pintrich 1996). In the areas of language arts, male and female students offer comparable self-assessments, although objective indicators reveal that female students are actually higher achieving in these fields (Pajares 2002).

Many of these misconceptions persist into adulthood, percolating up even to high-level professionals who have succeeded in traditionally male domains (Beyer and Bowden 1997; Beyer 1990). Hannah Bowles, Linda Babcock, and Kathleen McGinn (2004, 20) found that, controlling for a series of job related functions and previous work experience, female MBAs accepted salary offers that were 5.5 percent lower than the offers accepted by their male counterparts (see also Bowles, Babcock, and McGinn 2004).[5] In the absence of clear compensation standards, women are also more likely than men to work harder and make fewer errors for equivalent pay (Major, McFarlin, and Gagnon 1984) and to express lower career-entry and career-peak pay expectations (Bylsma and Major 1992).

Gender differences exist not only in how women and men perceive their objective skills, but also in the confidence they exude regarding their credentials, backgrounds, and willingness to engage in competition. Social psychologists find that, in general, men are more likely than women to express confidence in skills they do not possess and overconfidence in skills they do possess (Kling et al. 1999). Men tend to be more self-congratulatory, whereas women tend to be more modest about their achievements (Wigfield, Eccles, and Pintrich 1996). Men tend to overestimate their intelligence, whereas women tend to underestimate theirs (Furnham and Rawles 1995; Beloff 1992). Men often fail to incorporate criticism into their self-evaluations, whereas women tend to be strongly influenced by negative appraisals of their capabilities (Roberts 1991). Further, a series of experiments comparing professional performance in competitive and noncompetitive environments reveals that men are more likely than women to seek out competitive environments and to exude confidence when competing (Niederle and Vesterlund 2007; Gneezy, Niederle, and Rustichini 2003).

In a study pertaining to game-show performance, for instance, Sheila Brownlow, Rebecca Whitener, and Janet Rupert (1998) demonstrate the manner in which gender differences in attitudes toward competition work to women's detriment on the popular game show *Jeopardy*. In the first round of the game, "masculine" categories, such as politics and sports,

---

[5] For related findings from the 1970s and 1980s, see Stevens, Bavetta and Gist 1993; Callahan-Levy and Meese 1979.

TABLE 6.1. *Eligible Candidates' Perceptions of Their Qualifications to Run for Office*

| Eligible candidates who self-assess as ... | Women | Men |
| --- | --- | --- |
| Not at all qualified | 28%** | 12% |
| Somewhat qualified | 33** | 27 |
| Qualified | 25** | 34 |
| Very qualified | 14** | 26 |
| N | 1,640 | 1,853 |

*Notes:* Results are based on the 2001 survey data. Significance levels of chi-square test comparing women and men: ** p < .01.

outnumber "feminine" ones, like art and literature. Further, Daily Double questions, which allow contestants to wager up to their full amount of earnings, disproportionately appear in masculine subject areas. Women are just as likely as men to answer questions correctly in the traditionally masculine categories, but they tend to avoid choosing them. Thus, men's greater access to the Daily Doubles allows them to enter the Final Jeopardy round with about $650 more than women. Women and men perform equally well in Final Jeopardy and are equally likely to wager all of their earnings, but women's tendency to shy away from masculine categories early on detracts from their game-show success.

Our analysis provides compelling evidence that women's inclination to undervalue their skills and experiences transcends into the electoral arena. After all, many of the patterns identified by researchers in other disciplines are only exacerbated by a culture that tends to reinforce traditional sex-role expectations and women's marginalization in politics. We asked respondents to place themselves on a continuum from "not at all qualified" to "very qualified" to launch a candidacy. The survey results reveal that men are nearly twice as likely as women to consider themselves "very qualified" to seek an elective position (see Table 6.1). Women are more than twice as likely as men to assert that they are "not at all qualified" to run for office. Similar gender gaps appear when we consider women and men's assessments of whether they are qualified to perform the job of an elected official. Whereas 80 percent of men contend that they are "qualified" or "very qualified" to do the job of an officeholder, fewer than two-thirds of women assess themselves this way. Women are more than twice as likely as men to rate themselves as "not at all qualified" to perform the job.

This pattern persists when we turn to the likelihood of winning a race. As illustrated by the data presented in Table 6.2, women are only half as

TABLE 6.2. *Eligible Candidates' Perceptions of Their Likelihood of Winning a Political Race*

| Eligible Candidates who think winning a race for the first office they sought would be... | Women | Men |
|---|---|---|
| Very unlikely | 31%** | 19% |
| Unlikely | 44 | 43 |
| Likely | 22** | 30 |
| Very likely | 3** | 7 |
| N | 1,405 | 1,543 |

*Notes:* Results are based on the 2001 survey data. Number of cases includes only those women and men who never ran for office. Significance levels of chi-square test comparing women and men: ** $p < .01$.

likely as men to think they would meet electoral success if they ran for office. They are 63 percent more likely than men to view the likelihood of winning any political contest as "very unlikely." The gender gaps in these perceptions, which exist across professions, are not a result of women envisioning running for higher offices than men. In fact, women are more likely than men to refer to local offices when assessing their qualifications and prospects for success (see Chapter 3, Table 3.6).

Because we wanted to move beyond abstract assessments of qualifications to run for office and pinpoint the specific components of the qualifications gap, we included in the 2008 survey a series of questions about a variety of politically relevant skills. The data presented in Table 6.3 allow for comparisons between women and men's self-assessments on skills that are generally considered important in electoral politics. Regarding all five of the political skills about which we inquired, women are less likely than men to perceive themselves as possessing the skill. Men, for instance, are more than 60 percent more likely than women to think they could raise enough money to run for office; and they are almost 30 percent more likely than women to state they are knowledgeable about public policy issues. These perceptual differences are striking in light of women and men's actual skills and professional experiences. In terms of the key skills necessary to run for office, women and men in the sample report comparable levels of experience. Thirty-three percent of women and 35 percent of men have conducted extensive policy research; 65 percent of women and 69 percent of men regularly engage in public speaking; and 69 percent of women and 64 percent of men report experience soliciting funds and raising money.

Throughout the course of our interviews, a clear link emerged between the broad gender gap in self-perceived qualifications we identified and

TABLE 6.3. *Gender Differences in Eligible Candidates' Perceptions
of Political Skills*

|                                                | Women | Men |
|------------------------------------------------|-------|-----|
| Knowledgeable about public policy issues       | 46%** | 59% |
| Professional experience relevant to politics   | 66**  | 74  |
| Good public speaker                            | 57**  | 66  |
| Good fundraiser                                | 13**  | 21  |
| Good self-promoter                             | 17*   | 21  |
| N                                              | 913   | 1,095 |

*Notes:* Results are based on the 2008 survey data. Entries indicate the percentage
of respondents who self-assess as possessing the skill. Sample sizes vary slightly
because some respondents omitted answers to some questions. Significance levels
of chi-square tests comparing women and men: ** $p < .01$; * $p < .05$.

women's greater inclination to underestimate their skills more generally.
Richard Rose, an engineering professor from New Jersey, believes that
"men tend to vastly overestimate their abilities and their competence. We
tend to think we're brilliant. Women tend to downplay their own intelligence. It's sociocultural." Charlotte Lipman, an instructor at a liberal
arts college, agreed: "Men do not recognize any inferiority. Women pick
on what they can't do, including myself. Think about women's speech.
Women's jokes make fun of themselves. Men don't do that. They make
fun of other men or of women." Attorney Jeremy Lawson offered a similar
outlook: "Male [bravado] makes men say they're qualified for anything
even when they're not. Women are more honest with themselves."

Several respondents provided more specific examples of women's self-
doubts within the context of their professional environments. A partner
in a Midwest law firm identified "innate confidence" as the leading gender
difference in the associates with whom she works:

> New women and men come into the firm every year. In most cases, the
> women are more capable and qualified than the men. But men have con-
> fidence and women just don't. For instance, a woman will walk into the
> office and say, "I did the memo, I'm not sure if it's good. I'll do it again if
> you don't like it." Men will say, "Here's the memo," throw it on my desk,
> and not even look to me for approval.

Gloria Baxter offered a similar observation as she reflected on her experiences interacting with lawyers when she was a New Haven, Connecticut,
city court judge. She remembered that the women lawyers were "always
more prepared than the men, but far less confident in the courtroom.
They always had more evidence to make their points, more case law
as a reference. Women just didn't have the confidence to bullshit their

way through anything the way men did." Spokane high school principal Rebecca Sobel identified this pattern in the field of education, too:
"The women teachers I worked with underestimated how qualified they
were to advance to more powerful positions. They were much less likely
than men to become administrators because they just didn't think their
records were strong enough. Their records were always stronger than the
men who applied."

We might extrapolate from the fields of law, business, and education
to the realm of politics, as did this attorney from Georgia:

> If I'm working with two male colleagues, they peacock around and always
> try to take credit for every aspect of everything we do. When I work with
> women, we're more apt to work together. We don't care as much about
> our egos. But ego translates into confidence. So, when you turn to politics,
> which requires the highest levels of confidence, you see men who probably
> aren't that qualified and women who just don't think they have what it
> takes to be in politics.

A female attorney from California also sensed gender differences in eligible candidates' perceptions of their abilities to enter politics: "I think
that men overestimate what they're capable of doing and accomplishing.
Women are more honest. So, if women don't think they're qualified to
run for office, they're probably not. And if men think they are qualified,
they're probably not."

Women's greater likelihood to underestimate their qualifications to
enter politics is particularly important because of the extent to which
these self-perceptions influence levels of political ambition. Table 6.4
presents a model of whether a respondent ever considered running for
office; we supplement the baseline model with a measure of respondents'
self-perceived qualifications to seek elective office. The regression results
indicate that qualifications carry the most relative explanatory power
predicting political ambition. Moreover, the statistically significant interaction between the sex of the respondent and his or her self-assessed
qualifications demonstrates that women rely more heavily than men on
these self-perceptions.[6]

Because of the inclusion of the interaction term, the coefficient (and
predicted probability) associated with the sex variable – in and of itself –

---

[6] We included an interaction term between the sex of the respondent and the qualifications
measure because we expected women to be more concerned than men with appearing
credible and thereby more likely to look to their professional credentials to legitimize
their entry into politics (Sanbonmatsu 2002; Kahn 1996; Fowler and McClure 1989).
Regression analyses performed separately on the samples of women and men further
justify the inclusion of the interaction term. The same factors predict women and men's

TABLE 6.4. *The Impact of Self-Perceived Qualifications on Considering a Candidacy (Logistic Regression Coefficients, Standard Errors, and Change in Probabilities)*

|  | Coefficient (Standard Error) | Maximum Change in Probability (Percentage Points) |
|---|---|---|
| **Baseline Indicators** | | |
| Sex (female) | −1.28 (.27)** | 14.8 |
| Age | −.03 (.01)** | 15.9 |
| Education | .05 (.05) | − |
| Income | −.16 (.04)** | 16.9 |
| Race (White) | .49 (.13)** | 11.7 |
| Democrat | .22 (.12) | − |
| Republican | .11 (.13) | − |
| Political interest | .04 (.04) | − |
| Political participation | .17 (.03)** | 27.9 |
| Political knowledge | .05 (.05) | − |
| Political efficacy | .09 (.05) | − |
| Recruited by political actor | .78 (.12)** | 15.1 |
| Received encouragement from personal source | 1.62 (.11)** | 38.2 |
| **Qualifications** | | |
| Self-perceived qualifications | .48 (.07)** | 31.6 |
| Self-perceived qualifications * sex | .26 (.10)** | 52.5 |
| Constant | −1.92 (.45)** | |
| Pseudo-R² | .48 | |
| Percentage correctly predicted | 78.2 | |
| N | 3,118 | |

*Notes:* Results are based on the 2001 survey data. Maximum changes in probabilities are based on the logistic regression results. Probabilities were calculated by setting all continuous independent variables not under consideration to their means and dummy variables not under consideration to their modes. The change in probability reflects the independent effect a statistically significant variable exerts as we vary its value from its minimum to maximum. For age, we varied the values from one standard deviation above to one standard deviation below the mean. Because of the inclusion of the interaction term, the coefficient (and predicted probability) associated with the sex variable – in and of itself – does not accurately capture the gender gap in political ambition. We must assess the joint effect of the principal components and the interaction term. Men's likelihood of considering a run for office increases by 32 percentage points as they move along the continuum from perceiving themselves as "not at all qualified" to "very qualified" to seek an elected position. Women gain a 53 percentage point boost in considering a run when they self-assess as "very qualified." Significance levels: ** p < .01.

FIGURE 6.1. The Substantive Effect of Self-Perceived Qualifications on Considering a Candidacy.

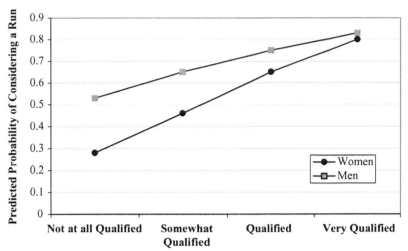

*Notes:* The predictions are based on setting the variables included in the regression equation presented in Table 6.4 to their respective means. Dummy variables were held constant at their modes.

does not accurately capture the gender gap in political ambition. Thus, we must assess the joint effect of the principal components and the interaction term, which we can do by graphing women and men's predicted probabilities of considering a candidacy at various levels of self-perceived qualifications. Figure 6.1 displays the substantive impact self-perceived qualifications exert on the likelihood of considering a political candidacy. Men's likelihood of considering a run for office increases by 32 percentage points as they move along the continuum from perceiving themselves as "not at all qualified" to "very qualified" to seek an elected position. The impact of self-perceived qualifications on women's predicted likelihood of considering a candidacy is substantially greater; women gain a 53 percentage point boost in considering a run when they self-assess as "very qualified." Put somewhat differently, a woman who thinks she is "not at all qualified" is approximately only half as likely as a similarly situated man to express political ambition. Women and men who consider themselves highly qualified for political office are nearly equally likely to consider running.

considerations of a candidacy, but the magnitude of the coefficient on self-perceived qualifications for women is much greater than it is for men.

Together, these results demonstrate that the gender gap in the baseline model of political ambition (Chapter 3) narrows dramatically when we control for self-perceived qualifications and the manner in which these perceptions interact with the sex of the eligible candidate. Further, the results indicate that women are doubly disadvantaged. Not only are they less likely than men to conclude that they are qualified to run for office, but women also accord more weight to their self-doubts when considering a candidacy.

## Explanations for the Gender Gap in Self-Perceived Qualifications

Across the board, women in our sample, regardless of profession, income level, party affiliation, and age, are significantly less likely than their male counterparts to view themselves as qualified to enter the electoral arena and more likely than men to doubt their political skills. As a result, women are substantially less likely than men to consider running for office. Because women's self-assessments are a complex phenomenon, we rely on both quantitative measures and evidence from our interviews to pinpoint the roots of the gender differences in these self-assessments. This mixed-method approach reveals three elements of the gendered psyche, each of which contributes to the gender gap in eligible candidates' self-perceived qualifications.

### The Sexist Environment

When Madeline Rogero ran for the Knox County Commission in 1990, a male member of her own party suggested that she save the money she would spend on the campaign and "buy herself something nice to wear."[7] Examples of such overt sexism have been on the decline in electoral politics, but as we discussed in Chapter 2, Hillary Clinton's experiences in the 2008 presidential election reinvigorated concerns that the political environment remains rife with gender bias. Sarah Palin's recent experiences serve as another case in point. From the moment the former Alaska governor burst on to the national political stage in August 2008 as John McCain's running mate, several commentators and organizations began tracking what they identified as a torrent of sexist media coverage and derision directed toward Palin (Carroll and Dittmar 2010).[8] This type of

---

[7] David Hunter, "Is Knoxville Election for New Mayor a Case of David vs. Goliath?" *Knoxville (TN) News Sentinel*, March 31, 2003, B5. Ms. Rogero continued her campaign and won the race.

[8] For a good summary of the treatment Palin received during the 2008 campaign up through her resignation as governor in 2009, see Marie Cocco, "Like Hillary, Palin

coverage also characterized Palin's 2009 resignation as governor. Rick Sanchez of CNN, for example, speculated that Palin might be pregnant again; *Vanity Fair*'s Todd Purdum referred to Palin as "the first indisputably fertile female to dare to dance with the big boys."[9]

Although the aforementioned examples are egregious, several of the eligible candidates we interviewed conveyed instances of gender bias and discrimination that persist in many traditionally male-dominated environments. Herb Timmons, for example, laments the fact that only two of the twenty-five partners in his Nashville law firm are women. He explained that even though female associates are regularly hired, they often feel forced to leave: "Due to the sexism and the backwards attitudes of many people in the office, the women who come in are treated poorly and think they'll never get promoted. It makes sense that they don't end up staying long." In another example, a family rights activist from Connecticut recalled an incident in which a Republican town committee chair refused to support campaign training for women because their political success would "go against traditional roles and norms." Roughly one-third of the women and men we interviewed also mentioned subtler forms of sexism in their own work environments. A female attorney from Missouri observed that many of the male partners in her law firm regularly golf or attend football games with the younger male associates. She explained that because women are often not included in these "bonding events," they do not benefit from early mentoring:

> [Women] are often left out and feel less supported. They learn to adjust and achieve success without this encouragement. But even though women eventually build a sense of self-confidence, it takes them years to get to the place that the men associate lawyers are their first days out of law school.

A small body of research finds that when women are not fully integrated in public life, they often withdraw.[10] Eligible women candidates' reluctance to consider a candidacy and question their qualifications, therefore, may be rooted, at least in part, in the male-dominated public spheres they navigate in their daily lives.

Faces Media Sexism," *RealClearPolitics.Com*, July 7, 2009, http://www.realclearpolitics.com/articles/2009/07/07/a_trashing_as_old_as_suffrage_97321.html (accessed August 14, 2009).

[9] Carol Jenkins, "WMC Statement on Recent Sexism in the Media Against Sarah Palin," July 6, 2009, http://womensmediacenter.com/wordpress/?p=845 (accessed August 13, 2009).

[10] Political scientists have identified this pattern both in the bureaucracy (Dolan 2000; Naff 1995) and in elective offices (Blair and Stanley 1991).

When we asked respondents to move beyond their own work environments and consider whether they believe women still face significant gender bias in the electoral arena, the levels of perceived sexism were striking. The examples of bias identified in our interviews ranged from claims of overt bias against women at the polls (a phenomenon that aggregate-level studies of vote shares and electoral outcomes do not substantiate) to subtler instances of gender stereotyping. For our purposes, however, perceived bias is just as important as documented bias, as both convey to women that they might face hostility if they enter the political arena. And as indicated in Figure 6.2, an overwhelming majority of respondents, across professions, do not think that women and men have an equal chance of succeeding when running for high elective office.

Between the two waves of the study, the perceived degree of gender bias and the gender gap therein remained largely unchanged. In 2008, 87 percent of female respondents and 76 of male respondents agreed that the electoral environment was more difficult for women than men. Similarly, despite the fact that women who actually run for office raise just as much money as their male opponents, eligible candidates do not perceive the electoral environment this way. The 2008 survey data reveal that 64 percent of women and 38 percent of men contend that it is more difficult for women than men to raise money for a political campaign. In fact, 12 percent of women stated outright that they are not qualified to run for office simply because they are the wrong sex. In addition, even though the women and men are geographically matched, women are approximately 25 percent more likely than men to judge their local and congressional elections as "highly competitive."

Existing in traditionally sexist professional environments leads many eligible women candidates to conclude that they need to be more qualified than men to compete evenly. Sheila Dimes, an educator from California, is convinced that "when they violate traditional gender roles, women have to do things twice as well to be considered half as good as men." Karen Doyle, a history professor from Washington, concurred: "Women don't think they're not as qualified as men to succeed. It's just that we perceive, even subconsciously, that we have to be twice as qualified to be successful." Carla Harper-Dowd, a linguistics professor from North Carolina, offered one of the most poignant examples of this sentiment when she explained, "Because women have historically served in secondary positions, they have learned to internalize this subordinate status." She concluded that women who break out of this status, "either by running for office, or by leaving an abusive relationship, or by receiving a promotion

FIGURE 6.2. Eligible Candidates' Perceptions of Gender Bias in the Political Arena.

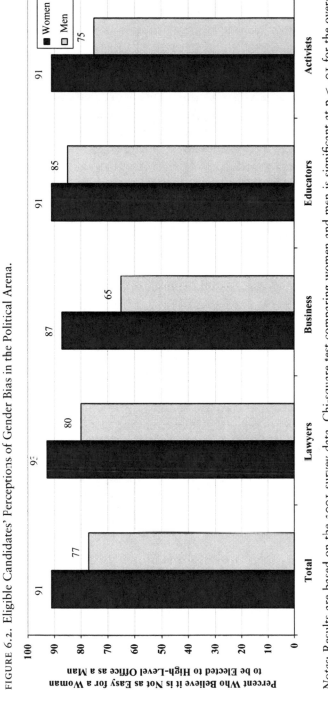

*Notes:* Results are based on the 2001 survey data. Chi-square test comparing women and men is significant at p < .01 for the overall sample and in each profession. Sample sizes: for women, N = 1,669; for men, N = 1,875.

at work – tend to be met with resentment. This negative feedback makes them think they need to be twice as competent as men in comparable positions." Cathy Finke, a businesswoman from the Northeast, believes that "professional women need a tremendous amount of confidence to survive in a man's world, especially in light of the unspoken requirement that women be twice as good as men." Overall, more than one-quarter of the women with whom we spoke referenced the fact that women need greater qualifications than their male counterparts to succeed.

The experiences of women who have succeeded in the political arena corroborate eligible candidates' impressions that women in politics are held to a higher bar than men. In her study of Arizona state legislators, for example, Beth Reingold (1996) found women more likely than men to mention the value of hard work and knowledge for political success. She concluded that these gendered references suggest that "fewer Arizona women than men felt that they had the latitude or ability to be successful without working extremely hard... confirm[ing] the popular notion that women have to work harder than men to be equally successful and respected" (Reingold 1996, 475). As former Texas Governor Ann Richards famously commented in support of the idea that public women have to meet a higher standard, "Ginger Rogers did everything Fred Astaire did, only backwards and in high heels."

Comments from the respondents, coupled with the data collected from the 2008 survey, indicate that perceptions of a sexist environment convey to women heightened levels of electoral competition and a more challenging campaign trail to traverse. These circumstances lead many women to conclude – perhaps rightfully so – that they have to be more qualified than men to compete successfully against them.[11] Because of the higher standards imposed on women – both internally and externally – they are more likely than men to conclude that they are not qualified to run for office.

### Gender Differences in Defining Political Qualifications
Considering that many women feel they are judged more harshly than men when they enter traditionally masculine domains, it is understandable that women rely on a more exhaustive set of criteria when assessing whether they are qualified to run for office. In particular, we find that

---

[11] Roberta Sigel (1996, 54) identifies a similar sentiment among the general public. In her survey of New Jersey voters, Sigel found that 85 percent of women believed that "to get ahead, a woman must be better than a man." Eighty-one percent agreed that "women get less recognition than men for the same accomplishments."

women are more likely than men to look to their professional and political experiences when evaluating their suitability to pursue public office. They are also more likely than men to doubt that their personality attributes qualify them to run.

Turning first to the weight eligible candidates place on their professional backgrounds, forty-five of the one hundred women we interviewed contend they are qualified to run for office. Of these forty-five women, thirty-eight stated very specific credentials. Like many respondents, Hilda Morganthau, an attorney from Wyoming, cited her years of professional service as qualifications to enter politics: "I have eighteen years of experience working for two governors and serving on a statewide board. I am certainly qualified to seek a state-level position." Laura Thompson, an attorney from Arlington, Virginia, employed the same type of calculus in assessing her qualifications:

> I have worked with the local, state, and federal government for twenty-five years and I have been the government affairs liaison between organizations and legislative bodies during that time. I'm currently the chair of a partnership, which is a seven-county economic development corporation. I don't know what other experiences someone could have.

Political experience was also a reference point for many women educators, among them Millicent Tillman. The North Carolina college administrator served in three gubernatorial administrations and as a trustee for the public school system. She contends that her "immediate proximity to political life" qualifies her to run for office.

Women who do not cite previous political experiences as credentials for a candidacy tend to refer to specific aspects of their current professions that would transfer to the political arena. For a Washington attorney, more than thirty years of experience means that she "knows more about the details of the local law and the political system than most." In addition, her job requires that she be "well read and up to date on political issues at the local, state, federal, and international levels." Carol Stewart has dealt with the public as a teacher and a principal for thirty years. She, too, invoked the experiences she acquired "on the job" as credentials for running for political office:

> I often call state representatives about budgetary and education issues. This has taught me to understand the difficult role of the states in times of budget cuts. My experiences in schools have also taught me how to deal with different types of people and understand their varying situations. So, I think that I would be qualified to run for office and serve the people.

According to Elizabeth Dixon, the executive director of a statewide organization devoted to children's issues and education, "Running an organization is probably not terribly different from sitting on a city council, or even in the state legislature." More specifically, she cited her abilities to "negotiate, build coalitions, retain facts, and develop coherent arguments" as skills that would transfer well to the political sphere. These statements embody the sentiments of the majority of women who self-assessed as "qualified" to run for office. Nearly all drew similarities between the political arena and their current professional positions. Nearly all offered abridged versions of their résumés. And nearly all stated the importance of concrete experiences in dealing with public officials or groups that influence the policy process.

All of the credentials women name as qualifying seem reasonable. Several men we interviewed offered a similar degree of specificity when stating why they consider themselves qualified to run for office. Sam Parker mentioned that his success in business and oversight of a staff of six thousand employees positions him to "manage a small town or county." Managing a four-year, fifty-thousand-student operation with a "tremendous budget" conferred political qualifications to a male college administrator from Florida. Attorneys Michael Rudman (Minnesota), Jeffrey Townsend (California), and John Serlen (New York) stated that their legal training qualifies them to run for office. Philip Nichols, a middle school principal from the Midwest, was convinced that, "compared to running a school with one thousand teenagers, politics would be a cakewalk."

Sixty-seven of the one hundred men interviewed considered themselves qualified to run for office; however, only twenty-seven offered specific linkages between their professions and the political environment. References to passion, leadership, and vision trumped references to concrete experiences. Kenneth McCarthy, a litigator from Tulsa, Oklahoma, captured this distinction well when he explained that he is qualified to run for office because "all you need is the desire to serve. I've got that. You can learn the details of policymaking later." Grant Cummings, the president of a branch of the Massachusetts Family Institute, made a similar claim: "I'm as qualified as anyone. I have tons of passion for the issues. And I can lead. Everything else would fall into place." With a somewhat more cavalier attitude, Washington, D.C., attorney Jared Schneider stated, "You bet I'm qualified. What do you need to know more than that you want to serve? With good aides and advisers, anyone with real passion is qualified." Many other men echoed these sentiments:

> Sure, I'm qualified. I'm of high moral character. (John Sussman, Attorney, Oregon)

> Yeah, I'm absolutely qualified. I get along well with people and I like people and want to do the best I can for them. (Russell Gordon, Businessman, New York)

> I'm a true leader with a vision of how I'd like to see the world. What else does someone need? A legal background, maybe? Well, I've got that, too. (Bill Smithfield, Attorney, New Mexico)

> To be qualified, you need to show that you can win a fight. You need to show that you can tough it out and make it through trying times. I can do that. (Joseph Simpson, Political Activist, Delaware)

> I understand the pros and cons of leadership and the responsibility that goes along with it. I understand how important it is to go out and take the pulse of the community on issues. I know how to lead. (Louis Shaw, Political Activist, Illinois)

Put simply by Bob Muller, a high school principal from Wisconsin, "I think anyone is qualified. This is a democracy."

The second gender difference we uncovered in respondents' definitions of a "qualified" candidate pertains to personality attributes. Many women who knowingly possessed the educational, professional, and community experience to run for office concluded that they were not qualified to enter electoral politics because they had the "wrong temperament," "not enough gumption," or an "aversion to criticism." Susan Kagan, for example, has worked in a legal environment for more than thirty years and is very involved in her community. She acknowledged that she has "a large network of people and know[s] a lot of experts in a lot of different arenas." Ultimately, though, she does not think she is qualified to run for office because she lacks "political savvy and the thick skin you need." Gina Van Morse, a Vermont attorney, is also aware of her objective qualifications, but she focused on her inability to withstand criticism. After chronicling her professional and political experiences, she explained that having "thick skin" is probably the most important trait people need to run for office: "In order to get to the point where you show that you're educated, a good listener, passionate, any of those things, you need to have been able to endure the campaign. That's unfortunate – I don't have it." Meghan Penner, the owner of a small business in Illinois, placed herself in the same category. She explained, "I'm not qualified to run for office. My feelings get hurt too easily and I second-guess myself too quickly. That wouldn't serve anyone well." Darla Mulrue, a professor from Kansas, offered a similar assessment:

> I have good communication skills, am educated, tend to be willing to compromise, and have a desire to be informed, even about those issues that don't directly affect me. These are the kinds of qualities elected officials should have.... But I'm not qualified to run because I can't take criticism well. And criticism is what you get when your personal life becomes politicized.

Dina Moore, the director of a health care association in Pennsylvania, summarized the manner in which women often consider the severity of the attacks launched at candidates and politicians too much to bear:

> I am not qualified to run for office because I could not endure the scrutiny and criticism. I tell this to young women in my field all the time. When you start off, you have grape skin, virtually none at all and easily injured. Time and experience have given me orange peel skin. Thick enough to be a success in most fields. But politics is different. You need watermelon skin for that. That way, unless you're dropped really hard, they won't see the juices flow. I don't have it.

The ability to withstand criticism was not the only personal trait about which eligible candidates doubted their ability to exude. Respondents also expressed a disdain for the practice of politics. Juanita Rivera, a health-care executive, commented "I don't like the BS of politics. You can't say what you mean.... [Y]ou have to smile and cut bad deals. I just wouldn't want to behave like a politician." Patricia Wilcox, a political activist from New Hampshire, would never consider running for office because she does not want to "water down" her positions and compromise on the issues that motivated her political activism: "For the most part, you have no choice but to cut deals if you want to accomplish anything in politics. What's the point of that? That's not progress. It would make me lose my mind. I couldn't do it." Like many eligible candidates, Professor Michelle Reed referenced her refusal to pander to special-interest groups as the main reason she would not think about entering electoral politics:

> I am very much interested in politics. And of course, I am very interested in all issues that play a role in current events – you know, the war, the economy. But I'd never run. I'm very blunt, and I stick to my views. I wouldn't crumble for special interest groups. I wouldn't be very effective at navigating the political waters.

TABLE 6.5. *Gender Differences in Eligible Candidates' Perceptions of Political Traits*

|  | Women | Men |
|---|---|---|
| Does not have thick skin | 48%** | 29% |
| Does not like to make deals to get things done | 32* | 25 |
| Has a lot of skeletons in his or her closet | 10 | 11 |
| N | 913 | 1,095 |

*Notes:* Results are based on the 2008 survey data. Entries indicate the percentage of respondents who self-assess as possessing the trait. Sample sizes vary slightly because some respondents omitted answers to some questions. Significance levels of chi-square tests comparing women and men: ** $p < .01$; * $p < .05$.

Sacramento County political activist Alexander Casey concurred: "I don't kiss babies and I don't kiss ass. Basically, I wouldn't want to compromise my public policy convictions – that's why I'd be getting involved in the first place. But that's what you need to do to be a viable candidate."

Although personality traits, such as leadership skills and passion, lead many men to conclude that they are qualified to run for office, very few of the men we interviewed felt that their temperaments and personalities detracted from their electoral viability. Indeed, responses to the new questions we included in the 2008 survey substantiate this point empirically. The second-wave data reveal that women are nearly two-thirds more likely than men to doubt that they have "thick enough skin" to run for office. Women are also significantly more likely than men to eschew the deal making that is often necessary to garner success in the political sphere (see Table 6.5).

Regardless of their actual qualifications and politically relevant skills – which are almost identical – women are more likely than men to place weight on previous experiences and a broad set of concrete credentials. In addition, they are more likely than men to conclude that their personalities are not well suited to the political arena. The gender gap in self-perceived qualifications, therefore, can certainly be attributed, at least in part, to the more complex criteria women invoke when determining whether they are suited to hold public office.

### Different Yardsticks for Gauging Political Qualifications

We develop an even deeper understanding of the gender gap in assessments of qualifications to run for office when we consider the yardstick against which eligible candidates compare themselves. Kate Lyman, an attorney from New Mexico, articulated the impression that "women are not as connected as men to the culture of politics and those in power.... Men are often rubbing elbows with each other. At the end of the day, they go have a drink or they play golf. Women go home to check on the family." As we demonstrate in Chapter 3, women and men are equally likely to have firsthand exposure to the political process and contact with politicians. But perhaps as a result of traditional family role orientations, women's connections to the electoral arena may be somewhat more tenuous. Accordingly, women are less likely than men to evaluate themselves relative to current officeholders. Instead, women are more likely to hold themselves to an idealized standard.

Many of the men we interviewed compared their experiences and backgrounds to those of current officeholders and concluded that they were at least as qualified to seek public office. Art Menlo, a lawyer for the Nebraska Civil Liberties Union, concluded that his training as a mediator and "wealth of experience" in political advocacy mean that he is "smarter and more qualified than [his] current representative in Congress." Ted Simpson, who is affiliated with a policy institute, believes that his investment experience and business degree make him "as qualified as anyone for any kind of office.... Look around. There are a lot of people making our laws and dictating our rights with no experience whatsoever, let alone in the fields where it really matters." Professor Randall White's background in education, coupled with his "formal training" and "life learning experiences" position him to be "as qualified and more qualified as those holding office."

Several of the men who compared themselves to candidates and elected officials did not even reference the specific credentials they possessed that politicians lacked. More than one-third conveyed the sentiment that they were "at least as good as what's out there." David Ball, an activist from South Carolina, estimated that "about 75 percent of current politicians are not qualified." Employing that standard, he believes that he "must be qualified." Several eligible men candidates, across professions, agreed:

> Have you seen what is out there? I must be qualified. (Edward Benton, Principal, Mississippi)

> I see tons of people who are less qualified than I am out there, so I think I must be. (Jerome Morrow, Attorney, California)

> I've lived in the same community for thirty years. Bill Frist, a leader in the Senate [was] my senator, and ten years ago he was just a doctor at

Vanderbilt, just down the block from here. I don't even think he lived here as long as I have. (Albert Michaels, Businessman, Tennessee)

I am much smarter and a lot more honest than the people currently in office. It's such a circus – all of politics is. Who is not qualified? (Oliver Winters, Political Activist, New Hampshire)

I'm bright. I have a mind for public service. I'm just as qualified as my senator is! (Bill Smithfield, Attorney, New Mexico)

Look at most of the people who are currently in office. I have at least their ability to communicate and provide effective leadership. (Ben Finkelstein, Attorney, Washington)

Stuart Williams, a business owner from Wyoming, was one of the only men who drew a different conclusion: "When I look around, I am increasingly stunned that there are a lot of politicians who know less than I do. But that doesn't really make me feel any more qualified. Just stunned at the stupidity of the people who are our elite."

By contrast, although women's levels of political knowledge, interest, and engagement are comparable to men's, women rarely assessed themselves relative to current officeholders and candidates. When women determined whether they were qualified to seek public office, they envisioned an extremely accomplished, well-rounded candidate – one who is educated, has political experience, community connections, professional ties, and possesses the personality traits and qualities necessary to run a successful campaign and endure the scrutiny and criticism it entails. The thoughts of the director of a Nevada branch of the Sierra Club and practicing attorney highlight this point: "Although I can easily speak about certain issues, I would never feel qualified to hold office. I could never offer analysis on every issue just off the top of my head." Melissa Green, a reproductive rights activist in Florida, attributed her perceived lack of qualifications to the fact that she "really doesn't know about other issues well enough. I know that many people learn the details about policy issues when they get in office. I would feel unready to assume any position if I didn't know about everything prior to the election." Samantha Weisman, an attorney for the National Organization of Women's Legal Defense Fund in New York, also called attention to her "limited experience." Her commitment to issues and her wealth of nonprofit sector experience are "not enough"; she has never worked in government or business. Janet Williams, a sociology professor, could "never be qualified enough to run for office." She asked, "How could I ever get to the point where I would know enough to represent everyone's interests? I couldn't pretend to."

Cheryl Perry is perhaps the most obvious example of a woman holding herself to a bar that might be impossible to reach. Despite the fact that she is very active in her profession and in the bar association, Ms. Perry asserted: "There are many more committees that I am not on than that I do serve on." Although she has almost a decade of courtroom experience, she went on to note: "I do not win all the time. It's not like I'm a superstar litigator. I just don't exude the success required to run for office."

Women contend that candidates and officeholders must hold a breadth of experience, whereas men, who have always operated within the public sphere, appear more likely to conclude that they can readily succeed in politics. Summarized well by Colorado attorney Ellen Chapman, "Men get how [the political process] works. You can be completely unqualified and completely successful. You learn when you get there. Women think they need to do all of the learning before they try to get there. Maybe they still do. That's just too formidable a barrier." Kathleen Courtney Hochul, a town board member in Hamburg, New York, agreed: "[Women] almost have to have a grey hair or two before it dawns on us that, hey, we're as qualified, if not more so, than the men."[12]

## Conclusion

The findings highlighted in this chapter are among the most important contributions of the study. Despite nearly identical levels of political participation, campaign experience, and proximity to the political system, women are far less likely than men to envision themselves as qualified, viable candidates for elective office. Further, the 2008 survey results allow us to identify with far greater specificity the central components of the gender gap in self-assessed qualifications to run for office. The data indicate that the gender gap in self-perceived qualifications exists not only at the abstract level, but also on every specific measure of political acumen about which we asked. Because women are less likely than men to conclude that they are qualified to run for office, they are less likely than men to consider running. Overall, the gender gap in self-perceived qualifications serves as the most potent explanation we uncover for the gender gap in political ambition.

The exact source of women and men's different beliefs about their own qualifications to run for office are multifaceted. Some women's

---

[12] Dick Dawson, "Women Make Gains, But Progress Is Slow," *Buffalo (NY) News*, March 19, 2000, 1C.

self-doubts can be linked to their perceptions of a sexist political environment dominated by a masculinized ethos. Other women's self-assessed qualifications are the product of a stringent definition of *qualified* that encompasses both essential political background experiences and personal traits. Still other women hold themselves to an extremely high bar in assessing their readiness to pursue elective office. These manifestations of the gendered psyche illustrate that, to consider themselves qualified to run for office, women must overcome a series of complex perceptual differences and doubts that result from long-standing patterns of traditional gender socialization.

Given the heavy weight that potential candidates place on their self-evaluations when considering a candidacy, these perceptual differences translate into perhaps the most difficult hurdle women must overcome in the quest to establish gender parity in electoral politics. Whereas a gender gap in political recruitment can ultimately be closed if political parties and interest groups mobilize and support women's candidacies, the changes required to close the gender gap in the perceptions we uncovered involve dismantling some of the most deeply embedded and socialized beliefs that both women and men hold about what political candidates look like and what performing that role entails.

# 7

# Taking the Plunge

## *Deciding to Run for Office*

Deciding whether to run for office can be very difficult, even for high-profile potential candidates or experienced politicians. In 2002, for example, *Time* magazine named Minneapolis FBI agent Coleen Rowley one of its "Persons of the Year." Ms. Rowley gained notoriety when she called attention to the FBI's refusal to seek a national security warrant to search suspected terrorist Zacarias Moussaoui's possessions before the September 11, 2001, attacks occurred. Because of Ms. Rowley's national security expertise, Democratic Party officials and members of Minnesota's congressional delegation encouraged her to challenge Congressman John Kline (R-MN) in 2004. Despite widespread support for her candidacy, Ms. Rowley declined the invitation. Having never before even considered a candidacy, she explained that she lacked the characteristics necessary to be a retail politician: "As a child, I only sold sixteen boxes of Girl Scout cookies. I was the lowest in the whole troop."[1] The Democrats continued to push Ms. Rowley to seek office, though, and their sustained recruitment efforts ultimately paid off. In 2006, she ran for Congress.[2] It took several years, but Coleen Rowley transformed from someone who had never conceived of herself as a candidate to someone who enthusiastically embraced the role.

Louise Slaughter's ultimate decision to run for a seat in the U.S. House of Representatives was similarly drawn out and difficult. Linda Fowler

---

[1] "FBI Whistleblower Says She Won't Run for Congress," *Associated Press State and Local Wire*, November 26, 2003.

[2] Jill Lawrence, "Parties Set Hopes on Well-Known Newcomers," *USA Today*, June 7, 2006. Rowley lost the 2006 race to John Kline by a margin of fifty-six to forty.

and Robert McClure (1989) describe in riveting detail the process by which Slaughter, a Democratic New York state legislator, came to run for Congress. Leading up to the 1984 congressional election, Slaughter had strong support within the local party organization, high name recognition, and enthusiastic backing from the Democratic Congressional Campaign Committee and several prominent national political action committees. Although this broad base of support meant that she could have had her party's nomination without a primary, Slaughter decided not to enter the race (Fowler and McClure 1989, 103). She was deterred by her freshman status in the state legislature, her small campaign chest in her previous legislative race, and her family obligations. It was not until two years later, when presented with a similar degree of support and encouragement, that she sought the seat in New York's 30th congressional district. Louise Slaughter has been a member of the U.S. House since 1986 and currently serves as chair of the Rules Committee.

Individuals deliberating an initial run for office might face an even more difficult decision process than did Coleen Rowley and Louise Slaughter, both of whom enjoyed high levels of name recognition and support for their candidacies. Most first-time candidates are moving into uncharted waters and are often unsure of what a candidacy would entail and whether they could endure it. James Fillmore, a lawyer from Indiana whom we interviewed for this study, questioned whether he could withstand the spotlight: "I have thought about [running] quite a bit.... Could I do it? Would I be good at making speeches? Do I want to be in the public eye? Is it too much of a sacrifice? These are hard issues for me to resolve." Harriet Goodwin, a political activist from South Carolina, also referred to the angst involved in the decision process, concluding: "I am too old now – but I thought about running at many different times across my life. I always made excuses, but I guess looking back now, I just never had the nerve."

Entering the electoral arena involves the courageous step of putting oneself before the public, only to face intense examination, loss of privacy, possible rejection, and disruption from regular routines and pursuits. For high-level positions, candidates often need to engage in months of full-time campaigning; and success may mean indefinitely suspending one's career. At the local level, the political stakes may not be as high, but the decision to enter even a city council or school board race can involve holding oneself up before neighbors and community members (Shaw 2004; Golden 1996). Further, local races can turn into very competitive, nasty contests (Grey 2007). In a 2007 campaign for the school board in

Orchard Prairie, Washington, for example, candidates regularly found their campaign signs torn down, and residents regularly found nasty campaign literature stuffed in their mailboxes. Remarkably, all of this occurred in a school district with only one school and seventy students.[3] Regardless of whether the candidacy is situated at the local, state, or federal level, deciding to enter electoral politics is a complex endeavor.

In this chapter, we turn to the second stage of the candidate emergence process and examine the factors that distinguish those who choose to run for office from those who think about running, but do not. The overt gender differences evident in the first stage of the process (considering a candidacy) begin to fade. This finding does not mean, however, that gender plays no role. Foremost, because women are far less likely than men to consider running for office – both in 2001 and 2008 – fewer women than men ever face the decision to enter an actual race. Accordingly, they are less likely than men to launch a candidacy. But even among eligible candidates who have considered entering the electoral arena, gender differences in ambition emerge. Data from the second wave of the study allow us to evaluate systematically women and men's attitudes about participating in the essential activities of a campaign. We find that that women are significantly more likely than men to be deterred by the toll a campaign often takes on candidates and their families. Moreover, when we turn to future interest in office holding, gender differences persist, further dampening any degree of optimism surrounding women's representation.

## Why Would Anyone Run for Office? Negative Perceptions of the Electoral Environment and the Campaign Process

Americans hold a high degree of cynicism toward elected officials and disdain for the political process. According to a 2008 Gallup poll, only 12 percent of Americans have "a great deal" of confidence in the members of Congress.[4] That same year, fewer than 50 percent of citizens reported any degree of trust for members of Congress.[5] These attitudes are consistent with survey research that finds that a majority of Americans do not believe that elected officials are qualified for the positions they hold (Knowledge

---

[3] Sara Leaming, "School Board Campaign Spices Up Usually Tranquil Orchard Prairie," *Spokane (WA) Spokesman-Review*, October 20, 2007.

[4] Jeffrey M. Jones, "Confidence in Congress: Lowest Ever for Any U.S. Institution," Gallup Poll, June 20, 2008, http://www.gallup.com/poll/108142/confidence-congress-lowest-ever-any-us-institution.aspx (accessed December 20, 2009).

[5] Jeffrey M. Jones, "Trust in Government Remains Low," Gallup Poll, September 18, 2008.

Networks 2002) and that more than 75 percent of Americans do not believe that members of Congress act honestly and ethically.[6]

Relatively negative attitudes about the political environment and the electoral arena are not restricted to mass population samples; many eligible candidates we surveyed drew similar conclusions. Forty percent contend that most current officeholders are not "well intentioned" in their desire to enter public service. Thirty-five percent do not think that the majority of elected officials are qualified to hold elective office. By the time of the 2008 survey, respondents' attitudes toward politics had become even more negative. Sixty-eight percent of eligible candidates reported having developed animosity toward the Bush administration, and 60 percent had grown increasingly frustrated with the Democrats in Congress. Overall, 62 percent of the women and men in the sample stated that they had become more cynical about politics since the time we first surveyed them in 2001.

These opinions certainly stem from a series of factors. Relatively short-term political and economic circumstances, for instance, can leave a significant imprint on individuals' attitudes toward government (Cook and Gronke 2005), as can presidential behavior and approval ratings or a change in congressional leadership (Keele 2007). The aftermath of September 11, 2001; the war in Iraq; the failed government response to Hurricane Katrina; and the polarized, gridlocked government with which so many Americans have grown frustrated, therefore, likely contribute to the record-low presidential and congressional approval ratings documented by national pollsters.[7] Moreover, these events shape attitudes toward state and local governments (Gartner and Segura 2008; Maestas et al. 2008). In short, the hyperpartisan bickering that dominates Washington, coupled with polarizing political leaders on both sides of the aisle and controversial government actions at home and abroad, have taken their toll as far as the status of politics is concerned.

In addition, the negative political advertising that saturates high-level competitive elections has turned politics into a blood sport that focuses on destroying the opponent (Mark 2006; Swint 2006; Kamber 2003). Further, the mainstream television networks and newspapers, in response to increasing competition from the Internet and cable news, incorporate

---

[6] Pew Center for People and the Press, "Disapproval of GOP Congressional Leaders, but Democrats Fare No Better," March 24, 2005.

[7] See, e.g., Kathleen Hunter, "Public Approval of Congress Hits New Low: Poll," *CQ Politics*, July 8, 2008; and Rasmussen Reports, "President Bush Job Approval: Another Month, Another Record Low Approval for President Bush," July 2, 2008.

TABLE 7.1. *Eligible Candidates' Preferred Means of Influencing the Policy Process*

| If you felt strongly about a government action or policy, how likely would you be to . . . | Women | Men |
|---|---|---|
| Give money to a political candidate who favors your position? | 72%* | 75% |
| Directly lobby or contact government officials? | 66 | 66 |
| Volunteer for a candidate/group that favors your position? | 60 | 58 |
| Organize people in the community to work on the issue? | 44 | 41 |
| Run for office? | 9 | 11 |
| N | 1,582 | 1,793 |

*Notes:* Results are based on the 2001 survey data. Entries represent the percentage of respondents who answered "likely" or "very likely." Number of cases varies slightly, as some respondents omitted answers to some questions. Significance levels of chi-square test comparing women and men: * $p < .05$.

scandal and partisan conflict into the central aspects of political reporting (Graber 2010; Fox, Van Sickel, and Steiger 2007; Sabato 2000). The emergence of openly partisan reporting adds to the contentious atmosphere in the presentation of politics (Jamieson and Capella 2008; Cohen 2006). It is no surprise, therefore, that broad national sentiment tends not to identify politics as a noble calling.

As we would expect, when women and men choose to participate politically, they tend to seek means other than running for office. The data presented in Table 7.1 indicate that the most viable means of political activism for the women and men in our sample are contributing time or money to candidates who favor their positions or lobbying already-elected government officials. Many also contend that working behind the scenes, or in nonelective positions, is a better way than running for office to affect public policy. Lara Berman, an attorney from Idaho, summarizes this position well. She explained that, although she does not choose to run for office, making her services available to women and minorities who otherwise would not consider using the legal system offers her "daily opportunities to promote change in the community." Many eligible candidates commented that working as activists, rather than as officeholders, affords them more opportunities to "focus on the issues," "talk to real people about their problems," "lobby the high ranking officials who have real political clout," and "avoid the inane aspects of politics." These responses are not gendered; the comparisons in Table 7.1 reveal that women and men offer the same rankings for the best means through which to implement change in their communities. For both sexes, as the political activity becomes more complex or "costly," the less likely respondents are to embrace it.

Negative attitudes about specific features of the campaign process also cloud individuals' willingness to engage in the activities associated with running for office. Throughout the course of our interviews, disdain for the political process and what entering an actual political contest might entail was readily apparent. More than three-quarters of the eligible candidates with whom we spoke expressed some degree of negativity about several aspects of running for office. In particular, fundraising and the potential loss of privacy emerged as the most common deterrents.

Turning first to fundraising, eligible candidates are well aware of the exorbitant amount of money needed to run a competitive federal race. In the ten most competitive congressional districts in the 2010 election cycle, incumbents seeking reelection to the U.S. House of Representatives each raised more than $2.5 million as of April 2009. The April 2009 finance reports to the Federal Election Commission for the five most competitive U.S. Senate races reveal average incumbent fundraising receipts of roughly $8 million.[8] These levels of campaign spending undoubtedly affect eligible candidates' interest in running for office. The sentiments of Matthew Halloway, the executive director of a Montana branch of the Sierra Club, reflect many respondents' concerns about the vast amounts of money required to run for office: "I read that Dianne Feinstein has to raise $10,000 a day just to stay competitive. That degree of fundraising would be too difficult for me. I would not even be willing to give it a shot." Concern over the amount of money needed to run for office trickles down to the local level as well. Carrie Hodge, a political activist, believes that the costs of campaigns make running for office "too daunting to think about. And it's not only Congress. All campaigns have become so expensive." Indeed, in just one example, the last three election cycles in Sunnyvale, California – a relatively small city with a population of only 138,000 residents – saw the average city council candidate spend $31,000 on the campaign trail. The winners in each race spent, on average, $43,000.[9]

---

[8] Elana Schor, "Campaign Contributions up Despite Economic Downturn: Tightest Races Draw More Money in First Quarter Than Last Cycle," *Washington Independent*, April 17, 2009, http://washingtonindependent.com/39299/campaign-contributions-up-despite-economic-downturn (accessed August 21, 2009).

[9] Office of the Mayor and Council, "Public Financing of City Council Elections," October 7, 2008, http://www.sunnyvale.ca.gov/NR/rdonlyres/9E16B7D0-B908-4A27-8637-01F339ABE951/0/107StudySessionReport.pdf (accessed August 23, 2009).

Also necessary for a viable candidacy is a willingness to endure a loss of privacy. Even individuals who seek local level offices often reference the unwelcome intrusion into one's personal life that can accompany a political campaign and public service. In April 2008, Alabama's *Mobile Register* surveyed roughly four hundred city residents about their interest in running for office. Only 12 percent of those surveyed expressed any interest in a future run. And among the 88 percent with no ambition to enter the electoral arena, loss of personal privacy was a leading reason.[10] Cathy Lipsett, a former member of the school board in Marietta, Georgia, also explained that serving as an elected official can be "emotionally draining," in large part because of the invasion into one's personal life: "It's a scrutiny of everything you do, everything you say. You never know what's going to end up in the newspaper. Or if something you say will come back at you."[11] Sandy Freedman, the former mayor of Tampa, Florida, offered a similar outlook when she reflected on the "demeaning, almost ridiculous" campaign process: "There is a loss of privacy, a feeling that nothing is off limits.... I think [we] are already seeing candidates of a lesser quality in many cases because people don't want to put themselves through this."[12]

Overall, the eligible candidates with whom we spoke identified the potential loss of privacy as a primary reason not to run for office. Stacy Blick-Newell, a businesswoman from northern California, follows politics very closely, but would never run for office because that involves "giving up the right to privacy that our country still affords us." Missouri trial lawyer Adriana Hunter is convinced that she could endure the scrutiny that accompanies a political campaign. She explained, however, that she does not care to subject herself to it. "Why punish myself if I don't have to?" Ben Finkelstein, an attorney from Washington, asked a similar question: "If you run, you're treated horribly, your life ravaged like a piece of meat fed to hungry vultures. Who could deal with that? Who'd want to deal with that?"

The women and men we interviewed frequently associated the loss of privacy with the contemporary news media's willingness to delve into almost all aspects of a candidate's life. In the words of an Arizona

---

[10] "Ethics Training Could Ease Voters' Distrust," *Mobile (AL) Register*, April 21, 2008, A06.

[11] Mary MacDonald, "Small Cities Face Politician Paucity," *Atlanta Journal-Constitution*, September 15, 2001, 1C.

[12] George Coryell, "Election Losers Find Life Goes On," *Tampa (FL) Tribune*, September 10, 2000, 1.

businessman, "Running means there's no privacy in your life. The press is merciless in the search to exploit anything to sell papers." Jean Grund, an activist from Idaho, elaborated when she described a Mormon talk-radio show that has a "huge listener-ship." She explained that anyone who runs for office – regardless of the position – has to go on the show for exposure:

> There are these two women hosts who are absolutely awful. They focus on things that have nothing to do with your qualifications. It's all about irrelevant issues and your scandalous past. Without fail, the first question they ask is your opinion on abortion. Then they ask if you've had an abortion, why you murdered your unborn child, whether you'd let your daughter have an abortion. These kinds of questions seem odd to ask of candidates running for county assessor, don't you think? I refuse to endure it.

For a female attorney from Colorado, being subjected to "press speculations, nefarious background checks, and all kinds of commentary without having the opportunity to respond" are sufficient deterrents to running for office. Florida business owner George Ortega explained that he would never run because "the press launches personal attacks and places your life under a microscope."

Many respondents noted that, even if they were willing to bear the loss of privacy, they could never ask their families to endure it. Bill Whitford, for instance, is a businessman from Arkansas who has thought about running for office "many times." He has always decided against it, though, because the campaign process could "destroy [his] family." He commented, "I would like to think that I don't have skeletons, but I'm sure they'd find them, between business interests, my wife, my children. Everything could be ruined for them and for me." The director of a Southern branch of the American Civil Liberties Union explained, "When you move from behind the scenes to the actual political scene, your life becomes a fishbowl. I can't do that – either to myself or my family."

Whereas other forms of political activism afford individuals a sense of privacy, running for office knows no boundaries. Nancy Davidson, a professor from Georgia, captured this distinction well:

> I am very interested in politics. I read three newspapers, watch the news everyday, and always listen to talk radio. I also always vote and am active around issues. I was recently a plaintiff in an ACLU case, I belong to women's rights organizations, whenever there's a pro-choice march or protest, I participate. But I wouldn't run for office because there are too many skeletons in my closet. I'm fifty years old – do the math; I've been

around the block and all it takes is one disgruntled boyfriend to expose someone's past.

The words of a California attorney represent, almost verbatim, many respondents' conclusions: "The intrusion into one's privacy that comes with a campaign is such that one would have to be insane to run for office."

Cincinnati high school teacher Barry Carter's explanation for why he would never run for office embodies the culmination of factors referenced by the eligible candidates we interviewed. Mr. Carter concluded that American politicians have a "psychological quirk" that causes them to enter such an undesirable profession:

> Most people I know who would be good candidates are unwilling to spend the time, money, and media scrutiny necessary to effectively run. It's just something they'd never do because it's too awful a process. No degree of civic duty or sense of obligation would lead a sane person to enter the trenches. This leaves the pool of office seekers to consist almost entirely of over achieving, emotionally stunted student body presidents. I'm just not one of those people.

Neither is Amanda Reese, a political activist from Colorado. Although she thought "very seriously" about running for state representative, she decided against entering the race for a variety of reasons: "I don't like being lied to or about. I don't like the arm-twisting that goes on at the state capitol. I don't like the deal making. . . . If I had to sum it up, I'd say I decided not to run because I don't want to have to interact daily with lying, egotistical, manipulative, crybaby scum."

To gauge more accurately and systematically the extent to which the nuts and bolts of campaigning deter eligible candidates from running for office, we included in the 2008 survey a battery of questions pertaining to eight aspects of electoral politics. Five of the activities about which we asked refer to the mechanics of a campaign; three focus on the personal toll a campaign might take. We asked respondents the extent to which they would feel comfortable undertaking each activity. We also asked whether negative feelings eligible candidates reported about any specific aspect of electoral politics would ultimately deter them from running for office. The data presented in Table 7.2 confirm the general trends we uncovered in the interviews and also reveal that women are statistically more likely than men to view all eight aspects of running for office so negatively that they serve as deterrents to running for office. Overall, 67 percent of women, compared to 54 percent of men, were deterred by at least one typical campaign activity (difference significant at $p < .05$). These

TABLE 7.2. *Eligible Candidates' Willingness to Engage in Campaign Activities*

| | Percentage Responding "So negative it would deter me from running for office." | |
|---|---|---|
| | Women | Men |
| **Mechanics of the Campaign** | | |
| Soliciting campaign contributions | 29%* | 21% |
| Dealing with party officials | 15* | 11 |
| Going door-to-door to meet constituents | 19* | 14 |
| Dealing with members of the press | 15* | 10 |
| Potentially having to engage in a negative campaign | 45* | 30 |
| **Personal Aspects of the Campaign** | | |
| Potentially hindering professional goals | 19* | 15 |
| Spending less time with your family | 33* | 25 |
| Loss of privacy | 46* | 37 |
| N | 866 | 1,029 |

*Notes:* Results are based on the 2008 survey data. Number of cases varies slightly as some respondents omitted answers to some questions. Significance levels of chi-square test comparing women and men: * $p < .05$.

findings are similar to research conducted in the early 1990s that found women less likely than men to be drawn to the rigors of an electoral contest (National Women's Political Caucus 1994; Staton/Hughes Research Group 1992). The new 2008 data reveal that, despite the increased number of women in politics, women's attitudes about entering the electoral arena remain more pessimistic than those of men.

Notably, the overwhelming majority of respondents – women and men alike – would be more likely to express interest in a political position if they did not have to campaign at all. In fact, 73 percent of women and 69 percent of men report that they would be more likely to seek a position of political power if they could do so without engaging in campaign activities. Despite the general disinclination toward the mechanics and personal trade-offs involved in running for office, however, women are significantly more likely than men to assert that their negative feelings toward the various aspects of a campaign prevent them from entering the electoral arena.

## Gender and the Decision to Enter a Race

Despite the widespread negative views of campaigning and the electoral process, the results of the first wave of the survey revealed that 320 members of our sample of the candidate eligibility pool stepped forward as candidates and ran for office at some point in their lives. When taken as a proportion of the entire sample, 12 percent of men and 7 percent of women launched a candidacy (see Chapter 3). By the time we completed the second wave of the data collection in 2008, fifty-four additional respondents emerged as candidates (forty-one of whom won their races). Thus, we have a unique opportunity to assess the factors that transform politically engaged citizens into actual candidates, as well as the manner in which patterns of traditional gender socialization influence the calculus.

In beginning an empirical analysis of who launches an actual candidacy, it is important first to paint a portrait of the eligible candidates who reach this second stage of the candidate emergence process. A greater proportion of men than women face the decision to run for office because women are significantly less likely than men to have considered running. Table 7.3 presents a fully specified model of who considers a candidacy. Because of the inclusion of interaction terms, the coefficient (and predicted probability) associated with the sex variable – in and of itself – does not accurately reflect the gender gap in political ambition (or the lack thereof). Like the analysis presented in Chapter 6, we can assess the extent to which the model explains the gender gap only by looking beyond the negative coefficient on sex and generating predicted probabilities.

The results we presented in Chapters 4, 5, and 6 offer substantial leverage not only in predicting whether a respondent has considered running for office, but also in accounting for and explaining the gender gap in political ambition. The logistic regression results reported in Table 7.3 translate to mean that, all else equal, a woman who self-assesses as "very qualified" to run for office and has received the suggestion to run from a family member and an electoral gatekeeper is only 3 percentage points less likely than a similarly situated man to consider running (0.86 predicted probability, compared to 0.89). But all else is not equal; women's greater likelihood of perceiving themselves as unqualified to run for office, coupled with their stronger reliance on these self-perceptions, points to the pervasive nature of the gendered psyche in the political realm. Undoubtedly, traditional family role orientations and a masculinized ethos fuel these perceptions, as women are significantly less likely than men to receive encouragement to run for office, both from personal sources and political actors. Women are more likely than men to weed themselves out of the candidate emergence process.

Performing a series of simple simulations highlights the power of this winnowing process and calls attention to the dramatic changes that would

TABLE 7.3. *The Fully Specified Model of Who Considers Running for Office (Logistic Regression Coefficients, Standard Errors, and Change in Probabilities)*

| | Coefficient (Standard Error) | Maximum Change in Probability (Percentage Points) |
|---|---|---|
| **Baseline Indicators** | | |
| Sex (female) | −1.28 (.28)** | 11.7 |
| Education | .03 (.05) | − |
| Income | −.19 (.04)** | 17.2 |
| Race (White) | 50 (.13)** | 11.1 |
| Political interest | .04 (.04) | − |
| Political participation | .13 (.03)** | 24.5 |
| Political knowledge | .08 (.06) | − |
| Political efficacy | .08 (.05) | − |
| **Political Socialization** | | |
| "Political" household | .09 (.05) | 14.4 |
| Parent ran for office | .36 (.14)** | 5.7 |
| Ran for office as a student | .34 (.10)** | 7.3 |
| **Family Structures, Roles, and Support** | | |
| Age | −.03 (.01)** | 13.7 |
| Marital status (married) | .18 (.15) | − |
| Responsible for majority of household tasks | .05 (.11) | − |
| Responsible for majority of child care | .08 (.16) | − |
| Received encouragement from personal source | 1.63 (.11)** | 38.5 |
| **Political Parties and Recruitment** | | |
| Democrat | .21 (.12) | − |
| Republican | .09 (.13) | − |
| Recruited by political actor | .73 (.12)** | 12.2 |
| **Qualifications** | | |
| Self-perceived qualifications | .47 (.07)** | 22.6 |
| Self-perceived qualifications * female | .26 (.10)* | 44.8 |
| Constant | −2.47 (.52)** | |
| Pseudo-$R^2$ | .50 | |
| Percentage Correctly Predicted | 78.6 | |
| N | 3,029 | |

*Notes:* Results are based on the 2001 survey data. Maximum changes in probabilities are based on the logistic regression results. These probabilities were calculated by setting all continuous independent variables not under consideration to their means and dummy variables not under consideration to their modes. For age, we varied the predicted probabilities from one standard deviation above to one standard deviation below the mean. Because of the inclusion of the interaction term, the coefficient (and predicted probability) associated with the sex variable – in and of itself – does not accurately capture the gender gap in political ambition. We must assess the joint effect of the principal components and the interaction term. Significance levels: ** $p < .01$; * $p < .05$.

be necessary to close the gender gap in considering a candidacy. Given the current levels of recruitment, self-perceived qualifications, and all other variables used to predict whether an individual has ever considered running for office, the regression results presented in Table 7.3 project that 57 percent of men and 40 percent of women will emerge from the eligibility pool and consider a candidacy.[13] We can simulate new projections of the percentage of women who would consider running for office by increasing the proportion of women who were tapped to run for office or who self-assessed as "very qualified" to run.

Turning first to recruitment, the simulation results indicate that if all of the women in the pool of eligible candidates received the suggestion to run for office from an electoral gatekeeper, then, assuming no changes in any other variables, the gender gap in considering a candidacy would decrease considerably. Yet even extremely high levels of political recruitment cannot fully mitigate the gender disparities in the first stage of the candidate emergence process. If more than twice as many women than men were recruited to run for office (100 percent of women compared to 43 percent of men), then 52 percent of women (compared to 57 percent of men) would consider a candidacy. Hence, fewer women than men would still reach the next stage of the candidate emergence process.

Another way to minimize the gender gap in considering a candidacy would be through modifying self-perceived qualifications to run for office. But here, too, the degree of sweeping change needed to attain an equal number of women and men to consider running for office is daunting. If every woman in the eligibility pool self-assessed as "very qualified" to run, then more women than men would reach the second stage of the candidate emergence process (70 percent of women compared to 57 percent of men). Gaining this moderate edge in political ambition, though, depends on women being four times as likely as men to consider themselves "very qualified" to run for office.

These simulations indicate that only a combination of profound changes – not only in terms of how women in the eligibility pool perceive themselves, but also in terms of how their professional, political, and personal networks perceive them – can begin to lessen the gender gap in considering a candidacy. Barring such change, women will continue to

---

[13] These percentages differ somewhat from the actual percentages of women and men who considered running for office because our projections are based on holding all independent variables at their means for the subsample of men and the subsample of women.

be less likely than men to consider running for office, so they will remain less likely than men even to reach the second stage of the candidate emergence process.

Currently, the women who do reach the second stage look a lot like the men, but a lot different from the women in the overall candidate eligibility pool. Consider external support for a candidacy by an electoral gatekeeper (Figure 7.1A). In the overall pool of eligible candidates, 43 percent of men, compared to 32 percent of women, received the suggestion to run for office from a party leader, elected official, or political activist. Among those respondents who considered a candidacy, women and men are equally likely to have received encouragement (60 percent of men compared to 57 percent of women). Of those who actually ran for office, more than four out of every five women and men received the suggestion from a political actor. Similar patterns emerge in terms of support from personal sources (Figure 7.1B) and self-perceived qualifications (Figure 7.1C). Thus, because only respondents who have considered running for office can enter actual electoral contests, we might expect fewer gender differences at this stage of the process.

Table 7.4 reports the logistic regression coefficients predicting who launches a candidacy, controlling for the baseline correlates of political ambition, as well as the gauges of traditional gender socialization we analyzed in predicting who considers running for office. Prior to explicating the findings, it is important to acknowledge that our model does not include a measure of eligible candidates' perceived likelihood of winning. Many studies find that officeholders' motivations to seek higher office are guided by how they assess their likelihood of winning, as they are unwilling to sacrifice their current levels of power if they are not confident they will acquire more of it.[14] A study geared to investigate the initial decision to run, however, cannot easily tap into the perceived likelihood of winning, as it requires a retrospective assessment. Of the women and men in the sample who actually sought elective positions, 52 percent of men and 51 percent of women contend that they would have been "likely" or "very likely" to win their race. For similar reasons, we do not include as an explanatory variable respondents' attitudes about engaging in campaigns. Individuals who ran for office expressed more negative attitudes

---

[14] As we discussed in Chapter 2, a wide body of literature employs objective indicators of the likelihood of winning a race as chief predictors of static, progressive, and discrete ambition. See, e.g., Maestas et al. 2006; Stone, Maisel and Maestas 2004; Stone and Maisel 2003; Kazee 1980, 1994; Rohde 1979; Black 1972; Schlesinger 1966.

FIGURE 7.1A. Gender Differences in Political Recruitment throughout the Candidate Emergence Process.

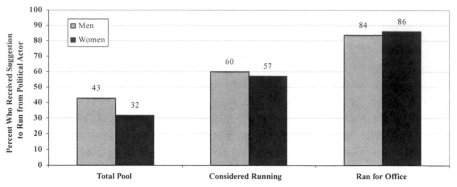

FIGURE 7.1B. Gender Differences in Personal Support throughout the Candidate Emergence Process.

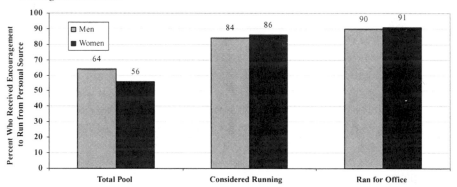

FIGURE 7.1C. Gender Differences in Self-Perceived Qualifications throughout the Candidate Emergence Process.

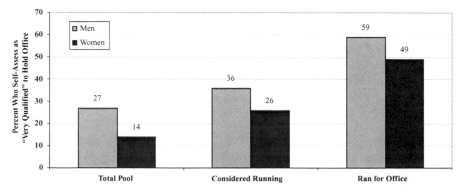

than did women and men who never launched a candidacy, probably a result of actual candidates' firsthand experiences. Among individuals who ran for office, though, women were no more likely than men to reflect negatively on the candidate emergence and campaign process.

The results that emerge from our regression analysis indicate that older respondents, as well as those with high levels of political activism and encouragement from political actors, are more likely to run for office. Eligible candidates who consider themselves qualified to run for office are also more likely to launch a candidacy.

Higher incomes, in contrast, depress the likelihood of running. For the 27 percent of respondents with household incomes that exceed $200,000, a political career may represent a particularly costly endeavor. Mary King, former supervisor of Alameda County, California, serves as an example of an individual forced to deal with the financial trade-offs involved in holding elective office. She chose not to seek reelection because she could earn more money in the private sector:

> The job pays about $54,000 a year, you work seven days a week, you can't make any outside income without it being one kind of conflict or another, and the job can be very, very trying. I had to start thinking about retiring, as a single parent who had sent my kids through school.... I had to think, how am I going to take care of myself and take my skills and transfer them into something that is going to be more professionally lucrative?[15]

Many eligible candidates choose not to run for office for similar reasons. David Carroway, for example, has been practicing law in Kentucky for thirty years. He explained that he cannot run, even though he thinks about it often: "My job allows me a lot of comfort. If I ran, I'd have to take off a great deal of time and that would put too big a dent in my pocket." Hilda Morganthau has practiced law in Wyoming for eighteen years. She, too, could never run for office because "the financial hit would be devastating." Attorneys Tom Corwin (Oklahoma), John Desmond (Colorado), and Barbara Judson (California) were among the twenty-six out of sixty-eight lawyers we interviewed who noted that the financial ramifications and opportunity costs that accompany a political candidacy would be too much to bear. Several businesspeople and executives expressed similar views. Summarized well by a small business owner from Lubbock, Texas, "I couldn't run for any kind of office, even if it

[15] James Kellybrew, "An Exclusive Interview with Alameda County Supervisor Mary King," *Gibbs Magazine*, August 12, 2004, http://www.gibbsmagazine.com/Mary%20King.htm (accessed December 20, 2009).

TABLE 7.4. *The Fully Specified Model of Who Runs for Office (Logistic Regression Coefficients, Standard Errors, and Change in Probabilities)*

| | Model 1 | | Model 2 | |
|---|---|---|---|---|
| | Coefficient (Standard Error) | Maximum Change in Probability (Percentage Points) | Coefficient (Standard Error) | Maximum Change in Probability (Percentage Points) |
| **Baseline Indicators** | | | | |
| Sex (female) | -.32 (.20) | — | -.65 (1.71) | — |
| Education | -.04 (.09) | — | -.06 (.09) | — |
| Income | -.20 (.07)** | 3.9 | -.24 (.09)** | 4.9 |
| Race (White) | -.06 (.21) | — | -.06 (.21) | — |
| Political interest | .09 (.06) | — | .17 (.08)* | 3.0 |
| Political participation | .15 (.05)** | 3.6 | .19 (.06)** | 4.6 |
| Political knowledge | .10 (.14) | — | .10 (.14) | — |
| Political efficacy | .04 (.08) | — | .04 (.08) | — |
| **Political Socialization** | | | | |
| "Political" household | -.13 (.08) | — | -.14 (.08) | — |
| Parent ran for office | -.10 (.21) | — | -.08 (.21) | — |
| Ran for office as a student | -.11 (.17) | — | -.10 (.17) | — |
| **Family Structures, Roles, and Support** | | | | |
| Age | .05 (.01)** | 4.0 | .05 (.01)** | 4.7 |
| Marital status (married) | .38 (.29) | — | .38 (.29) | — |
| Responsible for majority of household tasks | .24 (.20) | — | .23 (.21) | — |
| Responsible for majority of child care | .44 (.29) | — | .41 (.29) | — |
| Received encouragement from personal source | -.18 (.29) | — | -.19 (.30) | — |

| | Coefficient (SE) | Maximum Change | Coefficient (SE) | Maximum Change |
|---|---|---|---|---|
| **Political Parties and Recruitment** | | | | |
| Democrat | .08 (.21) | — | .09 (.21) | — |
| Republican | .18 (.22) | — | .22 (.22) | — |
| Recruited by political actor | .99 (.23)** | 4.9 | .83 (.28)** | 3.8 |
| **Self-Perceived Qualifications** | .62 (.11)** | 6.2 | .69 (.15)** | 6.9 |
| **Structural Variables** | | | | |
| Interested in high-level office | -.10 (.17) | — | -.10 (.17) | — |
| Political culture factor score | .18 (.08)* | 2.4 | .14 (.09) | — |
| **Interactions** | | | | |
| Income * female | | | .12 (.14) | — |
| Political participation * female | | | -.14 (.11) | — |
| Age * female | | | -.00 (.02) | — |
| Recruited by political actor * female | | | .54 (.47) | — |
| Self-perceived qualifications * female | | | -.18 (.22) | — |
| Political culture * female | | | .15 (.17) | — |
| Political interest * female | | | .24 (.13) | — |
| Constant | -7.74 (.99)** | | -8.24 (1.12)** | |
| Pseudo-R$^2$ | .28 | | .29 | |
| Percentage Correctly Predicted | 84.7 | | 85.3 | |
| N | 1,507 | | 1,507 | |

*Notes:* Results are based on the 2001 survey data. Maximum changes in probabilities are based on the logistic regression results. These probabilities were calculated by setting all continuous independent variables not under consideration to their means and dummy variables not under consideration to their modes. For age, we varied the predicted probabilities from one standard deviation above to one standard deviation below the mean. The change in probability reflects the independent effect a statistically significant variable exerts as we vary its value from its minimum to maximum (e.g., the change in probability for recruited by a political actor reflects the fact that a respondent who was recruited is 4.9 percentage points more likely than one who was not to run for office). Significance levels: ** $p < .01$; * $p < .05$.

153

was part-time. I'd have to take time off of work and that'd mean having
to give up everything I've worked so hard to achieve."

Perhaps the most striking result to emerge from the regression analysis is that, as we move throughout the candidate emergence process, the
effects of gender dissipate. Most of the traditional gender socialization
variables, such as a politicized upbringing, family structures, the division
of household and child-care responsibilities, and support from family
and friends, are statistically insignificant. Even sex itself does not predict
whether an eligible candidate enters an actual race. The "average" male
respondent has a 0.13 predicted probability of entering a race; an eligible
woman candidate's likelihood is roughly 0.10. Moreover, women and
men who reach this stage of the candidate emergence process rely on a
comparable decision structure (Table 7.4, column 3).[16] The lack of significance for each interaction term indicates that the variables that predict
men's likelihood of entering an electoral contest also predict women's
likelihood; and the magnitude of each variable's effect is not conditioned
by sex.

Although sex does not predict the likelihood of entering a race, it continues to exert a substantial effect through self-perceived qualifications.
Twenty-six percent of women who reach this stage consider themselves
"very qualified" to run for office, compared to 36 percent of men (difference significant at $p < .01$). When an eligible candidate considers himself or herself highly qualified, the likelihood of launching a candidacy
increases by more than 63 percent. Even though both women and men
rely heavily on their perceived qualifications when determining whether
to turn the consideration of a candidacy into an actual campaign, women
continue to be disadvantaged by their self-assessments.

### A Side Note on Political Culture and Structural Factors

Several studies suggest that the political environment has a gendered
effect on citizens' attitudes about entering the political system. David
Hill (1981) finds, for example, that, among citizens who choose to run
for office, women are more likely to emerge as candidates in states that
established an early pattern of electing women to the state legislature,

---

[16] When we performed the regression analysis separately on the subsamples of women
and men, we uncovered few differences. In an attempt to determine whether any of the
differences were statistically significant, we interacted with sex all variables that were
significant predictors of entering a race in the separate equations we performed on the
subsamples of women and men.

support women's participation in public affairs, and do not have a tradition of sex discrimination in income, or gender disparities in educational achievement. Women are less likely to run for office in states with a traditional culture (Rule 1990; Nechemias 1987), such as those located in the south (Fox 2010). The political geography and sociodemographic profile of a locality, district, or state, therefore, can affect women's representation (see Palmer and Simon 2008). Hence, it is important to note that the indirect role gender plays in the second stage of the candidate emergence process withstands controls for political culture, which we measure as a factor analytic composite of the percentage of women serving in the state legislature and the percentage of the state's Democratic presidential vote share.[17] Eligible candidates are more likely to emerge in more Democratic states and in states with a greater percentage of women in the state legislature. The interaction between political culture and sex, however, is not statistically significant, perhaps because women in the sample who live in particularly traditional environments have already overcome numerous obstacles in achieving professional success.[18]

Moreover, as we discussed in Chapter 2, structural variables that tap into the political contexts in which respondents live also might affect the initial decision to run for office. When we include in the fully specified model measures of legislative professionalization, the size and openness of the state's political opportunity structure, whether the state imposed term limits, and whether the respondent's party identification is congruent with the majority of the residents in the state, none of the variables achieves conventional levels of statistical significance.[19] This is not altogether surprising, as fewer than 4 percent of the women and men who considered running for office actually sought a statewide or congressional office. When we restrict the sample only to individuals who expressed interest in seeking a state or federal office and predict whether the respondent actually ran, several of the coefficients on the structural variables approach

---

[17] This variable correlates highly with Elazar's (1984) political culture measure ($r = .60$; $p < .01$), which is widely used throughout the women and politics literature. We employ our measure because it is more current.

[18] Perhaps for similar reasons, political culture does not predict whether an eligible candidate has considered running for office, whether he or she has been recruited to run, or whether he or she self-assesses as "qualified," nor does it interact statistically with the sex of the eligible candidate in any of these cases. Within the general population, however, women's levels of political proselytizing (Hansen 1997) and political interest (Burns, Schlozman, and Verba 2001) correlate with the presence of women elected officials.

[19] For a more detailed discussion of the influence structural variables exert on this sample of the eligibility pool's candidate emergence process, see Fox and Lawless 2005.

borderline significance in the expected direction. More important for our purposes, however, is that interaction terms between the sex of the respondent and the structural variables are never statistically significant.

We cannot capture the extent to which structural variables play a role in the initial decision to run for office, though, because we lack indicators of the local political context. The total number of local governmental units by state – which serves as the one local structural variable we can measure – is statistically insignificant, as is its interaction with sex. But we do not have gauges of the partisan composition of local constituencies, or information pertaining to the size and levels of incumbency associated with local offices, such as school board and city council.

Despite the limited quantitative evidence we can provide to tap into the extent to which structural variables affect the initial decision to run for office at the local level, the comments relayed by the eligible candidates we interviewed clearly indicate their effect. And as was the case for state level and federal level offices, we are confident that, at the local level, the effect of structural variables, such as incumbency, is not gendered. Eligible candidates with whom we spoke frequently mentioned that they would not run for office if they had to face a strong incumbent or if they were not politically in sync with their communities. Attorney Ellen Chapman noted, for instance, that Denver, Colorado, is becoming increasingly conservative. She explained that she could not run for the city council or any other municipal position: "I am definitely not in sync with this new majority. I would be unelectable." Professor Renee Gersten would also never run, even though she would "love to do it," because her views are not congruent with her town's residents: "They'd burn me or throw me in jail before they'd elect me. It's not worth it to run." Phil Bensen, a history professor at a large university in the South, feels the same way: "I don't fit in here politically. I'd like to run, but I'd never get elected locally, so it would be a waste of my time." In contrast, Amy Pittman, an attorney from Oklahoma, concluded: "My values and views are in line with the people in my community. This makes me more likely to run, not just because I could win, but because I wouldn't have to compromise my views. I'm just waiting for someone on the city council to retire." Texas businessman Mark Barnswell expressed a similar opinion when he explained that part of the reason he thinks about running for office "so often" is that he "is such a good fit policy-wise with the electorate." The president of an Indiana-based anti-choice organization noted that, like him, his community is 70 percent Republican. He plans to run for county commissioner "as soon as the guy in office retires." Structural variables

TABLE 7.5. *Eligible Candidates' Future Interest in Running for Office*

| | 2001 | | 2008 | |
|---|---|---|---|---|
| | Women | Men | Women | Men |
| Definitely want to run for office in the future | 3% | 4% | 3% | 3% |
| Would be willing to run if the opportunity presented itself | 15* | 19 | 14 | 17 |
| No current interest in running, but would not rule it out forever | 54 | 56 | 49 | 52 |
| Absolutely no interest in a future run for office | 28** | 21 | 34** | 28 |
| N | 1,621 | 1,829 | 899 | 1,078 |

*Notes*: Results are based on the 2001 and 2008 survey data. Significance levels of chi-square test comparing women and men: ** p < .01; * p < .05.

and strategic considerations very likely affect the decision to run for office at the local level, but women and men appear equally likely to rely on these factors.

## Prospective Interest in Running for Office

Gender affects not only whether respondents ever considered running or ran for office, but also whether they are interested in running in the future. Table 7.5 presents the breakdown of women and men's interest in a future candidacy in 2001 and 2008. The 2001 data reveal that women are significantly less likely than men to express interest in running for office at any point in the future. When we combine respondents who have a "definite desire to run in the future" with those who have a "willingness to run if the opportunity presented itself," men are 28 percent more likely than women to express prospective interest in seeking office. The gender gap in prospective interest narrowed by the time of the 2008 survey. Women are still less likely to express interest in a future run, but the gender difference fails to achieve statistical significance. It is important to recognize, though, that between the two waves of the survey, aggregate levels of interest in running for office at some point in the future declined. And women remain statistically more likely than men to write off a future candidacy altogether.

Among the eligible candidates we interviewed, the most frequently cited scenario that might lead to a future candidacy was increased passion for a particular issue or policy. Lisa Cantwell, the owner of a small business located outside of San Diego, California, put it this way: "The conservative direction our country has taken has made me consider running for office. It's made me a lot more angry and I have come to realize that good people are bowing out of politics. If this continues, I might run." Cecilia Dan also described political ideology as a potentially motivating factor:

> In Idaho, we enjoy a Republican majority in the House and Senate. In my county, it's becoming more mixed, with liberal hippies moving in from Boise. . . . If conservative voices begin to be silenced by these city people, I might have to get in there and do something about it.

Other eligible candidates cited more specific policies that could motivate a future candidacy. Gregory D'Andrea, a college administrator from Minnesota, would run "if we continue to make budget cuts in education and the [National Rifle Association] continues to control all the gun legislation." He could envision himself getting "so fed up" that he would "have to do something." Oregon lawyer Rachel Peterson believes that "an eventual run for office is imminent," mostly because of her concern for civil liberties violations: "The recent developments are pushing me like I've never been pushed before." Our survey evidence reveals that more than 40 percent of eligible candidates state that they would be more likely to run for office if motivated by a particular policy issue.

Although women and men were equally likely to refer to issues that could motivate them to run for office, we uncovered significant gender differences in several of the other factors that might propel a candidacy. We presented respondents with a list of eleven items that might encourage them to run for office in the future. The data presented in Table 7.6 reveal that many of the patterns of traditional gender socialization that affect whether respondents ever considered running for office or ever ran for office also emerge when we turn to ambition to seek elective office in the future.

Foremost, the masculinized ethos that detracts from women's likelihood of having considered a candidacy will likely continue to affect their emergence as candidates. Table 7.6 indicates that the factors associated with an encouraging political environment are the most influential for all eligible candidates, regardless of sex. Men are statistically more likely than women to anticipate responding positively to recruitment and external support for a candidacy, but the substantive gender differences are relatively small. Attorney Jose Espinoza highlighted the importance

TABLE 7.6. *Factors That Might Encourage Eligible Candidates to Run for Office in the Future*

| Percentage of eligible candidates who would be more likely to run for office if . . . | Women | Men |
|---|---|---|
| **Encouraging Political Environment** | | |
| Campaigns were publicly financed | 60%** | 50% |
| Received the suggestion from party or community leader | 49* | 53 |
| There was a lot of support for the candidacy | 69 | 72 |
| **Encouraging Personal Environment** | | |
| Received the suggestion from a friend | 25** | 33 |
| Received the suggestion from spouse/partner | 32** | 42 |
| Had more free time | 66 | 70 |
| Had more financial security | 56* | 61 |
| **Credentials, Experience, and Self-Motivation** | | |
| Had more impressive professional credentials | 28** | 21 |
| Had more public speaking experience | 33** | 22 |
| Had previous experience working on a campaign | 43** | 36 |
| Had more passions for political issues | 43 | 47 |
| N | 1,047 | 1,247 |

*Notes:* Results are based on the 2001 survey data. Cell entries represent the percentage of respondents who said that they would be more likely to run for office under the specified condition. N includes only those respondents who have never run for public office, but who have not ruled out entirely the prospects of a future candidacy. Significance levels of chi-square test comparing women and men: ** $p < .01$; * $p < .05$.

of external support when asked about the circumstances under which he could foresee running for office: "The only thing that would accelerate my running for office would be if an opportunity came about and there was substantial encouragement. If this were the case, I might take a chance and run even if it was not the best time for me." Olivia Bartlett, a political activist from Wisconsin, would run only after developing better connections and ties to the community. She believes that she needs a "better sense of the local political environment and who the players are." Similarly, Tom Johnson, a Virginia executive, noted that if many people came to him and demonstrated that he had grassroots support, then he would be more likely to run. As documented in Chapter 5, women are less likely than men to be encouraged to run for office.

That said, the emergence of women's organizations dedicated to increasing the number of female candidates bodes well for increasing women's presence in electoral politics in the years to come (see Chapter 5). In the second wave of the survey, we asked respondents whether they would be more inclined to consider a candidacy if they had access to reading materials, experts, webcasts, and training programs – four central tools on which women's organizations currently rely to bring more women into the political process. Across the board, women were at least as likely as men to respond positively to each resource. In fact, 25 percent of women (compared to 18 percent of men) would be more likely to think about running for office if they had the opportunity to attend a training program sponsored by a political organization (difference significant at $p < .05$). Women, therefore, are approximately 40 percent more likely than men to respond favorably to the notion of working with a political organization to develop the skills and connections to run for office at some point in the future. This finding certainly validates the work of women's groups and the methods they currently employ.

The data presented in Table 7.6 indicate that the masculinized ethos is not the only component of traditional gender socialization that will continue to impede women's candidate emergence. Traditional family role orientations likely also limit women's future ability to launch a candidacy. Women and men emphasize that free time is one of the most important factors that would encourage them to run for office in the future; the importance of more free time is second only to external support for a candidacy. As Colorado attorney Nina Henderson stated, "My current job is extremely time consuming. If that were somehow to change, I would consider running for office." Despite her high level of interest in politics, Maureen Martin, a high school principal from New Jersey, cannot run because of her job and family responsibilities. She commented that the only thing that would let her pursue a candidacy, even for a local office, would be "retirement." In light of the distribution of household and child-care responsibilities discussed in Chapter 4, women's prospects of accruing more free time seem far less likely than men's.

Finally, the gendered psyche leads men of all backgrounds and professions to be more likely than women to believe they already possess the experience needed to run for office. The bottom category presented in Table 7.6 focuses on eligible candidates' credentials, political experience, and self-motivation. Here, we uncover some of the sharpest gender differences that could lead to future candidacies. Women are 33 percent more likely than men to state that having more impressive credentials would heighten their likelihood of pursuing public office. They are 50 percent more likely than men to assert that more public speaking experience would increase their likelihood of running. And women are nearly 20 percent more likely than men to say they need additional campaign experience before running for office. Consistent with the respondents' remarks detailed in Chapter 6, women's self-doubts serve as deeply embedded obstacles to considering a candidacy, whether it be past, present, or future.

## Conclusion

At the second stage of the candidate emergence process – the decision to enter the first actual race – gender operates in a more subtle way than it does in considering a candidacy. Although some scholars might be tempted to interpret this finding as encouraging, we suggest that it must be evaluated within the context of the entire candidate emergence process. As a result of persistent patterns of traditional gender socialization, women are far less likely than men to consider a candidacy, so they are far less likely to face the decision to enter a race. And even when women do reach the second stage of the process, a greater proportion of women than men are held back by their negative self-assessments of their political qualifications, as well as their more negative perceptions of navigating the campaign trail.

The utility of our two-stage candidate emergence process is clear when we turn to two broad implications we can draw from it. First, the two-stage conception of political ambition allows us to identify more clearly the specific barriers to citizens' full inclusion in electoral politics. Research the focuses on the decision to enter specific political contests or that addresses actual candidates and officeholders' decisions to seek reelection, run for higher office, or retire from politics altogether overlooks many of the factors that affect political ambition. This is particularly relevant for the study of gender and elections, as well as women's underrepresentation, as many of the obstacles women face occur long before they enter political races.

Second, employing our conception of political ambition reveals that the end stage of the electoral process may not be as gender neutral as it is commonly described. Women who enter political races are not much different from men who run for office. Virtually all are supported by electoral gatekeepers and personal sources, and almost all consider themselves at least "qualified" to run. If women are more likely than men to doubt their own qualifications, though, then women who think they are "qualified" may actually be more qualified than men who self-assess this way. And if party leaders and other recruiters are less likely to encourage women to run, then women whom party leaders suggest for candidacy may also be more "qualified" than men they encourage. As long as women must meet higher standards, both self-imposed and external, then the apparent absence of voter bias against women candidates might reflect the higher average quality of women candidates, as compared to men.

# 8

# Gender and the Future of Electoral Politics

The most important and interesting question about women's political behavior is why so few seek and wield power. Women are numerous enough at the lowest level of politics – in the precincts, at the party picnics, getting out the vote, doing the telephoning, collecting the dollars – but remarkably scarce at the upper levels where decisions are made that affect the life of the community, state, nation.... Whether women have the capacity to participate fully in the power processes of society [and] why they have so rarely sought to do so... are empirical questions which can be answered only by systematic inquiry.

– Jeanne Kirkpatrick (1974, 23)

Women are active in politics in sizeable numbers – as party activists, as convention delegates, as staff members for other politicians, as community activists, as leaders in civic and community groups, as members of appointed boards and commissions. Yet few of these women seek elective office. Existing research has provided some clues as to why women might not run for office, but with very few exceptions, research has focused on women who became candidates for office or who were elected to office, not those who were dissuaded from running or who never considered running despite having qualifications and experience to do so. To develop a better understanding of why few women run for office, we need to examine what happens before primaries, i.e., the preprimary candidate selection process.

– Susan Carroll (1993, 214–15)

[U]nderstanding the factors that lead women to run for office and why women are discouraged from running is a neglected area of research. We miss half the story of women's representation if we only study women who run for office and ignore the women who do not run. The pre-candidacy stage remains as one of the great unexplored avenues of research.

– Kira Sanbonmatsu (2002, 792)

For the past thirty-five years, political scientists have issued the challenge to examine the initial decision to run for office and the gender dynamics that might underlie that process.[1] The first edition of this book took up that challenge. And in doing so, we uncovered three critical findings that provided dramatic evidence of gender's role in the candidate emergence process:

- Women are less likely than men to consider running for office.
- Women are less likely than men to run for office.
- Women are less likely than men to express interest in running for office in the future.

In this revised and expanded edition, we demonstrate that the gender gap in political ambition is roughly the same in 2008 as it was in 2001. In providing evidence for the enduring nature of the gender gap, we explain in far greater depth its roots. Moreover, in this edition, we rely on the second-wave survey data to offer a much more detailed account of women's recruitment experiences and perceptions of themselves as candidates for public office.

In light of the Citizen Political Ambition Panel Study, it is necessary not only to revise the prognosis for gender parity in political institutions, but also to recast the research agenda and areas of inquiry we pursue in the continued study of gender and U.S. politics. When women run for office, they win. But even educated, well-credentialed, professional women remain substantially less likely than men ever to emerge as candidates.

### Summarizing the Findings and Forecasting Women's Representation

Barbara Mikulski (D-MD), the longest serving woman in the U.S. Senate, hailed the results of the 2000 congressional elections. She explained that women candidates' successes pave the way for eventual gender parity in government: "Every Tom, Dick, and Harry is now going to be Hillary, Debbie, Jean, and Maria."[2] Six years later, politicians remained just as

---

[1] Gender politics scholars are not the only political scientists to identify the dearth of research pertaining to the initial decision to run for office. Donald Matthews (1984), Thomas Kazee (1994) and Walter Stone and L. Sandy Maisel (2003) also call attention to the little research that focuses on eligible candidates, despite its importance in helping political scientists develop a fuller understanding of the electoral process, candidate quality, and issues of representation.

[2] "More Women Go to Congress," *Houston (TX) Chronicle*, November 16, 2000, 7.

upbeat about women's electoral fortunes. According to Rahm Emanuel, who was chair of the Democratic Congressional Campaign Committee in 2006, female candidates were well positioned to compete and win in the most competitive districts: "In an environment where people are disgusted with politics in general, who represents clean and change? Women."[3] Indeed, noted professor and political analyst Larry Sabato predicted that 2006 would be the best year for women congressional candidates since 1992; he expected women to gain at least nine seats.[4] Even amid Hillary Clinton's presidential primary loss in 2008, Geraldine Ferraro voiced optimism when she reflected on Sarah Palin's place on the Republican ticket and women's prospects for political success: "I never thought I'd see another woman on a national ticket in this cycle after Hillary lost.... But it's like a ripple effect. Hillary's candidacy, my candidacy – they have a ripple effect far beyond the immediate results."[5]

Yet despite these assessments, as well as women's increasing presence in the professions from which most candidates emerge, significant gains in women's representation have not materialized in recent election cycles. We do not mean to minimize the past half century's evolution toward the social acceptance of women running for office. Prior to 1978, no woman whose career was not linked to the death of her spouse had ever served in the U.S. Senate (Gertzog 1995).[6] Currently, seventeen women serve in the Senate and seventy-five occupy positions in the House of Representatives. The 1992 "Year of the Woman" elections, alone, produced a 70 percent increase in the number of women serving in the U.S. Congress (from thirty-two to fifty-four).

But just as important as identifying the progress women have made is placing these advancements in the proper context. After steadily climbing for almost twenty years, the number of women state legislators has increased by less than two percentage points since 1992. The number of women serving in statewide elective office has actually declined in the past ten years. And the total number of women filing to run for the

---

[3] Robin Toner, "Women Wage Key Campaigns for Democrats," *New York Times*, March 24, 2006, A1.

[4] Sabato's prediction, like those of Barbara Mikulski and Rahm Emanuel, was wrong. Women gained only three congressional seats that cycle. Anushka Asthana, "A Political Opportunity for Women; Advocates Predict Gains in Congress and Push for More Participation," *Washington Post*, October 7, 2006, A9.

[5] Lois Romano, "Ideology Aside, This Has Been the Year of the Woman," *Washington Post*, October 24, 2008, A01.

[6] Historically, many women entered Congress as widows of congressmen. For more on congressional widows, see Palmer and Simon 2003; Solowiej and Brunell 2003.

U.S. House and Senate has increased only marginally throughout the past several election cycles. Even up through the the 2008 elections, more women filed to run for Congress in 1992 than ever have since.

Women's increasing presence in the candidate pipeline and voters' willingness to elect women candidates are certainly necessary for moving toward gender parity in elected bodies. But our empirical evidence, coupled with the words of the eligible candidates with whom we spoke, suggests that even if women were much better represented in the candidate eligibility pool, they would still be less likely than men to run for office. Women's full inclusion in our political institutions requires more than open seats and a steady increase in the number of women occupying the professions that most often precede political careers. It depends on closing the gender gap in political ambition.

The gender gap in political ambition is linked to three deeply embedded aspects of traditional gender socialization. Traditional family role orientations, a masculinized ethos, and the gendered psyche overlap, interact, and simultaneously affect eligible candidates' inclinations to pursue public office. The three-part conception we developed lends specificity to traditional gender socialization's pervasive effects, as well as to the sociocultural, institutional, and psychological obstacles women must overcome to emerge as candidates. Table 8.1 summarizes and categorizes our empirical and qualitative evidence. Juxtaposing the backgrounds and political experiences of two eligible candidates we surveyed and interviewed for this study illustrates our broad range of findings and underscores the value of our conception.

First, consider Jill Gruber, a forty-five-year-old high school principal. Although she rarely discussed politics with her parents when growing up, Ms. Gruber is very politically involved as an adult. Not only does she try to attend school board and city council meetings, but she is also an active member of several political organizations that focus on the environment and education. Ms. Gruber's political activism is somewhat limited by her lack of free time; she has three school-age children and performs more of the household tasks and child care than does her spouse, who is an elementary school principal. No friend or family member ever suggested that Ms. Gruber run for office. No colleague ever encouraged a candidacy. And no party official, officeholder, or fellow political activist ever mentioned that she should consider entering electoral politics. Though she has not considered running for office, Ms. Gruber is open to the idea "at some point down the road when the children are grown." But she doubts she could win. She does not view herself as qualified to seek most offices and she does not think she "know[s] the right people."

TABLE 8.1. *Summary of Findings Categorized by the Three-Part Conception of Traditional Gender Socialization*

**Evidence of Traditional Family Role Orientations among Eligible Candidates:**
- Within their childhood homes, women were less likely than men to discuss politics with their parents and less likely than men to be encouraged to run for office by their parents.
- Women are older than men when they first consider running for office.
- Women in the candidate eligibility pool are less likely than men to be married and have children.
- Women in marital relationships are more likely than men to be responsible for the majority of the household tasks.
- Women with children are more likely than men to be responsible for a majority of the child care.
- Women, across generations, are forced to reconcile career and family with political ambition in ways that men are not.
- Women receive less encouragement than men to run for office from family members and friends.

**Evidence of a Masculinized Ethos among Eligible Candidates:**
- Across profession and party, women are less likely than men to be recruited to run for office by party leaders and elected officials.
- An overwhelming majority of eligible candidates identify a sexist corporate culture.
- A majority of eligible candidates identify bias against women in the electoral arena.
- Women attorneys, educators, and political activists are less likely than men to be encouraged to run for office by colleagues.
- Across professions, women are less likely than men to be recruited to run for office by members of party organizations (e.g., party leaders and elected officials).
- Women are less likely than men to be recruited to run for office frequently.
- Women are less likely than men to be recruited to run for office by multiple electoral gatekeepers.
- The recruitment disadvantage is particularly pronounced for Republican women, most of whom do not benefit from the recent emergence of progressive women's organizations that bring Democratic women into the electoral process.

**Evidence of the Gendered Psyche among Eligible Candidates:**
- Among eligible candidates with equal credentials, women are less likely than men to believe they are qualified to run for office.
- The gender gap in self-perceived qualifications exists not only at the abstract level, but also on specific measures of political skills.
- Many women's self-doubts about their qualifications can be linked to their perceptions of a sexist political environment dominated by a masculinized ethos.
- Women's lower self-assessments are also the product of a stringent definition of *qualified* that encompasses both essential political background experiences and personal traits.
- Women think women must be twice as good as men to compete evenly in the political arena.
- Among eligible candidates who doubt their qualifications, women are less likely than men to consider a candidacy.
- Women are less likely than men to think they would win if they ran for office.

Now consider Sam Skylar, a forty-seven-year-old university administrator. Mr. Skylar's parents regularly encouraged him to be politically
active, so from an early age, he has been involved with several political
interest groups. Like Jill Gruber, Mr. Skylar is married and has three children who still live at home, but his spouse, a divorce attorney, performs
more of the child care and household duties. Mr. Skylar thinks about
running for office frequently and discusses his options with friends and
coworkers often. Recently, a friend on the city council urged him to run
for the state legislature and offered his full support. Mr. Skylar has not
decided when or if he will run, but he is confident that he will win if he
chooses to throw his hat into the ring. He is convinced that his "years
of administrative and leadership experience" would make him "a great
policy maker."

Jill Gruber and Sam Skylar's experiences highlight the far-reaching
manner in which traditional gender socialization can inhibit women's
emergence as candidates and facilitate men's. Traditional family role orientations, embodied by heterosexual marriage in which women assume
the majority of household labor and child-care responsibilities, continue to dominate family structures and arrangements among adults in
the United States. This distribution of labor leads many women to conclude that entering politics would restrict their ability to fulfill existing
personal and professional obligations. A masculinized ethos in many public and private institutional settings reinforces traditional gender roles.
Political organizations and institutions that have always been controlled
by men continue to operate with a gendered lens that promotes men's
participation in the political arena and does not sufficiently encourage
women to break down barriers in traditionally masculine spheres and
environments. The gendered psyche imbues many women with a sense
of doubt as to their ability to thrive in the political sphere. The same
deeply internalized attitudes about gender roles and women and men's
receptivity in the political arena lead men to envision and, in some cases,
embrace the notion of running for public office.

The gendered roles and perceptions that pervade early family life and
persist into the professional environments of successful career women
and men are not a thing of the past. The gender gap in ambition is
larger among respondents younger than the age of forty than it is for
those older than sixty. Relatively young women who are well situated
to pursue a future political career – whether local, state, or federal – are
significantly less likely than relatively young men to consider running for
office. Moreover, a June 2009 national survey of students taking the Law

TABLE 8.2. *Pre-Law Students' Attitudes toward Running for Office*

| Would you consider running for political office at some point in your career? | Women | Men |
| --- | --- | --- |
| Definitely Yes | 10% | 20% |
| Probably Yes | 24 | 38 |
| Probably No | 43 | 31 |
| Definitely No | 23 | 12 |

*Notes:* Data are based on Kaplan Test Prep and Admissions' survey to 2,955 Kaplan students who took the June 2009 Law School Admission Test. Chi-square test comparing women and men is significant at p < .01 for all comparisons.

School Admission Test revealed a sizable gender gap in political ambition. Male and female test takers were quite similar when asked whether potential earnings played a role in their pursuit of a law degree (24 percent of women, compared to 29 percent of men, stated that earning potential "very much" affected their interest in law school). But women were only half as likely as men to report that they would "definitely" consider using the law degree as a stepping-stone to a political career in the future. Women were almost twice as likely as men to write off that possibility altogether (see Table 8.2).[7] The enduring effects of traditional gender socialization that transcend all generations make sweeping increases in women's representation unlikely.

The prognosis for increasing women's representation is also dampened by the lack of a coherent women's movement. Hillary Clinton's presidential campaign – particularly the media coverage she garnered – certainly elevated issues of sexism and gender consciousness into the national discourse.[8] But her candidacy did not bring with it the kind of rallying cry to elect more women that accompanied the Equal Rights Amendment or the Clarence Thomas confirmation hearings (see Kornblut 2010). In fact, Clinton's candidacy was frequently cited as evidence of the dramatic strides the United States has made toward attaining gender equity. Perhaps the only issue that motivates some degree of unified

[7] We thank Russell Schaffer and Kaplan Test Prep and Admissions for making these data available.

[8] For a discussion with prominent scholars and feminists about the role gender plays in political life, see Amanda Fortini, "The Feminist Reawakening: Hillary Clinton and the Fourth Wave," *New York*, April 14, 2008, http://nymag.com/news/features/46011/ (accessed December 20, 2009).

political action for women's rights focuses on reproductive freedom. A broad network of pro-choice groups – such as Planned Parenthood Action Fund, NARAL Pro-Choice America, National Women's Political Caucus, EMILY's List, and Wish List – enjoy considerable influence in political circles, especially among Democrats. But motivating activism even on this issue can be difficult. Sarah Weddington (1993, 241), who argued *Roe v. Wade* before the U.S. Supreme Court, observes: "The fact that many do not remember the horrors of illegal abortion makes our job of motivating young people harder.... To the extent that advocates of choice perceive a crisis, to that extent will reproductive freedom become a priority." No issues or circumstances currently represent the "crisis" necessary to mobilize widespread political action on behalf of women's rights.

Finally, the context of electoral politics in the United States compounds many of the difficulties women face in navigating the candidate emergence process. In many countries where women constitute 40 percent of the members of the national legislature, for instance, electoral rules, such as the use of quotas and proportional party list systems, facilitate women's candidacies and attempt to mitigate a history of patriarchy. Entrepreneurial candidacies, in contrast, define electoral competition in the United States. To compete effectively in this system, women must shed completely the vestiges of traditional gender socialization. They must build networks of support within political institutions that are operated by men and accustomed to working with male candidates. Men must simply emphasize the qualities, traits, and networks they were socialized to possess and pursue. Consequently, political institutions and public life remain more accessible and inclusive to men than to women. Barring radical structural change in the institutions of politics and the family, achieving gender parity in U.S. government is not on the horizon.

It is also critical to note that women's representation in the Republican Party is particularly precarious. Seventy-one Democratic and twenty-one Republican women hold seats in the U.S. Congress. This means that 77 percent of the women in the U.S. House and Senate are Democrats. Seventy-one percent of female state legislators across the country are Democrats. Moreover, whereas Democrats have experienced steady increases in the number of women in most elective offices over the past three decades, Republicans have not. In fact, more Republican women served in state assemblies – which are key launching pads to higher political office – in 1989 than do today. As we pointed out in Chapter 5, Republican women's underrepresentation is exacerbated by the growing network of women's organizations that do an excellent job encouraging progressive women to enter the electoral arena. The Republicans simply have no such network of organizations.

Although the Republicans are increasingly becoming a party of men, this was not always the case. The Republican Party was the first to support the Equal Rights Amendment. It was the first major party from which a woman (Margaret Chase Smith) sought the presidency. With Nancy Kassebaum's successful election in 1978, it was the first major party to send a woman to the U.S. Senate in her own right (as opposed to through the death of her husband). And in the mid-1980s, Republican women actually outnumbered Democratic women in the U.S. Congress. The future prognosis for women's representation depends on Republicans working to ameliorate the problems they have attracting, recruiting, and electing women to public office.

Framed in this light, the gender gap in political ambition raises grave concerns over the quality of democratic governance and political legitimacy. A central criterion in evaluating the health of democracy in the United States is the degree to which all citizens are encouraged and willing to engage the political system and run for public office. As gender politics scholar Sue Thomas (1998, 1) argues, "A government that is democratically organized cannot be truly legitimate if all its citizens . . . do not have a potential interest in and opportunity for serving their community and nation." The inclusion of women in the candidate emergence process is also intertwined with fundamental issues of political representation. As we detailed in Chapter 1, a compelling body of evidence suggests that particular sociodemographic groups are best able to represent the policy preferences of that group. In addition, political theorists ascribe symbolic or role model benefits to a more diverse body of elected officials (Amundsen 1971; Pitkin 1967; Bachrach 1967). If interest in seeking office is in any way restricted to citizens with certain demographic profiles – in this case, men – then serious questions emerge regarding the quality of descriptive, symbolic, and substantive representation.

## Recasting the Study of Gender and Elections

Since the 1970s, one simple question has guided much of the research on gender and elections: why do so few women occupy elective office? In an attempt to answer this question, gender politics scholars employed a multifaceted and eclectic approach. They surveyed and interviewed candidates and elected officials to assess levels of discrimination against women. They combed fundraising receipts and vote totals to determine how women fare at the polls and in the campaign process. They analyzed institutional barriers, such as the incumbency advantage and women's proportions in the professions that lead to political careers, to uncover structural obstacles women face. But they did not address eligible candidates' political ambition. The results of the Citizen Political Ambition Panel Study make clear that the gender gap in political ambition serves as one of the strongest explanations for women's underrepresentation. And our two-stage conception of the candidate emergence process reveals many critical obstacles and influences that affect eligible candidates long before they face the decision to enter an actual race. Considering the fundamental role gender plays in the precandidacy stage of the electoral process, we propose five avenues of future research to pick up where our study leaves off.

Researchers might begin by studying gender differences in early family, education, and career experiences that can affect the candidate emergence process. For most people, choosing to run for office is not a spontaneous decision; rather, it is the culmination of a long, personal evolution that often stretches back into early family life. From an early age, do women and men develop different conceptions of what political careers embody and entail? In school, does American political history's focus on men's accomplishments leave enduring effects on the psyches of young women and men? When women first enter the workforce, do they have strong role models and mentors to encourage their professional achievement and facilitate their political ambition? Women's greater sense of self-doubt pertaining to their abilities to enter the political arena is one of the most complex barriers to their emergence as candidates. In continuing to explore the origins of these doubts and assess the cognitive and contextual processes that affect whether and how women and men come to view themselves as candidates, early socialization merits investigation. And in conducting these analyses, researchers may want to focus on high school and college students. Many gendered attitudes about running for office and the electoral environment are in place long before women and men find themselves in the candidate eligibility pool. Investigating these gender differences at their source, as opposed to relying on retrospective assessments of events that occurred decades earlier, may prove fruitful.

Second, we must build on the research that already speaks to the double bind women face and sort out the manner in which it impedes their political ambition. The bind appears more complicated than we might have imagined. Women's marital and parental status do not exert a statistically significant effect on their likelihood of considering a candidacy. Yet most of the women we interviewed believe that having children and caring for them poses one of the greatest barriers to women's entrance into elective office. Under what circumstances can women foresee simultaneously running for office and being a spouse and parent? To what extent must men reconcile their careers, their families, and their political ambition? Can opting out of the candidate pipeline serve to catalyze women's political interest and involvement at the local level? Can a range of experiences shaped by parenthood be reframed so as to bolster women's sense of qualifications to run for office?[9] A wide range of questions about whether and how politics can merge with family and household responsibilities merits investigation.

Third, gender differences in perceptions play a critical role in the candidate emergence process; and because perceptions dictate behavior, they are just as important as reality. Nearly two decades ago, Timothy Bledsoe and Mary Herring (1990) uncovered empirical evidence to suggest that gender differences in perceptions inhibit women's ambition to seek higher office. More recently, Marianne Githens (2003) called for research that examines the manner in which gender differences in perceptions of the political opportunity structure affect the decision to run for office. We have only begun to understand how women and men's perceptions of themselves as candidates and the electoral arena affect the decision to run for office. Are there gender differences in how perceptions of personal skills, traits, and the costs associated with running for office and perceptions of gender bias in electoral competition affect political ambition? Are there gender differences in how women and men view the opportunity structure associated with different levels of office? Do women perceive an easier campaign and political environment when they consider pursuing positions that are more typically occupied by women? Only by answering these questions can we begin to gauge prospects for a perceived level electoral playing field.

Fourth, if we are to gain a fuller understanding of the roots of women's lower levels of political ambition, then we must study how ambition evolves. Although many patterns of traditional gender socialization dampen women's opportunities to run for office, there is growing acceptance of women candidates, even at the highest levels. As women

---

[9] Cathy Benko and Anne C. Weisberg (2007) suggest that when work becomes less of a ladder, women will gain the flexibility to reconcile their families and careers in a way that values not only their experiences as mothers, but also their drive for professional success once their child-care duties abate. See also Lisa Belkin, "The Senator Track," *New York Times Magazine*, January 4, 2009, 9.

gain greater exposure to women in politics, do they become more likely to consider running for office? Are they less likely to view the political environment as sexist and more likely to believe they can overcome adversity in male-dominated spheres? What are the long-term implications of Hillary Clinton and Sarah Palin's candidacies? Did these women serve as lightning rods to fuel women's political ambition? Or did their experiences depress levels of interest in running for office? Among our survey respondents, women are significantly more likely than men to report feeling inspired by other women in politics. And these feelings transcend party. For example, among Democrats, 59 percent of women, as opposed to 38 percent of men, consider Hillary Clinton "inspirational." Republicans are obviously less likely to view Hillary Clinton this way, but female Republicans are still much more likely than their male counterparts to offer this assessment (17 percent of women compared to 4 percent of men). We uncover similar patterns when we turn to Nancy Pelosi and Condoleezza Rice. It may take time for the presence of women in such high levels of political power to trickle down to the candidate eligibility pool and inspire future candidacies. Only by tracking women and men's political ambition over time can we assess these dynamics.

Finally, our research points to the importance of determining the specific factors that might spur ambition among eligible women candidates. What types of recruitment messages are particularly effective in encouraging women's candidacies? Can the dissemination of information that shows that women actually perform as well as men at the polls combat women's negative attitudes and pessimistic expectations about the electoral process? What specific steps can political parties, electoral gatekeepers, and political activists take to improve women's self-assessments of themselves as candidates? Although this type of research carries clear normative implications for organizations and individuals working to increase the number of women candidates in electoral politics, it will also shed even more light on the nuances of how women are socialized to think about the electoral process.

These new avenues of research must be complemented with investigations that continue to track women's electoral success when they do emerge as candidates. Future investigators, however, must be very careful when generating broad assessments from end-stage analyses. We must withstand the temptation to conclude that, because there are no gender differences in general election vote totals and campaign fundraising receipts, the electoral process is gender neutral. When women become candidates and make it to Election Day, they perform as well as men.

But aggregate-level studies of electoral outcomes and fundraising ignore the more stringent selection process involved in women's candidate emergence. In addition to higher self-imposed standards, women, across professions, are less likely than men to be tapped as candidates by party organizations, elected officials, colleagues, and peers. A pervasive, albeit subtler, form of discrimination persists through the continued manifestations of traditional gender socialization in the electoral arena.

We began this book by asking why highly accomplished and politically minded women like Cheryl Perry and Tricia Moniz demonstrated no ambition to run for office, whereas their similarly situated male counterparts, Randall White and Kevin Kendall, confidently spoke about their prospects of entering the political sphere as candidates. We end the revised edition of this book with an answer to that question: deeply embedded patterns of traditional gender socialization pervade U.S. society and continue to make politics a much less likely path for women than for men.

# Appendix A

## The Citizen Political Ambition Panel Study
## Sample Design and Data Collection

We drew the candidate eligibility pool from a national sample of women and men employed in the four professions that most often precede state legislative and congressional candidacies: law, business, education, and politics. In assembling the sample, we created two equally sized pools of candidates – one female and one male – that held the same professional credentials. Because we wanted to make nuanced statistical comparisons within and between the subgroups of men and women in each profession, we attempted to compile a sample of nine hundred men and nine hundred women from each.

We drew the names of lawyers and business leaders from national directories. We obtained a random sample of 1,800 lawyers from the 2001 edition of the *Martindale-Hubble Law Directory*, which provides the addresses and names of practicing attorneys in all law firms across the country. We stratified the total number of lawyers by sex and in proportion to the total number of law firms listed for each state. We randomly selected 1,800 business leaders from *Dun and Bradstreet's Million Dollar Directory, 2000–2001*, which lists the top executive officers of more than 160,000 public and private companies in the United States. Again, we stratified by geography and sex and ensured that men and women held comparable positions.

No national directories exist for our final two categories. To compile a sample of educators, we focused on college professors and administrative officials, as well as public school teachers and administrators. Turning first to the higher education subsample, we compiled a random sample of six hundred public and private colleges and universities from the roughly four thousand schools listed in *U.S. News and World Report*'s *America's*

*Best Colleges 2001*, from which we selected three hundred male and three hundred female professors and administrative officials. Because we did not stratify by school size, the college and university portion of the sample yielded a greater number of educators from smaller schools; however, we found that the size of the institution was not a significant predictor of political ambition. We then compiled a national sample of 1,200 public school teachers and principals (600 men and 600 women). We obtained the sample through an Internet search of public school districts, from which we located the websites of individual schools and the names of their employees. This technique might result in a bias toward schools that had the resources to provide computers in 2001. A 2001 study by the U.S. Department of Education, however, found that 98 percent of public schools had Internet access and 84 percent had a web page (Cattagni and Westat 2001).

Our final eligibility pool profession – political activists – represents citizens who work in politics and public policy. We created a list of political interest groups and national organizations with state and/or local affiliates and sought to strike a partisan and ideological balance. We randomly selected state branch and local chapter executive directors and officers of organizations that focus on the environment, abortion, consumer issues, race relations, civil liberties, taxes, guns, crime, social security, school choice, government reform, and women's issues. This selection technique, which provided a range of activists from a broad cross-section of occupations, yielded 744 men and 656 women, thereby making the activist subsample smaller than the other three groups.

We employed standard mail survey protocol in conducting the study. Eligible candidates received an initial letter explaining the study and a copy of the questionnaire. Three days later, they received a follow-up postcard. Two weeks later, we sent a follow-up letter with another copy of the questionnaire. We supplemented this third piece of correspondence with an email message when possible (for roughly one-half of the lawyers, educators, and political activists). Four months later, we sent all men and women from whom we did not receive a survey another copy of the questionnaire. The final contact was made the following month, when we sent, via email, a link to an online version of the survey. The survey was conducted from July 2001 to August 2002.[1]

---

[1] In light of calls for increased public service and community engagement following the events of September 11, 2001, we compared attitudes toward running for office between individuals who returned the questionnaire before and individuals who returned the

From the original sample of 6,800, 554 surveys were either undeliverable or returned because the individual was no longer employed in the position. From the 6,246 remaining members of the sample, we received responses from 3,765 individuals (1,969 men and 1,796 women). After taking into account respondents who left the majority of the questionnaire incomplete, we were left with 3,614 completed surveys, a for a usable response rate of 58 percent, which is higher than that of typical elite sample mail surveys and substantially greater than the expected response rate of 40 percent (Johnson, Joslyn, and Reynolds 2001).[2]

Six months after collecting the data, we sent a summary of the results to all respondents. We asked individuals to return an enclosed postcard indicating whether we could contact them for a follow-up interview. Of the 3,765 respondents who participated in the study, 1,219 agreed to be interviewed and 374 refused. We did not hear from the remaining sample members. After stratifying by sex and occupation, we randomly selected one hundred men and one hundred women for phone interviews, which we conducted in July and August 2003. The interviews ranged from thirty minutes to ninety minutes in length.

In early 2008, we completed the second wave of the panel study. Through extensive Internet searches and phone calls, we obtained current address information for 2,976 members (82 percent) of the original sample of respondents who had completed the questionnaire in 2001. After employing standard mail survey protocol, we heard from 2,060 men and women, 2,036 of whom completed the questionnaire. This represents a 75 percent response rate for the second wave of the panel.[3] Controlling for sex, race, and profession, individuals who expressed some degree of political ambition in 2001 were no more likely than respondents who had never considered a candidacy to complete the 2008 survey (regression results not shown).

---

questionnaire after the terrorist attacks. We uncovered no differences in political ambition or interest in seeking public office.

[2] Response rates within the four subsamples were as follows: lawyers, 68 percent; business leaders, 45 percent; educators, 61 percent; political activists, 68 percent. Nonresponse is probably inversely correlated with interest in running for political office, but does not differ between women and men.

[3] Response rates for the 2008 survey varied less by profession than was the case in 2001: lawyers, 77 percent; business leaders, 59 percent; educators, 71 percent; political activists, 73 percent. High response rates for the second wave are to be expected, as each respondent had already demonstrated a propensity to complete the questionnaire. The rates we calculate take into account 205 undeliverable surveys.

# Appendix B

## The First-Wave Survey (2001)

This appendix includes a copy of the questionnaire completed by the members of the candidate eligibility pool sample. We modified some questions for the political activist subsample and asked for elaboration regarding those respondents' levels of political activity and issue advocacy.

\*   \*   \*   \*   \*   \*   \*   \*   \*   \*   \*   \*   \*

### INSTRUCTIONS

Thank you very much for participating in this survey. All of your answers are confidential. Please answer the questions to the best of your ability and then enclose the survey in the addressed, stamped envelope. If you would like a copy of the results, then please write your address on the back of the return envelope. Thank you.

**Part I – We would like to begin by asking you about your political attitudes and the ways you participate politically.**

1. Please mark your level of agreement with the following statements:

| | Strongly Disagree | Disagree | Neither Disagree nor Agree | Agree | Strongly Agree |
|---|---|---|---|---|---|
| Taxes are too high. | O | O | O | O | O |
| More gun control laws should be passed. | O | O | O | O | O |
| Abortion should always be legal in the first trimester. | O | O | O | O | O |

(Question 1 continued)

| | Strongly Disagree | Disagree | Neither Disagree nor Agree | Agree | Strongly Agree |
|---|---|---|---|---|---|
| The U.S. should move toward universal health care. | O | O | O | O | O |
| The government should take a more active role combating sexual harassment in the workplace. | O | O | O | O | O |
| Government pays attention to people when making decisions. | O | O | O | O | O |
| It is just as easy for a woman to be elected to a high-level public office as a man. | O | O | O | O | O |
| Waging a war against terrorism is the single most important goal the federal government should pursue in the next 10 years. | O | O | O | O | O |
| Most men are better suited emotionally for politics than are most women. | O | O | O | O | O |
| Within the corporate and business world, it is still more difficult for women to climb the career ladder. | O | O | O | O | O |
| Feminism has had a positive impact on social and political life in the United States. | O | O | O | O | O |
| Congress should enact hate crime legislation | O | O | O | O | O |

2. How would you describe your party affiliation?

   O Democrat
   O Republican
   O Independent
   O Other

3. How would you describe your political philosophy?

   O Liberal
   O Moderate
   O Conservative

4. How closely do you follow national politics?

   O Very Closely
   O Closely
   O Somewhat Closely
   O Not Closely

5. How closely do you follow politics in your community?

    ○ Very Closely
    ○ Closely
    ○ Somewhat Closely
    ○ Not Closely

6. Many people do not engage in many political or community activities. In which, if any, of the following activities have you engaged in the past year?

|  | Yes | No |
|---|---|---|
| Voted in the 2000 presidential election | ○ | ○ |
| Wrote a letter to a newspaper | ○ | ○ |
| Joined or paid dues to a political interest group | ○ | ○ |
| Contacted an elected official (by phone, email, letter, etc.) | ○ | ○ |
| Contributed money to a campaign | ○ | ○ |
| Volunteered for a political candidate | ○ | ○ |
| Joined a group in the community to address a local issue | ○ | ○ |
| Volunteered on a community project | ○ | ○ |
| Attended a city council or school board meeting | ○ | ○ |
| Served on the board of a non-profit organization | ○ | ○ |

7. When you think about politics, how important are the following issues to you when you are considering how to vote and whether to participate politically?

| | Very Important | Important | Not Very Important | Not At All Important |
|---|---|---|---|---|
| Abortion | ○ | ○ | ○ | ○ |
| Education | ○ | ○ | ○ | ○ |
| Health Care | ○ | ○ | ○ | ○ |
| Enviromment | ○ | ○ | ○ | ○ |
| Economy | ○ | ○ | ○ | ○ |
| Guns | ○ | ○ | ○ | ○ |
| Crime | ○ | ○ | ○ | ○ |
| Gay Rights | ○ | ○ | ○ | ○ |
| Foreign Policy | ○ | ○ | ○ | ○ |

8. Do you consider yourself a feminist?

    ○ Yes
    ○ No

9. Off the top of your head, do you recall the name of your member of the U.S. House of Representatives?

    ○ Unsure
    ○ Name: _____

10. Off the top of your head, do you recall the names of your U.S. senators?

    1. ◯ Unsure    ◯ Name: _____
    2. ◯ Unsure    ◯ Name: _____

11. Which statement best captures how you feel about people who run for political office?

    ◯ Most people who run for office are very well intentioned and genuinely hope to improve society.
    ◯ Most people who run for office are generally interested in their own fame and power.

12. If you felt strongly about a government action or policy, how likely would you be to engage in each of the following political activities?

| | Very Unlikely | Unlikely | Likely | Very Likely |
|---|---|---|---|---|
| Give money to a political candidate who favors your position | ◯ | ◯ | ◯ | ◯ |
| Volunteer for a candidate or group that favors your position | ◯ | ◯ | ◯ | ◯ |
| Organize people in the community to work on the issue | ◯ | ◯ | ◯ | ◯ |
| Directly lobby or contact government officials | ◯ | ◯ | ◯ | ◯ |
| Run for public office | ◯ | ◯ | ◯ | ◯ |

**Part II** – The next series of questions deals with your attitudes toward running for office. We realize that most citizens have never thought about running, but your answers are still very important.

1. Which of the following options do you think is the most effective way for you to get government to address a political issue?

    ◯ Run for office and become a policy maker
    ◯ Form a grassroots organization to lobby government
    ◯ Make monetary contributions to appropriate political leaders
    ◯ Support a candidate who shares your views

2. Generally speaking, do you think most elected officials are qualified for the positions they hold?

    ◯ Yes
    ◯ No

3. Have you ever held elective public office?

   ○ Yes: What office[s]: _____
   ○ No

If no, have you ever run for public office?

   ○ Yes: What office[s]: _____
   ○ No

4. If you have never run for office, have you ever thought about running for office?

   ○ Yes, I have seriously considered it.
   ○ Yes, it has crossed my mind.
   ○ No, I have not thought about it.

5. If you have ever thought about running for office, have you ever taken any of the following steps?

|  | Yes | No |
|---|---|---|
| Discussed running with party leaders | ○ | ○ |
| Discussed running with friends and family | ○ | ○ |
| Discussed running with community leaders | ○ | ○ |
| Solicited or discussed financial contributions with potential supporters | ○ | ○ |
| Investigated how to place your name on the ballot | ○ | ○ |

6. Regardless of your interest in running for office, have any of the following individuals ever suggested that you run for office?

|  | Yes | No |
|---|---|---|
| An official from a political party | ○ | ○ |
| A co-worker or business associate | ○ | ○ |
| An elected official | ○ | ○ |
| A friend or acquaintance | ○ | ○ |
| A spouse or partner | ○ | ○ |
| A member of your family | ○ | ○ |
| A non-elected political activist | ○ | ○ |
| Other; specify: _____ | ○ | ○ |

7. Would you be more likely to consider running for office if:

|  | No | Possibly | Yes |
|---|---|---|---|
| Someone from work suggested you run? | ○ | ○ | ○ |
| Someone from your political party or community suggested you run? | ○ | ○ | ○ |
| You had more free time? | ○ | ○ | ○ |
| A friend suggested you run? | ○ | ○ | ○ |

(Question 7 continued)

|  | No | Possibly | Yes |
|---|---|---|---|
| You had more impressive professional credentials? | O | O | O |
| A spouse/partner suggested you run? | O | O | O |
| You were more financially secure? | O | O | O |
| You had fewer family responsibilities? | O | O | O |
| There were issues you felt more passionate about? | O | O | O |
| You knew there was a lot of support for your candidacy? | O | O | O |
| You had previous experience working on a campaign? | O | O | O |
| You had more experience with public speaking? | O | O | O |
| Campaigns were publicly financed? | O | O | O |

8. Please assess how important you think it is that candidates for public office have the following experiences in their backgrounds:

|  | Not Important | Somewhat Important | Important | Very Important |
|---|---|---|---|---|
| Having worked in business | O | O | O | O |
| Having expertise on policy issues | O | O | O | O |
| Having a law degree | O | O | O | O |
| Having campaign experience | O | O | O | O |
| Having public speaking experience | O | O | O | O |

9. Overall, how qualified do you feel you are to run for public office?

- O Very Qualified
- O Qualified
- O Somewhat Qualified
- O Not At All Qualified

10. If you were to become a candidate for public office, how would you feel about engaging in the following aspects of a campaign?

|  | Very Positive | Positive | Negative | So negative, it would deter me from running |
|---|---|---|---|---|
| Attending fundraising functions | O | O | O | O |
| Dealing with party officials | O | O | O | O |
| Going door-to-door to meet constituents | O | O | O | O |
| Dealing with members of the press | O | O | O | O |
| The amount of time it takes to run for office | O | O | O | O |

11. We would now like to ask you about your interest in specific public offices.

1) If you were to run for office, which one would you likely seek first? (check one)

2) What offices might you ever be interested in running for? (check all that apply)

| | | |
|---|---|---|
| School Board | ○ | ○ |
| Mayor | ○ | ○ |
| State Legislator | ○ | ○ |
| Member of the U.S. House of Representatives | ○ | ○ |
| U.S. Senator | ○ | ○ |
| President | ○ | ○ |
| City, County, or Town Council | ○ | ○ |
| Governor | ○ | ○ |
| Statewide Office (i.e., Attorney General) | ○ | ○ |
| I would never run for any office | ○ | ○ |
| I have held elected office | ○ | ○ |

12. **If you were to become a candidate for public office, how likely do you think it is that you would win your first campaign?**

   ○ Very Likely
   ○ Likely
   ○ Unlikely
   ○ Very Unlikely

13. **Which best characterizes your attitudes toward running for office in the future?**

   ○ It is something I definitely would like to undertake in the future.
   ○ It is something I might undertake if the opportunity presented itself.
   ○ I would not rule it out forever, but I currently have no interest.
   ○ It is something I would absolutely never do.
   ○ I currently hold elected office.

14. **How have the recent attacks in New York and Washington, D.C., affected your attitudes about running for public office?**

   ○ They make me more likely to run.
   ○ They make me less likely to run.
   ○ They do not change my attitude.

---

**Part III – Finally, we would like to ask you some questions about your background and family life.**

---

1. **What is your sex?**     ○ Female     ○ Male

2. **What is your age?** _____

3. What is your race?
   - ○ White
   - ○ Black
   - ○ Asian
   - ○ Hispanic/Latino
   - ○ Native American
   - ○ Other (please specify): _____

4. In what type of area do you live?
   - ○ Major City
   - ○ Suburb
   - ○ Small Town
   - ○ Rural Area

5. What is your city and state of residence?

   _____

6. What is your current occupation?

   _____

7. What is your level of education?
   - ○ Never Completed High School
   - ○ High School Graduate
   - ○ Attended Some College (no degree attained)
   - ○ Completed College (B.A. or B.S. degree)
   - ○ Attended Some Graduate School (no degree attained)
   - ○ Completed Graduate Degree (check all that apply):
     ○ M.B.A.   ○ M.P.A.   ○ J.D.   ○ M.A.   ○ Ph.D.   ○ M.D.

8. In what category were your personal and household incomes last year?
   (check one for each column)

   |  | Personal income | Household income |
   |---|---|---|
   | under $ 25,000 | ○ | ○ |
   | $ 25,000 – $ 50,000 | ○ | ○ |
   | $ 50,001 – $ 75,000 | ○ | ○ |
   | $ 75,001 – $ 100,000 | ○ | ○ |
   | $ 100,001 – $ 200,000 | ○ | ○ |
   | over $ 200,000 | ○ | ○ |

9. What is your marital status?
   - ○ Single
   - ○ Unmarried, Living as a Couple
   - ○ Married
   - ○ Widowed
   - ○ Separated
   - ○ Divorced

10. If you are married or live with a partner and your spouse or partner considered running for elective office, how supportive would you be?

   ○ Very Supportive
   ○ Somewhat Supportive
   ○ Not Very Supportive

11. If you are married or live with a partner, which statement below best describes the division of labor on household tasks, such as cleaning, laundry, and cooking?

   ○ I am responsible for all household tasks.
   ○ I am responsible for more of the household tasks than my spouse/partner.
   ○ The division of labor in my household is evenly divided.
   ○ My spouse/partner takes care of more of the household tasks than I do.
   ○ My spouse/partner is responsible for all household tasks.
   ○ Other Arrangements; describe: _____

12. Do you have children?

   ○ Yes
   ○ No

   |                                                                 | Yes | No |
   |-----------------------------------------------------------------|-----|----|
   | If yes, do they live with you?                                  | ○   | ○  |
   | If yes, do you have children under the age of 6 living at home? | ○   | ○  |
   | If you do not have children, do you plan to start a family in the future? | ○ | ○ |

13. If you have children, which statement best characterizes your child-care arrangements?

   ○ I am the primary caretaker of the children.
   ○ I have more child-care responsibilities than my spouse/partner.
   ○ My spouse/partner and I share child-care responsibilities completely equally.
   ○ My spouse/partner has more child-care responsibilities than I do.
   ○ My spouse/partner is the primary caretaker of the children.
   ○ Other Arrangements; describe: _____

14. When you were in high school or college, did you ever run for office, such as class representative or president?

   ○ Yes
   ○ No

15. When you were growing up, how frequently did your parents discuss politics with you?

   ○ Frequently
   ○ Occasionally
   ○ Seldom
   ○ Never

16. **When you were growing up, was your father or mother more likely to discuss politics with you?**

    ○ Mother
    ○ Father
    ○ Both Spoke Equally
    ○ Neither

17. **When you were growing up, how frequently did your parents suggest that, someday, you should run for office?**

    ○ Frequently
    ○ Occasionally
    ○ Seldom
    ○ Never

18. **Did either of your parents ever run for elective office?**

    ○ Yes, Both Parents
    ○ Yes, My Father
    ○ Yes, My Mother
    ○ No

19. **Please answer these questions regarding levels of concern about politics in your past.**

|  | Not at all Concerned | Somewhat Concerned | Very Concerned |
|---|---|---|---|
| How concerned were the students in your high school about current events and politics? | ○ | ○ | ○ |
| When you were in high school, how concerned were you about current events and politics? | ○ | ○ | ○ |
| When you were growing up, how concerned were your parents with current events and politics? | ○ | ○ | ○ |
| How concerned were the students at your college or university about current events and politics? | ○ | ○ | ○ |
| When you were in college, how concerned were you about current events and politics? | ○ | ○ | ○ |

20. **When you were growing up, what description best characterizes the arrangements in your household?**

    ○ I grew up in a household where my father was the primary breadwinner and my mother was the primary caretaker of the household.
    ○ I grew up in a two-career household where my parents shared household duties evenly.
    ○ I grew up in a two-career household where my mother was responsible for most household duties.
    ○ I grew up in a two-career household where my father was responsible for most household duties.

(Question 20 continued)
  ○ I grew up in a single-parent household with my mother.
  ○ I grew up in a single-parent household with my father.
  ○ Other

21. **In thinking about your own life, how important are the following goals and accomplishments?**

| | Very Important | Important | Not very Important | Not At All Important |
|---|:---:|:---:|:---:|:---:|
| Earning a great deal of money | ○ | ○ | ○ | ○ |
| Rising to the top of my profession | ○ | ○ | ○ | ○ |
| Making my community a better place to live | ○ | ○ | ○ | ○ |
| Devoting time to my children | ○ | ○ | ○ | ○ |
| Playing a big part in charitable endeavors | ○ | ○ | ○ | ○ |
| Devotion to my religion | ○ | ○ | ○ | ○ |

Other: _____

---

Thank you very much for participating in this survey. If you would like to offer additional comments about your attitudes toward politics, or your political aspirations, then please feel free to enclose an additional page of comments.

# Appendix C

## The Second-Wave Survey (2008)

This appendix includes a copy of the questionnaire completed by the members of the candidate eligibility pool sample in the second wave of the study.

\*     \*     \*     \*     \*     \*     \*     \*     \*     \*     \*     \*     \*

### INSTRUCTIONS

Thank you very much for participating in our survey once again. All of your answers are confidential. Please answer the questions to the best of your ability and then enclose the survey in the addressed, stamped envelope. If you would like a copy of the results, then please write your address on the back of the return envelope. Thank you.

Part I – We would like to begin by asking you about your political attitudes and experiences.

---

1. Many people do not engage in many political or community activities. In the past year, did you ...?

|  | Yes | No |
|---|---|---|
| Vote in the 2006 congressional election | O | O |
| Write or email a letter to a newspaper about a political issue | O | O |
| Join or renew membership in a political organization | O | O |
| Contact an elected official (by phone, email, letter, etc.) | O | O |
| Contribute money to a candidate or political cause | O | O |
| Volunteer for a community project | O | O |

**2. How closely do you follow national politics?**

O Very Closely
O Closely
O Somewhat Closely
O Not Closely

**3. How closely do you follow politics in your community?**

O Very Closely
O Closely
O Somewhat Closely
O Not Closely

**4. How do you characterize the political leanings of the city or town where you live?**

O Heavily Democratic
O Leans Democratic
O Roughly Equal Balance
O Leans Republican
O Heavily Republican

**5. How do you characterize the political leanings of the state where you live?**

O Heavily Democratic
O Leans Democratic
O Roughly Equal Balance
O Leans Republican
O Heavily Republican

**6. How would you describe your party affiliation?**

O Strong Democrat
O Democrat
O Independent, Leaning Democrat
O Independent
O Independent, Leaning Republican
O Republican
O Strong Republican

**7. How would you describe your political views?**

O Liberal
O Moderate
O Conservative

**8. Which classification best describes you?**

O Strong Feminist
O Feminist
O Not a Feminist
O Anti-Feminist

9. In general, how competitive are elections for local offices in the area where you live?

- ○ Very Competitive
- ○ Competitive
- ○ Somewhat Competitive
- ○ Not at All Competitive
- ○ I Don't Know

10. In general, how competitive are congressional elections in the area where you live?

- ○ Very Competitive
- ○ Competitive
- ○ Somewhat Competitive
- ○ Not at All Competitive
- ○ I Don't Know

11. Either professionally, or outside of work, have you ever done any of the following things?

|  | Yes | No |
|---|---|---|
| Engaged in regular public speaking | ○ | ○ |
| Conducted significant research on a public policy issue | ○ | ○ |
| Solicited funds for an organization, interest group, or cause | ○ | ○ |
| Ran an organization, business, or foundation | ○ | ○ |
| Organized an event for a large group | ○ | ○ |

12. Thinking about your news habits, how often do you . . . ?

|  | Every Day | A Few Times a Week | A Few Times a Month | Rarely/Never |
|---|---|---|---|---|
| Read a print or online newspaper | ○ | ○ | ○ | ○ |
| Watch local television news | ○ | ○ | ○ | ○ |
| Listen to political talk radio | ○ | ○ | ○ | ○ |
| Watch C-SPAN | ○ | ○ | ○ | ○ |
| Watch the Fox News Channel | ○ | ○ | ○ | ○ |
| Watch CNN or MSNBC | ○ | ○ | ○ | ○ |
| Read political websites | ○ | ○ | ○ | ○ |

13. Are you at all inspired by any of the following contemporary political leaders? (check all that apply)

- ○ John McCain
- ○ Rudy Giuliani
- ○ Hillary Clinton
- ○ Bill Clinton

(Question 13 continued)
- ○ Condoleezza Rice
- ○ Mitt Romney
- ○ Nancy Pelosi
- ○ Barack Obama
- ○ George W. Bush
- ○ John Edwards
- ○ Al Gore
- ○ Bill Richardson

14. **Throughout the course of your life, have you ever . . . ?**

|  | Yes | No |
|---|---|---|
| Worked or volunteered for a candidate | ○ | ○ |
| Attended a city council or school board meeting | ○ | ○ |
| Attended a political party meeting, convention, or event | ○ | ○ |
| Observed or attended a state legislative committee meeting or floor session | ○ | ○ |
| Interacted with elected officials as part of your job | ○ | ○ |
| Interacted with elected officials socially | ○ | ○ |
| Had an elected official as a family member or friend | ○ | ○ |
| Served on the board of a non-profit organization or foundation | ○ | ○ |

15. **Please mark your level of agreement with the following statements:**

| | Strongly Disagree | Disagree | Neither Disagree nor Agree | Agree | Strongly Agree |
|---|---|---|---|---|---|
| Government pays attention to people when making decisions. | ○ | ○ | ○ | ○ | ○ |
| It is just as easy for women to be elected to high-level office as men. | ○ | ○ | ○ | ○ | ○ |
| It is just as easy for a Black person to be elected to high-level office as a White person. | ○ | ○ | ○ | ○ | ○ |
| Within the corporate and business world, it is still more difficult for women to climb the career ladder. | ○ | ○ | ○ | ○ | ○ |
| Within the corporate and business world, it is still more difficult for a Black person to climb the career ladder. | ○ | ○ | ○ | ○ | ○ |
| When women run for public office, it is more difficult for them to raise money than it is for men. | ○ | ○ | ○ | ○ | ○ |

Part II – The next series of questions concerns whether you have ever considered running for office.

1. Do you hold or have you ever held elective public office?

    ○ Yes
        What office[s]? _____
        What year[s] did you serve? _____
    ○ No

    **If no, have you ever run for public office?**

    ○ Yes
        What office[s]? _____
        What year[s]? _____
    ○ No

2. If you have never run for office, have you ever thought about running for office?

    ○ Yes, I have seriously considered it.
    ○ Yes, it has crossed my mind.
    ○ No, I have not thought about it (please skip to Part III).

3. How often do you think about running for office?

    ○ It is always in the back of my mind.
    ○ At least once a year.
    ○ Sporadically, over the years.
    ○ It has been many years since I last thought about it.

4. To the best of your recollection, how old were you when you first thought about running for office? _____

5. Have you ever taken any of the following steps that often precede a run for office?

| | Yes | No |
|---|---|---|
| Discussed running with party leaders or elected officials | ○ | ○ |
| Discussed running with friends and family | ○ | ○ |
| Discussed running with community leaders | ○ | ○ |
| Solicited or discussed financial contributions with potential supporters | ○ | ○ |
| Investigated how to place your name on the ballot | ○ | ○ |

Part III – Most citizens have never thought about running for office. But we're interested in your impressions and experiences even if you're not interested in these things.

1. Overall, how qualified do you feel you are to run for public office?

   ○ Very Qualified
   ○ Qualified
   ○ Somewhat Qualified
   ○ Not At All Qualified

2. Overall, how qualified do you feel you are to do the job of an elected official?

   ○ Very Qualified
   ○ Qualified
   ○ Somewhat Qualified
   ○ Not At All Qualified

3. Would you be more interested in public office if you were appointed, rather than had to engage in a campaign?

   ○ Yes
   ○ No

4. Has anyone been particularly persistent or influential in trying to get you to run for office?

   ○ Yes
   ○ No

   **If yes, was this person a man or woman?**

   ○ Man        ○ Woman

   **What was this person's relationship to you?** _____

5. Regardless of your interest in running for office, have any of the following ever suggested it to you?

|  | More than 5 Times | 3–5 Times | Once or Twice | Never |
|---|---|---|---|---|
| A friend or acquaintance | ○ | ○ | ○ | ○ |
| A co-worker or business associate | ○ | ○ | ○ | ○ |
| An elected official | ○ | ○ | ○ | ○ |
| An official from a political party | ○ | ○ | ○ | ○ |
| A spouse or partner | ○ | ○ | ○ | ○ |
| A member of your family | ○ | ○ | ○ | ○ |
| A non-elected political activist | ○ | ○ | ○ | ○ |
| A women's organization | ○ | ○ | ○ | ○ |
| Someone from your church, synagogue, mosque, etc. | ○ | ○ | ○ | ○ |

6. Have any of the following individuals ever discouraged you or tried to talk you out of running for office?

|  | Yes | No |
| --- | --- | --- |
| A friend or acquaintance | O | O |
| A co-worker or business associate | O | O |
| An elected official | O | O |
| An official from a political party | O | O |
| A spouse or partner | O | O |
| A member of your family | O | O |
| A non-elected political activist | O | O |

7. In thinking about your qualifications to run for office, do any of the following apply to you? (check all that apply)

- O I know a lot about public policy issues.
- O I have relevant professional experience.
- O I am a good public speaker.
- O I have connections to the political system.
- O I have or could raise enough money.
- O I am a good self-promoter.
- O My politics are too far out of the mainstream.
- O I don't like to make deals to get things done.

8. Turning to your interest in specific public offices...

1) If you were to run for office, which one would you seek first? (check one)

2) What offices might you ever be interested in running for? (check all that apply)

| | 1) | 2) |
| --- | --- | --- |
| School Board | O | O |
| Mayor | O | O |
| City, County, or Town Council | O | O |
| State Legislator | O | O |
| Governor | O | O |
| Statewide Office (i.e., Attorney General, Secretary of State) | O | O |
| Member of the U.S. House of Representatives | O | O |
| U.S. Senator | O | O |
| President | O | O |
| Judge | O | O |
| District Attorney | O | O |

9. Would any of the following resources make you more interested in running for office? (check all that apply)

○ Manuals and articles on campaigns and elections
○ Interviews with political operatives and elected officials
○ Webcasts on organizing, fundraising, and media skills
○ Training programs sponsored by political organizations

10. Lots of people have a negative view of what is entailed in running for office. How would you feel about ... ?

| | So Negative, It Would Deter Me from Running | | | |
| --- | --- | --- | --- | --- |
| | | | | Negative |
| | | | Wouldn't Bother Me | |
| | | Comfortable | | |
| Spending less time with family | ○ | ○ | ○ | ○ |
| Loss of privacy | ○ | ○ | ○ | ○ |
| Less time for personal interests | ○ | ○ | ○ | ○ |
| Hindering professional goals | ○ | ○ | ○ | ○ |

11. If you were to run for public office, how would you feel about engaging in the following aspects of a campaign?

| | So Negative, It Would Deter Me from Running | | | |
| --- | --- | --- | --- | --- |
| | | | | Negative |
| | | | Wouldn't Bother Me | |
| | | Comfortable | | |
| Soliciting campaign contributions | ○ | ○ | ○ | ○ |
| Dealing with party officials | ○ | ○ | ○ | ○ |
| Going door-to-door to meet constituents | ○ | ○ | ○ | ○ |
| Dealing with members of the press | ○ | ○ | ○ | ○ |
| Potentially having to engage in or endure a negative campaign | ○ | ○ | ○ | ○ |

12. If you were to run for public office, how likely do you think it is that you would win your first campaign?

○ Very Likely
○ Likely
○ Unlikely
○ Very Unlikely

13. In thinking about your qualifications to run for office, do any of the following apply to you? (check all that apply)

○ I don't have thick enough skin.
○ I have a lot of skeletons in my closet.
○ I worry about how a campaign would affect my family.
○ I am too old.
○ I am the wrong gender.
○ I am the wrong race/ethnicity.

## Part IV – Finally, we would like to ask you some questions about your background and family life.

1. What is your sex?　　　O Female　　O Male

2. What is your age? _____

3. What was your undergraduate major? _____

4. Did you attend a single-sex high school?
    O Yes
    O No

5. Did you attend an all women's college?
    O Yes
    O No

6. What is your religious affiliation? _____

7. How often do you attend religious services?
    O At Least Weekly
    O Monthly
    O Seldom
    O Never

8. In what category were your personal and household incomes last year? (check one for each column)

|  | Personal income | Household income |
|---|---|---|
| under $ 25,000 | O | O |
| $ 25,000 – $ 50,000 | O | O |
| $ 50,001 – $ 75,000 | O | O |
| $ 75,001 – $ 100,000 | O | O |
| $ 100,001 – $ 200,000 | O | O |
| over $ 200,000 | O | O |

9. What is your marital status?
    O Single
    O Unmarried, Living as a Couple
    O Married/Civil Union
    O Separated
    O Divorced
    O Widowed

10. If you are married or live with a partner, which of the following statements best describes the division of labor on household tasks (cleaning, laundry, and cooking)?

    ○ I am responsible for all household tasks.
    ○ I am responsible for more of the household tasks than my spouse/partner.
    ○ The division of labor in my household is evenly divided.
    ○ My spouse/partner takes care of more of the household tasks than I do.
    ○ My spouse/partner is responsible for all household tasks.
    ○ Other Arrangements; describe: _____

11. How many hours each week do you spend on these household tasks? _____

12. Do you have children?

    ○ Yes
    ○ No (skip to No. 16)

13. Do you have children living with you?

    ○ Yes
    ○ No

14. Do you have children under age 6 living with you?

    ○ Yes
    ○ No

15. Which statement best characterizes your child care, or characterized it when your children lived at home?

    ○ I am the primary caretaker of the children.
    ○ I have more child-care responsibilities than my spouse/partner.
    ○ My spouse/partner and I share child-care responsibilities completely equally.
    ○ My spouse/partner has more child-care responsibilities than I do.
    ○ My spouse/partner is the primary caretaker of the children.
    ○ Other Arrangements; describe: _____

16. When your children were (are) young, what were (are) your professional responsibilities?

    ○ I work(ed) full-time.
    ○ I work(ed) full-time, but scaled back my responsibilities.
    ○ I work(ed) part-time.
    ○ I am taking (took) a number of years off.

17. Since our last survey in 2001, have you...?

|  | Yes | No |
|---|---|---|
| Become more interested in politics | O | O |
| Become more cynical about politics | O | O |
| Become more concerned about global warming | O | O |
| Begun following foreign affairs more closely | O | O |
| Developed animosity toward the Bush Administration | O | O |
| Become frustrated with the Democrats in Congress | O | O |
| Known someone sent to Afghanistan or Iraq | O | O |

18. **Which statement best characterizes your attitudes toward running for office in the future?**

   O I definitely would like to do it in the future.
   O I might do it if the opportunity presented itself.
   O I would not rule it out forever, but I have no interest now.
   O It is something I would absolutely never do.

19. In the last six years, have you...?

|  | Yes | No |
|---|---|---|
| Had or adopted a child | O | O |
| Undergone a career change | O | O |
| Retired | O | O |
| Moved to a different town, city, state | O | O |
| Increased your religious devotion | O | O |
| Had children move out of the house | O | O |
| Had to care for a sick or aging parent | O | O |
| Taken on more responsibilities at work | O | O |
| Dealt with a serious personal or family illness | O | O |

Thank you very much for participating in this survey. If you would like to offer additional comments about your attitudes toward politics, then please feel free to enclose an additional page of comments.

# Appendix D

## The Interview Questionnaire

This appendix includes an outline of the topics addressed during the phone interviews we conducted. These interviews were free flowing, so the exact wording of each question varied.

**Introduction:** Thank you for agreeing to take the time to be interviewed. Most of the questions I'm going to ask deal with your attitudes about running for office. I want to emphasize that we're interested in your opinions and attitudes even if you tend not to be very interested in politics.

### Part I – Running for Public Office

1. Have you ever thought about running for any public office – that is, any office at the local, state, or federal level? Has it even ever crossed your mind?

   *If they have considered it:*
   - Is this something that you think about often? (Depending on the level of specificity in the answer, ask about the level of office.)
   - What makes you think you might want to do this? What's your motivation for wanting to get involved? Can you remember when you first realized that running for office was something that you might want to do?
   - Have you thought about it recently?

     *If yes:*
     - When was the most recent time you've thought about it?
     - Why did or didn't you decide to run?

- Do you think that, at some point in the future, you will run? Why is this or isn't this something you think you'll do?

  *If yes:*
  - What level of office(s) do you think you'd seek?
  - Why this office and not others?
  - Do you think you would win? Why?
  - Would you be willing to run even if you thought your likelihood of winning was quite low? If yes, why?

  *If they have already run for or held office:*
  - What office? Why did you decide to seek that particular office?
  - When?
  - Did you win?
  - Could you tell me a little bit about the campaign and the specific race you were involved in? Was it a close race, for example? Were there any aspects of the campaign that were particularly difficult? Surprising?

*If they have never considered it:*
- Are you interested in politics?
- Do you follow politics in your community? At the national level?
- When you say you've never considered running, does that mean it's something you could never see yourself doing? Why not?
- And this holds for all levels of office?

  *If they indicate that they could imagine running at some point in the future:*
  - What level of office(s) do you think you'd seek?
  - Why this office and not others?
  - Do you think you would win? Why?
  - Would you be willing to run even if you thought your likelihood of winning was quite low? If yes, why?

2. Is there anything that might make you more likely to run for office?
   - What type of circumstances or scenarios can you imagine might make you more likely?
   - What position(s) do you think you'd be more likely to seek?
   - What do you think are the most unappealing aspects about running?

3. Has anyone ever suggested or encouraged you to run for office?

*If yes:*
- Who? What were their relations to you? Family and friends versus party leaders, elected officials, colleagues, community activists?
- For what office?
- How many different times would you say someone has recommended that you run for office?
- How important is this kind of support to you in your deciding whether to enter a race?
- Whose support do you think is most important?
- So, overall, do you feel like you'd have a lot of support?

*If no:*
- Would receiving support or encouragement make you more receptive to considering a run?
- Whose support do you think is most important?

4. Do you think you are qualified to hold public office?

*If yes:*
- Why? What experiences and qualifications do you think position you to be a credible candidate?
- What about high-level office, like Congress? Do you think you are qualified for a position like that?
- What do you think are the most important qualifications/credentials in public officials and candidates?

*If no:*
- Why not? What experience are you missing?
- What do you think are the most important qualities and/or credentials in office holders and candidates?

5. Lots of people say that, in order to enter the political arena, you need to have thick skin. Do you think this is an accurate assessment?

*If yes:*
- Do you think you have what it takes to endure a possibly negative campaign and months of public scrutiny?

*If no:*
- Then how would you characterize the kinds of people who decide to run for office?

6. Others say that, in order to enter politics, you need to have a lot of confidence or ego strength. Do you think this is an accurate assessment?

   *If yes:*
   • Do you think you have these kinds of personality traits that seem necessary?

   *If no:*
   • Then how would you characterize the kinds of people who decide to run for office?

**Part II – Political Culture: I'd now like to turn to a few questions about the political environment you live in.**

1. Do you live in an area that tends to be liberal or conservative? Democrat or Republican? Very religious? Traditional? Urban, suburban, or rural?
2. Are your political views generally in sync with those in your community or out of sync? Do you think this plays a role in whether you'd ever be interested in running for local level office? How so?
3. Are you involved with your political party? At the local level? Statewide?
4. You might not know this, but are the political parties in your community strong? Do you know if they tend to recruit candidates, even for city council–type positions?

**Part III – Professional and Life Goals: Now I'd like to spend a couple of minutes talking about your career goals.**

1. Are you still working as a lawyer (or whatever)?

   *If yes:*
   • How long have you been working in your current profession?
   • Do you feel you still have a lot to accomplish within your profession? Like what?
   • How hard would it be for you to leave your profession and move on to something else if the opportunity presented itself?
   • If you had greater financial security, would you be more likely to consider leaving your current profession?
   • What other career ambitions do you have?

*If no:*
- When did you leave and what are you currently doing?
- How long have you been working in your current profession?
- Do you feel you still have a lot to accomplish within your profession? Like what?
- How hard would it be for you to leave your profession and move on to something else if the opportunity presented itself?
- If you had greater financial security, would you be more likely to consider leaving your current profession?
- What other career ambitions do you have?

2. Do you think that your current professional status affects your likelihood of running for office? That is, would your current job allow you the time necessary to campaign, fundraise, engage in the kinds of activities required to run?

3. Have you had any mentors help you achieve your professional success?

*If yes:*
- Who? What was the relation (mother, father, professor, supervisor, elected official)?
- What was this person's sex?

**Part IV – Perceptions of a Gendered Environment: Finally, I would like to ask you about some of the gender dynamics you may have witnessed in your professional life.**

1. Do you think that it is harder for women than men to succeed in your professional environment? Have you ever seen any patterns of sexism?
2. Within your work environment, have you ever noticed differences in the levels of confidence men and women exude?
3. Within your professional environment, have you ever identified differences in the ways that household responsibilities and/or children affect women and men?

# Appendix E

## Variable Coding

The following chart describes the variables included in the multivariate results presented and discussed throughout the book. Although many of these variables are referenced in more than one chapter, each is noted under the chapter in which it first appears.

| Variable | Range | Mean | Standard Deviation | Coding |
|---|---|---|---|---|
| Chapter 3 – "The Gender Gap in Political Ambition" | | | | |
| Sex (female) | 0, 1 | 0.47 | 0.50 | Indicates whether respondent is a woman (1) or a man (0). |
| Education | 1–6 | 5.42 | 1.03 | Indicates respondent's highest level of completed education. Ranges from less than high school (1) to graduate degree (6). |
| Income | 1–6 | 4.58 | 1.21 | Indicates respondent's annual household income. Ranges from less than $25,000 (1) to more than $200,000 (6). |
| Race (White) | 0, 1 | 0.83 | 0.38 | Indicates whether respondent is White (1) or not (0). |
| Democrat | 0, 1 | 0.45 | 0.50 | Indicates whether respondent self-identifies as a Democrat (1) or not (0). |
| Republican | 0, 1 | 0.30 | 0.46 | Indicates whether respondent self-identifies as a Republican (1) or not (0). |

*(continued)*

*(continued)*

| Variable | Range | Mean | Standard Deviation | Coding |
|----------|-------|------|--------------------|--------|
| Political knowledge | 0–3 | 2.43 | 0.98 | Indicates how many of respondent's members of Congress (House of Representatives and Senate) he or she can name. |
| Political interest | 2–8 | 5.53 | 1.66 | Indicates how closely respondent follows local and national news. Ranges from not closely (2) to very closely (8). |
| Political efficacy | 1–5 | 2.79 | 1.00 | Indicates whether respondent agrees that government officials pay attention to people like him or her. Ranges from strongly disagrees (1) to strongly agrees (5). |
| Political participation | 0–9 | 5.49 | 2.31 | Indicates level of respondent's political participation (over the course of the past year) based on the following activities: voted, contacted an elected official, joined or paid dues to an interest group, wrote a letter to a newspaper, contributed money to a campaign, volunteered for a candidate, volunteered on a community project, attended a political meeting, served on the board of a nonprofit organization. Lower numbers indicate lower levels of political engagement. |
| Considered running for elective office | 0, 1 | 0.51 | 0.50 | Indicates whether respondent ever considered running for local, state, or federal level office (1) or not (0). |
| Ran for elective office | 0, 1 | 0.09 | 0.29 | Indicates whether respondent ever sought local, state, or federal level office (1) or not (0). |

.

| Variable | Range | Mean | Standard Deviation | Coding |
|---|---|---|---|---|
| | | | | |

Chapter 4 – "Barefoot, Pregnant, and Holding a Law Degree"

| Variable | Range | Mean | Standard Deviation | Coding |
|---|---|---|---|---|
| "Political" household | 2–8 | 3.77 | 1.06 | Indicates "how frequently [respondent] discussed politics with parents when growing up" and "how often parents encouraged [him or her] to run for office someday." Higher numbers indicate a more political household. |
| Parent ran for office | 0, 1 | 0.14 | 0.35 | Indicates whether either of the respondent's parents ever ran for office (1) or not (0). |
| Ran for office as a student | 0, 1 | 0.55 | 0.50 | Indicates whether respondent ran for office in high school and/or college (1) or not (0). |
| Marital status (married) | 0, 1 | 0.75 | 0.44 | Indicates whether respondent is married (1) or not (0). |
| Children | 0, 1 | 0.76 | 0.43 | Indicates whether respondent has children (1) or not (0). |
| Children under age 6 living at home | 0, 1 | 0.14 | 0.35 | Indicates whether respondent has children under the age of 6 living at home (1) or not (0). |
| Responsible for majority of household tasks | 0–2 | 1.00 | 0.61 | Indicates whether respondent is responsible for less than half (0), half (1), or the majority (2) of the household tasks. |
| Responsible for majority of child care | 0, 1 | 0.11 | 0.32 | Indicates whether respondent is responsible for the majority of the child-care tasks (1) or not (0; which includes those respondents who have no children). |
| Age | 22–88 | 48.47 | 11.02 | Indicates respondent's age. |

Chapter 5 – "Gender, Party, and Political Recruitment"
(values based on second-wave data)

| Variable | Range | Mean | Standard Deviation | Coding |
|---|---|---|---|---|
| Percentage of women in the state legislature | .09–.38 | .24 | .06 | Indicates percentage of women in the state legislature where the respondent lives. |

*(continued)*

*(continued)*

| Variable | Range | Mean | Standard Deviation | Coding |
|---|---|---|---|---|
| Moralistic political culture | 0, 1 | .30 | .46 | Indicates whether respondent lives in a state with a moralistic political culture (1) or not (0). |
| Worked or volunteered on a campaign | 0, 1 | .65 | .48 | Indicates whether respondent worked or volunteered for a candidate or campaign (1) or not (0). |
| Attended a political meeting | 0, 1 | .79 | .41 | Indicates whether respondent attended a school board, city council, or local political meeting (1) or not (0). |
| Served on the board of an organization | 0, 1 | .71 | .46 | Indicates whether respondent served on the board of any organization or foundation (1) or not (0). |
| Attended political party meeting or event | 0, 1 | .64 | .48 | Indicates whether respondent attended any party meeting or event (1) or not (0). |
| Interacted with elected officials at work | 0, 1 | .66 | .47 | Indicates whether respondent interacts with elected officials as part of his or her job (1) or not (0). |
| Contact with women's organization(s) | 0, 1 | .15 | .35 | Indicates whether respondent has had contact with a women's organization (1) or not (0). |
| Received suggestion to run from an electoral gatekeeper (or recruited by political actor) | 0, 1 | 0.49 | 0.50 | Indicates whether a party official, nonelected activist, or elected official ever encouraged the respondent to run for office (1) or not (0). |
| Took at least one concrete step that precedes running for office | 0, 1 | .30 | .46 | Indicates whether respondent ever took a step that typically precedes running for office (1) or not (0). Steps include investigating how to get on the ballot, discussing running for office with potential contributors, supporters, and community members. |

| Variable | Range | Mean | Standard Deviation | Coding |
|---|---|---|---|---|
| | | | | |

### Chapter 6 – "I'm Just Not Qualified"

| Variable | Range | Mean | Standard Deviation | Coding |
|---|---|---|---|---|
| Received encourage-ment to run from personal source | 0, 1 | 0.60 | 0.49 | Indicates whether a friend, family member, or spouse/partner ever encouraged respondent to run for office (1) or not (0). |
| Self-perceived qualifications | 1–4 | 2.52 | 1.03 | Indicates respondent's level of self-perceived qualifications for holding elective office. Ranges from "not at all qualified" (1) to "very qualified" (4). |

### Chapter 7 – "Taking the Plunge"

| Variable | Range | Mean | Standard Deviation | Coding |
|---|---|---|---|---|
| Interested in high-level office | 0, 1 | 0.29 | 0.45 | Indicates whether respondent would ever consider running for federal or statewide office (1) or not (0). |
| Political culture factor score | −2.34–1.70 | 0.00 | 1.00 | Factor score derived from principal component analysis with varimax rotation. Indicates how moralistic respondent's political culture is. Percentage of women in the state legislature and percentage of the statewide vote Gore received in 2000 load on this factor. |

# Works Cited

Aberbach, Joel D., Robert D. Putnam, and Bert A. Rockman. 1981. *Bureaucrats and Politicians in Western Democracies*. Cambridge, MA: Harvard University Press.

Aldrich, John H. 2000. "Southern Parties in the State and Nation." *Journal of Politics* 62(3):643–70.

Alejano-Steele, AnnJanette. 1997. "Early Career Issues: Let the Juggling Begin." In *Dilemmas of a Double Life: Women Balancing Careers and Relationships*, ed. N. B. Kaltreider. Northvale, NJ: Jason Aronson.

Alexander, Deborah, and Kristi Andersen. 1993. "Gender as a Factor in the Attributions of Leadership Traits." *Political Research Quarterly* 46(3):527–45.

Alexander, Ruth M. 1988. "We Are Engaged as a Band of Sisters: Class and Domesticity in the Washingtonian Temperance Movement, 1840–1850." *Journal of American History* 75(December):763–85.

Alford, John, Carolyn L. Funk, and John R. Hibbing. 2005. "Are Political Orientations Genetically Transmitted?" *American Political Science Review* 99(2): 153–67.

———. 2008. "Twin Studies, Molecular Genetics, Politics, and Tolerance: A Response to Beckwith and Morris." *Perspectives on Politics* 6:793–97.

Almond, Gabriel Abraham, and Sidney Verba. 1963. *The Civic Culture; Political Attitudes and Democracy in Five Nations*. Princeton, NJ: Princeton University Press.

American Bar Association. 2008. "Women and the Law: Women in the Justice System." http://www.uslaw.com/library/article/ABAWomenJustice.html (December 10, 2009).

*America's Best Colleges 2001*. 2001. New York: U.S. News and World Report.

Amundsen, Kirsten. 1971. *The Silenced Majority: Women and American Democracy*. Englewood Cliffs, NJ: Prentice Hall.

Andolina, Molly W., Krista Jenkins, Cliff Zukin, and Scott Keeter. 2003. "Habits from Home, Lessons from School: Influences on Youth Civic Engagement." *PS: Political Science & Politics* 36:275–80.

Apter, Teri. 1993. *Working Women Don't Have Wives: Professional Success in the 1990s.* New York: St. Martin's Press.

Astin, Helen S., and Carole Leland. 1991. *Women of Influence, Women of Vision: A Cross-Generational Study of Leadership and Social Change.* San Francisco: Jossey-Bass.

Atkeson, Lonna Rae. 2003. "Not All Cues Are Created Equal: The Conditional Impact of Female Candidates on Political Engagement." *Journal of Politics* 65(4):1040–61.

Atkeson, Lonna Rae, and Nancy Carrillo. 2007. "More Is Better: The Influence of Collective Female Descriptive Representation on External Efficacy." *Politics & Gender* 3(1):79–101.

Bachrach, Peter. 1967. *The Theory of Democratic Elitism: A Critique.* Boston: Little, Brown.

Banerji, Shilpa. 2006. "AAUP: Women Professors Lag in Tenure, Salary." *Diverse Issues in Higher Education,* October 26, http://diverseeducation. com/article/6660/1.php (accessed December 21, 2009).

Barakso, Maryann, and Brian Schaffner. 2006. "Winning Coverage: News Media Portrayals of the Women's Movement, 1969–2004." *Harvard International Journal of Press/Politics* 11(4):22–44.

Barone, Michael, and Richard E. Cohen. 2008. *Almanac of American Politics.* Washington, D.C.: National Journal.

Baxter, Sandra, and Marjorie Lansing. 1983. *Women and Politics: The Visible Minority.* Ann Arbor: University of Michigan Press.

Beck, Paul Allen, and M. Kent Jennings. 1982. "Pathways to Participation." *American Political Science Review* 76(1):94–108.

Beckwith, Jon, and Corey A. Morris. 2008. "Twin Studies of Political Behavior: Untenable Assumptions?" *Perspectives on Politics* 6:785–91.

Beloff, H. 1992. "Mother, Father and Me: Our IQ." *Psychologist* 5:309–11.

Bendavid, Naftali. 2007. *The Thumpin': How Rahm Emanuel and the Democrats Learned to Be Ruthless and Ended the Republican Revolution.* New York: Doubleday.

Benko, Cathy, and Anne C. Weisberg. 2007. *Mass Career Customization: Aligning the Workplace with Today's Nontraditional Workforce.* Cambridge, MA: Harvard Business School Press.

Bergmann, Barbara. 1986. *The Economic Emergence of Women.* New York: Basic Books.

Berkman, Michael B., and Robert E. O'Connor. 1993. "Do Women Legislators Matter?" *American Politics Quarterly* 21(1):102–24.

Bernstein, Robert. 1986. "Why Are There So Few Women in the House?" *Western Political Quarterly* 39(1):155–64.

Beyer, S. 1990. "Gender Differences in the Accuracy of Self-Evaluation of Performance." *Journal of Personality and Social Psychology* 59:960–70.

Beyer, S., and Bowden, E. M. 1997. "Gender Differences in Self-Perceptions: Convergent Evidence from Three Measures of Accuracy and Bias." *Personality and Social Psychology Bulletin* 23(2):157–72.

Black, Gordon S. 1972. "A Theory of Political Ambition: Career Choices and the Role of Structural Incentives." *American Political Science Review* 66(1):144–59.

Blair, Diane D., and Jeanie R. Stanley. 1991. "Personal Relationships and Legislative Power: Male and Female Perceptions." *Legislative Studies Quarterly* 16(4):495–507.

Bledsoe, Timothy, and Mary Herring. 1990. "Victims of Circumstances: Women in Pursuit of Political Office." *American Political Science Review* 84(1):213–23.

Blumstein, Philip, and Pepper Schwartz. 1991. "Money and Ideology: Their Impact on Power and the Division of Household Labor." In *Gender, Family, and the Economy: The Triple Overlap*, ed. R. L. Blumberg. Newbury Park, CA: Sage.

Borelli, Maryanne, and Janet Martin. 1997. *Other Elites*. Boulder, CO: Lynne Rienner.

Bowles, Hannah R., Linda Babcock and Kathleen L. McGinn. 2004. "When Does Gender Matter in Negotiation? Tests of a Conceptual Framework." Manuscript, Harvard University.

Boxer, Barbara. 1994. *Politics and the New Revolution of Women in America*. Washington, D.C.: National Press Books.

Bratton, Kathleen. 2005. "Critical Mass Theory Revisited: The Behavior and Success of Token Women in State Legislatures." *Politics & Gender* 1(1):97–125.

Brown, Clifford W., Lynda W. Powell, and Clyde Wilcox. 1995. *Serious Money*. New York: Cambridge University Press.

Brownlow, Sheila, Rebecca Whitener, and Janet M. Rupert. 1998. "I'll Take Gender Differences for $1000! Domain-Specific Intellectual Success on 'Jeopardy'." *Sex Roles: A Journal of Research* 38(3):269–86.

Bullock, Charles, Susan MacManus, F. E. Atkins, L. J. Hoffman, and A. Newmark. 1999. "Winning in My Own Backyard: County Government, School Board Positions Steadily More Attractive to Women Candidates." In *Women in Politics: Outsiders or Insiders?* 3rd ed., ed. L. D. Whitaker. Upper Saddle River, NJ: Prentice Hall.

Burns, Nancy, Kay Lehman Schlozman, and Sidney Verba. 2001. *The Private Roots of Public Action: Gender, Equality, and Political Participation*. Cambridge, MA: Harvard University Press.

Burrell, Barbara. 1996. *A Woman's Place Is in the House: Campaigning for Congress in the Feminist Era*. Ann Arbor: University of Michigan Press.

———. 1998. "Campaign Finance: Women's Experience in the Modern Era." In *Women and Elective Office*, ed. S. Thomas and C. Wilcox. New York: Oxford University Press.

———. 2006. "Political Parties and Women's Organizations: Bringing Women into the Electoral Arena." In *Gender and Elections: Shaping the Future of American Politics*, ed. S. Carroll and R. Fox. New York: Cambridge University Press.

Burt-Way, Barbara J., and Rita Mae Kelly. 1992. "Gender and Sustaining Political Ambition: A Study of Arizona Elected Officials." *Western Political Quarterly* 44(1):11–25.

Bylsma, W. H., and B. Major. 1992. "Two Routes to Eliminating Gender Differences in Personal Entitlement: Social Comparisons and Performance Evaluations." *Psychology of Women Quarterly* 16(2):193–200.

Callahan-Levy, C., and L. A. Meese. 1979. "Sex Differences in the Allocation of Pay." *Journal of Personality and Social Psychology* 37(3):433–46.

Campbell, Angus, Philip E. Converse, Warren E. Miller, and Donald E. Stokes. 1960. *The American Voter.* New York: Wiley.

Campbell, David E., and Christina Wolbrecht. 2006. "See Jane Run: Women Politicians as Role Models for Adolescents." *Journal of Politics* 68:233–47.

Carroll, Susan J. 1985. "Political Elites and Sex Differences in Political Ambition: A Reconsideration." *Journal of Politics* 47(4):1231–43.

———. 1989. "The Personal Is Political: The Intersection of Private Lives and Public Roles among Women and Men in Elective and Appointive Office." *Women & Politics* 9(2):51–67.

———. 1993. "The Political Careers of Women Elected Officials: An Assessment and Research Agenda." In *Ambition and Beyond: Career Paths of American Politicians*, ed. S. Williams and E. Lascher. Berkeley, CA: Institute of Governmental Studies.

———. 1994. *Women as Candidates in American Politics*, 2nd ed. Bloomington: Indiana University Press.

Carroll, Susan J., and Kelly Dittmar. 2010. "The 2008 Candidacies of Hillary Clinton and Sarah Palin: Cracking the 'Highest, Hardest Glass Ceiling.'" In *Gender and Elections: Shaping the Future of American Politics*, 2nd ed., ed. S. Carroll and R. Fox. New York: Cambridge University Press.

Carroll, Susan, Debra L. Dodson, and Ruth B. Mandel. 1991. *The Impact of Women in Public Office: An Overview.* New Brunswick, NJ: Eagleton Institute of Politics' Center for American Women and Politics.

Carroll, Susan J., and Wendy S. Strimling. 1983. *Women's Routes to Elective Office: A Comparison with Men's.* New Brunswick, NJ: Center for the American Woman and Politics.

Catalyst. 2009. "Women CEOs of the Fortune 1000." http://catalyst.org/publication/322/women-ceos-of-the-fortune-1000 (accessed December 19, 2009).

Cattagni, Anne, and Elizabeth Farris Westat. 2001. *Internet Access in U.S. Public Schools and Classrooms: 1994–2000.* Washington, D.C.: U.S. Department of Education.

Center for American Women and Politics (CAWP). 2001. "Women State Legislators: Past, Present, and Future." http://www.cawp.rutgers.edu/research/topics/documents/StLeg2001Report.pdf (December 19, 2009).

———. 2008. "Gender Differences in Voter Turnout." http://www.cawp.rutgers.edu/fast_facts/voters/turnout.php (July 15, 2009).

———. 2009a. "Fast Facts." http://www.cawp.rutgers.edu/fast_facts/index.php (May 25, 2009).

———. 2009b. "Women in Elective Office." http://www.cawp.rutgers.edu/fast_facts/levels_of_office/documents/elective.pdf (July 17, 2009).

Clark, Janet. 1994. "Getting There: Women in Political Office." In *Different Roles, Different Voice*, ed. M. Githens, P. Norris and J. Lovenduski. New York: HarperCollins.

Clinton, Bill. 2004. *My Life.* New York: Alfred A. Knopf.

Clinton, Hillary Rodham. 2003. *Living History.* New York: Simon and Schuster.

Cohen, Jeff. 2006. *Cable News Confidential: My Misadventures in Corporate Media.* Sausalito, CA: PoliPointPress.

Coltrane, Scott. 2000. "Research on Household Labor: Modeling and Measuring the Social Embeddedness of Routine Family Work." *Journal of Marriage and the Family* 62(4):1208–33.

Conover, Pamela Johnston, and Virginia Gray. 1983. *Feminism and the New Right: Conflict over the American Family.* New York: Praeger.

Conway, M. Margaret. 1991. *Political Participation in the United States*, 2nd ed. Washington, D.C.: Congressional Quarterly.

Conway, M. Margaret, Gertrude A. Steuernagel, and David W. Ahern. 2004. *Women and Political Participation: Cultural Change in the Political Arena*, 2nd ed. Washington, D.C.: Congressional Quarterly.

Cook, Elizabeth Adell. 1998. "Voter Reaction to Women Candidates." In *Women and Elective Office*, ed. S. Thomas and C. Wilcox. New York: Oxford University Press.

Cook, Timothy E., and Paul Gronke. 2005. "The Skeptical American: Revisiting the Meanings of Trust in Government and Confidence in Institutions." *Journal of Politics* 67(3):784–803.

Costantini, Edmond. 1990. "Political Women and Political Ambition: Closing the Gender Gap." *American Journal of Political Science* 34(3):741–70.

Curran, Barbara A. 1995. *Women in the Law: A Look at the Numbers.* Chicago: American Bar Association Commission on Women in the Profession.

Curran, Barbara A., and Clara N. Carson. 1994. *The Lawyer Statistical Report: The US Legal Profession in the 1990s.* Chicago: American Bar Foundation.

Darcy, R., Charles D. Hadley, and Jason F. Kirksey. 1993. "Electoral Systems and the Representation of Black Women in American State Legislatures." *Women & Politics* 13(2):73–89.

Darcy, Robert, Susan Welch, and Janet Clark. 1994. *Women, Elections, and Representation*, 2nd ed. Lincoln: University of Nebraska Press.

Davis, Rebecca Howard. 1997. *Women and Power in Parliamentary Democracies: Cabinet Appointments in Western Europe.* Lincoln: University of Nebraska Press.

Davis, Richard, and Diana Marie Owen. 1998. *New Media and American Politics: Transforming American Politics.* New York: Oxford University Press.

Deckman, Melissa. 2007. "Gender Differences in the Decision to Run for School Board." *American Politics Research* 35(4):541–63.

Diamond, Irene. 1977. *Sex Roles in the Statehouse.* New Haven, CT: Yale University Press.

Djupe, Paul A., and Christopher P. Gilbert. 2006. "The Resourceful Believer: Generating Civic Skills in Church." *Journal of Politics* 68(1):116–27.

Djupe, Paul A., Anand E. Sokhey, and Christopher P. Gilbert. 2007. "Present but Not Accounted For? Gender Differences in Civic Resource Acquisition." *American Journal of Political Science* 51(4):906–20.

Dodson, Debra L. 1998. "Representing Women's Interests in the U.S. House of Representatives." In *Women and Elective Office*, ed. S. Thomas and C. Wilcox. New York: Oxford University Press.

Dodson, Debra L., and Susan J. Carroll. 1991. *Reshaping the Agenda: Women in State Legislatures*. New Brunswick, NJ: Eagleton Institute of Politics' Center for American Women and Politics.

Dolan, Julie. 2000. "The Senior Executive Service: Gender, Attitudes and Representative Bureaucracy." *Journal of Public Administration Research and Theory* 10(3):513–29.

Dolan, Kathleen. 2004. *Voting for Women: How the Public Evaluates Women Candidates*. Boulder, CO: Westview Press.

———. 1998. "Voting for Women in the 'Year of the Woman.'" *American Journal of Political Science* 42(1):272–93.

———. 2006. "Symbolic Mobilization? The Impact of Candidate Sex in American Elections." *American Politics Research* 34(6):687–704.

Dolan, Kathleen, and Lynne E. Ford. 1997. "Change and Continuity among Women State Legislators: Evidence from Three Decades." *Political Research Quarterly* 50(1):137–51.

Dolbeare, Cushing N., and Anne J. Stone. 1990. "Women and Affordable Housing." In *The American Woman*, ed. S. Rix. New York: W. W. Norton.

Douglas, Susan J. 1994. *Where the Girls Are: Growing Up Female with the Mass Media*. New York: Times Books.

DuBois, Ellen Carol. 1987. "Working Women, Class Relations, and Suffrage Militance: Harriot Stanton Blatch and the NY Woman Suffrage Movement, 1894–1909." *Journal of American History* 74(1):34–58.

Duerst-Lahti, Georgia. 1998. "The Bottleneck, Women as Candidates." In *Women and Elective Office*, ed. S. Thomas and C. Wilcox. New York: Oxford University Press.

———. 2006. "Presidential Elections: Gendered Space and the Case of 2004." In *Gender and Elections: Shaping the Future of American Politics*, ed. S. Carroll and R. Fox. New York: Cambridge University Press.

———. 2008. "Seeing What Has Always Been: Opening Study of the Presidency." *PS: Political Science and Politics* 41(4):733–7.

Duerst-Lahti, Georgia, and Cathy Marie Johnson. 1992. "Management Styles, Stereotypes, and Advantages." In *Women and Men of the States: Public Administrators at the State Level*, ed. M. E. Guy. Armonk, NY: M. E. Sharpe.

Duerst-Lahti, Georgia, and Rita Mae Kelly. 1995. *Gender, Power, Leadership and Governance*. Ann Arbor: University of Michigan Press.

*Dun and Bradstreet Million Dollar Directory, 2000–2001*. 2001. Parsippany, NJ: Dun's Marketing Services.

Eagly, Alice, and Linda L. Carli. 2007. "Women and the Labyrinth of Leadership." *Harvard Business Review*, September 1, 63–71.

Eagly, Alice, and Blair T. Johnson. 1990. "Gender and Leadership Style: A Meta-Analysis." *Psychological Bulletin* 108(2):233–56.

Elazar, Daniel J. 1984. *American Federalism: A View from the States*. New York: Harper and Row.

Elshtain, Jean Bethke. 1981. *Public Man, Private Woman*. Princeton, NJ: Princeton University Press.

Enloe, Cynthia. 2004. *The Curious Feminist*. Berkeley: University of California Press.

Evans, Sara M. 1997. *Born for Liberty: A History of Women in America*. New York: Free Press.

Eulau, Heinz, and Kenneth Prewitt. 1973. *Labyrinths of Democracy: Adaptations, Linkages, Representation, and Policies in Urban Politics*. Indianapolis: Bobbs-Merrill.

Falk, Erika. 2008. *Women for President: Media Bias in Eight Campaigns*. Champaign: University of Illinois Press.

Falkenheim, Jacquelina C., and Mark K. Feigener. 2008. "2007 Records Fifth Consecutive Annual Increase in U.S. Doctoral Awards." November, *NSF 09-307*. Arlington, VA: National Science Foundation.

Faludi, Susan. 1991. *Backlash: The Undeclared War Against American Women*. New York: Crown.

Fiber, Pamela, and Richard L. Fox. 2005. "A Tougher Road for Women: Assessing the Role of Gender in Congressional Elections." In *Gender and American Politics*, ed. S. Tolleson-Rinehart and J. Josephson. Armonk, NY: M. E. Sharpe.

Fiorina, Morris P., and Paul E. Peterson. 2002. *The New American Democracy*, 2nd ed. New York: Longman.

Flammang, Janet. 1985. "Female Officials in the Feminist Capital: The Case of Santa Clara County." *Western Political Quarterly* 38(1):94–118.

———. 1997. *Women's Political Voice: How Women Are Transforming the Practice and Study of Politics*. Philadelphia: Temple University Press.

Flanigan, William H., and Nancy H. Zingale. 2002. *Political Behavior of the American Electorate*, 10th ed. Washington, D.C.: Congressional Quarterly.

Fowler, Linda L. 1993. *Candidates, Congress, and the American Democracy*. Ann Arbor: University of Michigan Press.

Fowler, Linda L., and Jennifer L. Lawless. 2009. "Looking for Sex in All the Wrong Places: Press Coverage and the Electoral Fortunes of Gubernatorial Candidates." *Perspectives on Politics* 7(3):519–37.

Fowler, Linda L., and Robert McClure. 1989. *Political Ambition*. New Haven, CT: Yale University Press.

Fowlkes, Diane L., Jerry Perkins, and Sue Tolleson Rinehart. 1979. "Gender Roles and Party Roles." *American Political Science Review* 73(3):772–80.

Fox, Richard L. 1997. *Gender Dynamics in Congressional Elections*. Thousand Oaks, CA: Sage.

———. 2010. "Congressional Elections: Women's Candidacies and the Road to Gender Parity." In *Gender and Elections*, 2nd ed, ed. S. Carroll and R. Fox. New York: Cambridge University Press.

Fox, Richard L., and Jennifer L. Lawless. 2003. "Family Structure, Sex-Role Socialization, and the Decision to Run for Office." *Women & Politics* 24(4):19–48.

———. 2005. "To Run or Not to Run for Office: Explaining Nascent Political Ambition." *American Journal of Political Science* 49(3):659–76.

———. 2009. "Gaining and Losing Interest in Running for Public Office: Developing the Concept of Dynamic Political Ambition." Paper presented at the annual meeting of the American Political Science Association, Toronto, September 2–5.

Fox, Richard L., Jennifer L. Lawless, and Courtney Feeley. 2001. "Gender and the Decision to Run for Office." *Legislative Studies Quarterly* 26(3):411–35.

Fox, Richard L., and Zoe Oxley. 2003. "Gender Stereotyping in State Executive Elections: Candidate Selection and Success." *Journal of Politics* 65(3):833–50.

Fox, Richard L., and Robert Schuhmann. 1999. "Gender and Local Government: A Comparison of Women and Men City Managers." *Public Administration Review* 59(3):231–42.

———. 2001. "The Mentoring Experiences of Women and Men City Managers: Are Women Disadvantaged?" *American Review of Public Administration* 31(4):381–92.

Fox, Richard L., and Eric R. A. N. Smith. 1998. "The Role of Candidate Sex in Voter Decision-Making." *Political Psychology* 19(2):405–19.

Fox, Richard L., Robert Van Sickel, and Thomas Steiger. 2007. *Tabloid Justice: Criminal Justice in an Age of Media Frenzy*, 2nd ed. Boulder, CO: Lynne Rienner.

Frederick, Brian. 2009. "Are Female House Members Still More Liberal in a Polarized Era? The Conditional Nature of the Relationship between Descriptive and Substantive Representation." *Congress and the Presidency* 36(2):181–202.

Freeman, Jo. 2000. *A Room at a Time: How Women Entered Party Politics*. Lanham, MD: Rowman and Littlefield.

Freedman, Estelle. 2002. *No Turning Back*. New York: Ballantine Books.

Friedan, Betty. 1963. *The Feminine Mystique*. New York: W. W. Norton.

Fulton, Sarah A., Cherie D. Maestas, L. Sandy Maisel, and Walter J. Stone. 2006. "The Sense of a Woman: Gender, Ambition and the Decision to Run for Congress." *Political Research Quarterly* 59(2):235–48.

Furnham, A., and R. Rawles. 1995. "Sex Differences in the Estimation of Intelligence." *Journal of Social Behavior and Personality* 10:741–8.

Gaddie, Ronald Keith, and Charles S. Bullock. 2000. *Elections to Open Seats in the U.S. House: Where the Action Is*. Lanham, MD: Rowman and Littlefield.

Galinsky, Ellen, and James T. Bond. 1996. "Work and Family: The Experiences of Mothers and Fathers in the U.S. Labor Force." In *The American Woman, 1996 – 1997*, ed. C. Costello and B. K. Krimgold. New York: W. W. Norton.

Gartner, Scott Sigmund, and Gary M. Segura. 2008. "All Politics Are Still Local: The Iraq War and the 2006 Midterm Elections." *PS: Political Science and Politics* 41(1):95–100.

Gerrity, Jessica C., Tracy Osborn, and Jeanette Morehouse Mendez. 2007. "Women and Representation: A Different View of the District?" *Politics & Gender* 3(2):179–200.

Gertzog, Irwin N. 1995. *Congressional Women: Their Recruitment, Integration, and Behavior*, 2nd ed. Westport, CT: Praeger.

Ginzberg, Lori D. 1986. "Moral Suasion Is Moral Balderdash: Women, Politics, and Social Activism in the 1850s." *Journal of American History* 73(3):601–22.

Githens, Marianne. 2003. "Accounting for Women's Political Involvement: The Perennial Problem of Recruitment." In *Women and American Politics*, ed. S. Carroll. New York: Oxford University Press.

Githens, Marianne, and Jewel L. Prestage. 1977. *A Portrait of Marginality: The Political Behavior of the American Woman*. New York: Longman.

Gneezy, Uri, Muriel Niederle, and Aldo Rustichini. 2003. "Performance in Competitive Environments: Gender Differences." *Quarterly Journal of Economics* 118(3):1049–74.

Golden, Catherine. 1996. *Campaign Manager: Running and Winning*. Ashland, OR: OakStreet Press.

Goodliffe, Jay. 2001. "The Effect of War Chests on Challenger Entry in U.S. House Elections." *American Journal of Political Science* 45(4):830–44.

Graber, Doris A. 2010. *Mass Media and American Politics*, 8th ed. Washington, D.C.: CQ Press.

Grey, Lawrence. 2007. *How to Win a Local Election: A Complete Step-by-Step Guide*, 3rd ed. Lanham, MD: M. Evans.

Hansen, Susan B. 1997. "Talking about Politics: Gender and Contextual Effects on Political Proselytizing." *Journal of Politics* 59(1):73–103.

Hart, Daniel, Thomas M. Donnelly, James Youniss, and Robert Atkins. 2007. "High School Community Service as a Predictor of Adult Voting and Volunteering." *American Education Research Journal* 44(1):197–219.

Hess, F. 2002. *School Boards at the Dawn of the 21st Century*. Alexandria, VA: American School Boards Association.

Hess, Robert D., Judith V. Torney, and Jaan Valsiner. 2006. *The Development of Political Attitudes in Children*. Edison, NJ: Transaction Publishers.

Hill, David. 1981. "Political Culture and Female Political Representation." *Journal of Politics* 43(1):159–68.

Hirshman, Linda. 2006. *Get to Work: A Manifesto for Women of the World*. New York: Viking.

Hochschild, Arlie. 1989. *The Second Shift*. New York: Avon.

Huddy, Leonie, and Nayda Terkildsen. 1993a. "The Consequences of Gender Stereotypes for Women Candidates at Different Levels and Types of Office." *Political Research Quarterly* 46(3):503–25.

———. 1993b. "Gender Stereotypes and the Perception of Male and Female Candidates." *American Journal of Political Science* 37(1):119–47.

Hymowitz, Kay S. 2002. "The End of Herstory." *City Journal* 12(3):52–63.

Inter-Parliamentary Union. 2009. "Women in National Parliaments." http://www.ipu.org/wmn-e/classif.htm (June 29, 2009).

Jacobson, Gary. 2004. *The Politics of Congressional Elections*, 6th ed. New York: Longman.

Jamieson, Kathleen Hall. 1995. *Beyond the Double Bind*. New York: Oxford University Press.

Jamieson, Kathleen Hall, and Joseph N. Capella. 2008. *Echo Chamber: Rush Limbaugh and the Conservative Media Establishment*. New York: Oxford University Books.

Jenkins, Krista, and Susan J. Carroll. 2003. "Term Limits and the Representation of Women." *American Political Science Association Newsletter*, http://www.apsanet.org/~lss/Newsletter/jan03/Jenkins.htm (February 17, 2005).

Jennings, M. Kent. 2006. "The Gender Gap in Attitudes and Beliefs about the Place of Women in American Political Life: A Longitudinal, Cross-Generational Analysis." *Politics & Gender* 2(2):193–219.

Jennings, M. Kent, and Gregory B. Markus. 1984. "Partisan Orientations over the Long Haul: Results from the Three-Wave Political Socialization Panel Study." *American Political Science Review* 78(4):1000–18.

Jennings, M. Kent, and Richard G. Niemi. 1981. *Generations and Politics: A Panel Study of Young Adults and Their Parents.* Princeton, NJ: Princeton University Press.

Jewell, Malcolm E., and Sarah M. Morehouse. 2001. *Political Parties and Elections in American States,* 4th ed. Washington, D.C.: Congressional Quarterly.

Johnson, Janet B., Richard A. Joslyn, and H. T. Reynolds. 2001. *Political Science Research Methods,* 4th ed. Washington, D.C.: Congressional Quarterly.

Kahn, Kim Fridkin. 1996. *The Political Consequences of Being a Woman.* New York: Columbia University Press.

Kamber, Victor. 2003. *Poison Politics: Are Negative Campaigns Destroying Democracy?* New York: Basic Books.

Kathlene, Lyn. 1994. "Power and Influence in State Legislatures; the Interaction of Gender and Position in Committee Hearing Debates." *American Political Science Review* 88(3):560–76.

————. 1995. "Alternative Views of Crime: Legislative Policymaking in Gendered Terms." *Journal of Politics* 57(3):696–723.

Kathlene, Lyn, Susan E. Clarke, and Barbara A. Fox. 1991. "Ways Women Politicians Are Making a Difference." In *Reshaping the Agenda: Women in State Legislatures,* ed. D. Dodson and S. Carroll. New Brunswick, NJ: Eagleton Institute of Politics' Center for American Women and Politics.

Kazee, Thomas A. 1980. "The Decision to Run for the U.S. Congress: Challenger Attitudes in the 1970s." *Legislative Studies Quarterly* 5(1):79–100.

————. 1994. "The Emergence of Congressional Candidates." In *Who Runs for Congress? Ambition, Context, and Candidate Emergence,* ed. Thomas Kazee. Washington, D.C.: Congressional Quarterly.

Keele, Luke. 2007. "Social Capital and the Dynamics of Trust in Government." *American Journal of Political Science* 51(2):241–54.

Kerber, Linda. 1998. *No Constitutional Right to be Ladies.* New York: Hill and Wang.

Kirkpatrick, Jeanne J. 1974. *Political Woman.* New York: Basic Books.

Klein, Ethel. 1984. *Gender Politics.* Cambridge, MA: Harvard University Press.

Kling, Kristen C., J. Hyde, C. Showers, and B. Buswell. 1999. "Gender Differences in Self-Esteem: A Meta-Analysis." *Psychological Bulletin* 125(4):470–500.

Koch, Jeffrey W. 2000. "Do Citizens Apply Gender Stereotypes to Infer Candidates' Ideological Orientations?" *Journal of Politics* 62(2):414–29.

Kornblut, Anne E. 2010. *Notes from the Cracked Ceiling: Hillary Clinton, Sarah Palin, and What It Will Take for a Woman to Win.* New York: Crown.

Kousser, Thad. 2005. *Term Limits and the Dismantling of State Legislative Professionalism.* New York: Cambridge University Press.

Krook, Mona Lena. 2009. *Quotas for Women in Politics: Gender and Candidate Selection Reform Worldwide*. New York: Oxford University Press.

Kunin, Madeline May. 2005. *Living a Political Life*. New York: Knopf Doubleday.

Lane, Robert Edwards. 1959. *Political Life: Why People Get Involved in Politics*. Glencoe, IL: Free Press.

Lasswell, Harold. 1948. *Power and Personality*. Stanford, CA: Stanford University Press.

Lawless, Jennifer L. 2004a. "Politics of Presence: Women in the House and Symbolic Representation." *Political Research Quarterly* 57(1):81–99.

———. 2004b. "Women, War, and Winning Elections: Gender Stereotyping in the Post-September 11th Era." *Political Research Quarterly* 53(3):479–90.

———. 2009. "Sexism and Gender Bias in Election 2008: A More Complex Path for Women in Politics." *Politics & Gender* 5(1):70–80.

Lawless, Jennifer L., and Richard L. Fox. 2008. "Why Are Women Still Not Running for Public Office?" *Issues in Governance Studies No. 14*. Washington, D.C.: Brookings Institution.

Lawless, Jennifer L., and Kathryn Pearson. 2008. "The Primary Reason for Women's Under-Representation: Re-Evaluating the Conventional Wisdom." *Journal of Politics* 70(1):67–82.

Lawless, Jennifer L., and Sean M. Theriault. 2005. "Will She Stay or Will She Go? Career Ceilings and Women's Retirement from the U.S. Congress." *Legislative Studies Quarterly* 30(4):581–96.

Lee, Marcia Manning. 1976. "Why So Few Women Hold Public Office: Democracy and Sexual Roles." *Political Science Quarterly* 91:297–314.

Leeper, Mark. 1991. "The Impact of Prejudice on Female Candidates: An Experimental Look at Voter Inference." *American Politics Quarterly* 19(2):248–61.

Lerner, Gerda. 1986. *The Creation of Patriarchy*. New York: Oxford University Press.

Maestas, Cherie D., Lonna Rae Atkeson, Thomas Croom, and Lisa A. Bryant. 2008. "Shifting the Blame: Federalism, Media, and Public Assignment of Blame Following Hurricane Katrina." *Publius* 38(4):609–32.

Maestas, Cherie D., Sarah Fulton, L. Sandy Maisel, and Walter J. Stone. 2006. "When to Risk It? Institutions, Ambitions, and the Decision to Run for the U.S. House." *American Political Science Review* 100(2):195–208.

Maestas, Cherie D., L. Sandy Maisel, and Walter J. Stone. 2005. "National Party Efforts to Recruit State Legislators to Run for the U.S. House." *Legislative Studies Quarterly* 30(2):277–300.

Maisel, L. Sandy, and Walter J. Stone. 1998. "The Politics of Government-Funded Research: Notes from the Experience of the Candidate Emergence Study." *PS* 31(4):811–7.

Major, B., D. B. McFarlin, and D. Gagnon. 1984. "Overworked and Underpaid: On the Nature of Gender Differences in Personal Entitlement." *Journal of Personality and Social Psychology* 47(6):1399–1412.

Malbin, Michael J., Norman J. Ornstein, and Thomas E. Mann. 2008. *Vital Statistics on Congress 2008*. Washington, D.C.: Brookings Institution.

Mann, Thomas E., and Bruce E. Cain. 2005. "Introduction." In *Party Lines*, ed. Thomas E. Mann and Bruce E. Cain. Washington, D.C.: Brookings Institution.

Mansbridge, Jane. 1999. "Should Blacks Represent Blacks and Women Represent Women? A Contingent 'Yes.'" *Journal of Politics* 61(3):628–57.

Margolies-Mezvinsky, Marjorie. 1994. *Woman's Place: The Freshman Women Who Changed the Face of Congress*. New York: Crown.

Mark, David. 2006. *Going Dirty: The Art of Negative Campaigning*. Lanham, MD: Rowman and Littlefield.

*Martindale-Hubbell Law Directory, 2001*. 2001. New Providence, NJ: Martindale-Hubbell.

Mason, Mary Ann, and Marc Goulden. 2002. "Do Babies Matter? The Effect of Family Formation on the Lifelong Careers of Academic Men and Women." *Academe*, http://www.aaup.org/publications/academe/2002/02nd/02ndmas .htm (February 17, 2005).

Matland, Richard E. 1998. "Women's Representation in National Legislatures: Developed and Developing Countries." *Legislative Studies Quarterly* 23(1): 109–25.

Matthews, Donald R. 1984. "Legislative Recruitment and Legislative Careers." *Legislative Studies Quarterly* 9(4):547–85.

Mayhew, David. 1974. *The Electoral Connection*. New Haven, CT: Yale University Press.

McDermott, Monika L. 1997. "Voting Cues in Low-Information Elections: Candidate Gender as a Social Information Variable in Contemporary US Elections." *American Journal of Political Science* 41(1):270–83.

———. 1998. "Race and Gender Cues in Low-Information Elections." *Political Research Quarterly* 51(4):895–918.

McDonagh, Eileen. 2008. *The Motherless State: Women's Political Leadership and American Democracy*. Chicago: University of Chicago Press.

McGlen, Nancy E., Karen O'Connor, Laura Van Assendelft, and Wendy Gunther-Canada. 2005. *Women, Politics, and American Society*, 4th ed. New York: Longman.

McIntosh, Hugh, Daniel Hart, and James Youniss. 2007. "The Influence of Family Political Discussion on Youth Civic Development: Which Parent Qualities Matter?" *PS: Political Science & Politics* 40(3):495–9.

Mezey, Susan Gluck. 2003. *Elusive Equality*. Boulder, CO: Lynne Rienner.

Moncrief, Gary F., Peverill Squire, and Malcolm E. Jewell. 2001. *Who Runs for the Legislature?* Upper Saddle River, NJ: Prentice Hall.

Myers, Dee Dee. 2008. *Why Women Should Rule the World*. New York: Harper.

Myrdal, Alva. 1941. *Nation and Family: The Swedish Experiment in Democratic Family and Population Policy*. New York: Harper and Brothers.

———. 1968. *Nation and Family*. Cambridge: Massachusetts Institute of Technology Press.

Naff, Katherine C. 1995. "Subjective vs. Objective Discrimination in Government: Adding to the Picture of Barriers to the Advancement of Women." *Political Research Quarterly* 48(3):535–58.

National Association for Law Placement Foundation. 2009. "Women and Minorities in Law Firms by Race and Ethnicity." http://www.nalp.org/jan2009 womenminorities (June 30, 2009).

National Conference of State Legislatures. 2009a. "Full and Part-Time Legislatures." http://www.ncsl.org/?tabid=16701 (July 15, 2009).

———. 2009b. "The Term Limited States." http://www.ncsl.org/Default.aspx?TabId=14844 (May 30, 2009).

National Women's Political Caucus (NWPC). 1994. *Why Don't More Women Run?* Washington, D.C.: Mellman, Lazarus, and Lake.

Nechemias, Carol. 1987. "Changes in the Election of Women to U.S. State Legislative Seats." *Legislative Studies Quarterly* 12(1):125–42.

Niederle, Muriel, and Lise Vesterlund. 2007. "Do Women Shy Away from Competition? Do Men Compete Too Much?" *Quarterly Journal of Economics* 122(3):1067–1101.

Niemi, Richard G. 1974. *How Family Members Perceive Each Other: Political and Social Attitudes in Two Generations.* New Haven, CT: Yale University Press.

Niven, David. 1998. *The Missing Majority: The Recruitment of Women as State Legislative Candidates.* Westport, CT: Praeger.

———. 2006. "Throwing Your Hat out of the Ring: Negative Recruitment and the Gender Imbalance in State Legislative Candidacy." *Politics & Gender* 2(4):473–89.

Nixon, David L., and R. Darcy. 1996. "Special Elections and the Growth of Women's Representation in the House of Representatives." *Women & Politics* 16(Winter):96–107.

Norrander, Barbara, and Clyde Wilcox. 2008. "The Gender Gap in Ideology." *Political Behavior* 30(4):503–23.

Norris, Pippa. 1994. "The Impact of the Electoral System on Election of Women to National Legislatures." In *Different Roles, Different Voices*, ed. Marianne Githens, Pippa Norris, and Joni Lovenduski. New York: HarperCollins.

O'Connor, Karen. 2002. *Women and Congress.* Binghamton, NY: Haworth Press.

Okin, Susan Moller. 1989. *Justice, Gender, and the Family.* New York: Basic Books.

Owen, Diana, and Jack Dennis. 1988. "Gender Differences in the Politicization of American Children." *Women & Politics* 8(Summer):23–43.

Pajares, Frank. 2002. "Gender and Perceived Self-Efficacy in Self-Regulated Learning." *Theory into Practice* 41(2):116–25.

Palmer, Barbara, and Dennis Simon. 2003. "Political Ambition and Women in the U.S. House of Representatives, 1916–2000." *Political Research Quarterly* 56(2):127–38.

———. 2008. *Breaking the Political Glass Ceiling: Women and Congressional Elections*, 2nd ed. New York: Routledge.

Paolino, Phillip. 1995. "Group-Salient Issues and Group Representation: Support for Women Candidates in the 1992 Senate Elections." *American Journal of Political Science* 39(2):294–313.

Pasek, Josh, Lauren Feldman, Daniel Romer, and Kathleen Hall Jamieson. 2008. "Schools as Incubators of Democratic Participation: Building Long-Term Political Efficacy with Civic Education." *Applied Developmental Science* 12(1):26–37.

Pateman, Carole. 1988. *The Sexual Contract*. Stanford, CA: Stanford University Press.

Patterson, Thomas E. 1994. *Out of Order: An Incisive and Boldly Original Critique of the News Media's Domination of America's Political Process*. New York: Random House.

Pitkin, Hanna F. 1967. *The Concept of Representation*. Berkeley: University of California Press.

Prewitt, Kenneth. 1970. "Political Ambitions, Volunteerism, and Electoral Accountability." *American Political Science Review* 64(1):5–17.

Prinz, Timothy S. 1993. "The Career Paths of Elected Politicians: A Review and Prospectus." In *Ambition and Beyond: Career Paths of American Politicians*, ed. S. Williams and E. Lascher. Berkeley, CA: Institute of Governmental Studies.

Rausch, John D., Mark Rozell, and Harry L. Wilson. 1999. "When Women Lose: A Case Study of Media Coverage of Two Gubernatorial Campaigns. *Women & Politics* 20(4):1–22.

Reingold, Beth. 1996. "Conflict and Cooperation: Legislative Strategies and Concepts of Power among Female and Male State Legislators." *Journal of Politics* 58(2):464–85.

_____. 2000. *Representing Women: Sex, Gender, and Legislative Behavior in Arizona and California*. Chapel Hill: University of North Carolina Press.

Renshon, Stanley A. 1975. "Temporal Orientations and Political Life: The Psychology of Political Impatience." *British Journal of Political Science* 7(2):262–72.

Roberts, T. 1991. "Gender and the Influences of Evaluation on Self-Assessment in Achievement Settings." *Psychological Bulletin* 109(2):297–308.

Rohde, David W. 1979. "Risk-Bearing and Progressive Ambition: The Case of the U.S. House of Representatives." *American Journal of Political Science* 23(1):1–26.

Rosenthal, Cindy Simon. 1995. "The Role of Gender in Descriptive Representation." *Political Research Quarterly* 48(3):599–612.

_____. 1998. *When Women Lead*. New York: Oxford University Press.

Rosenwasser, Shirley M., and Norma G. Dean. 1989. "Gender Roles and Political Office: Effects of Perceived Masculinity/Femininity of Candidate and Political Office." *Psychology of Women Quarterly* 13(June):77–85.

Roth, Louise Marie. 2006. *Selling Women Short: Gender and Money on Wall Street*. Princeton, NJ: Princeton University Press.

Roy, Robin E., Kristin S. Weibust, and Carol T. Miller. 2007. "Effects of Stereotypes about Feminists on Feminist Self-Identification." *Psychology of Women Quarterly* 31(2):146–56.

Rule, Wilma. 1981. "Why Women Don't Run: The Critical Contextual Factors In Women's Legislative Recruitment." *Western Political Quarterly* 34(March):60–77.

_____. 1987. "Electoral Systems, Contextual Factors, and Women's Opportunity for Election to Parliament in Twenty-Three Democracies." *Western Political Quarterly* 40(3):477–98.

_____. 1990. "Why More Women Are State Legislators: A Research Note." *Western Political Quarterly* 43(2):437–48.

Sabato, Larry J. 2000. *Feeding Frenzy: Attack Journalism and American Politics.* Baltimore: New Lanahan Editions in Political Science.

Saint-Germain, Michelle A. 1989. "Does Their Difference Make a Difference? The Impact of Women on Public Policy in the Arizona State Legislature." *Social Science Quarterly* 70(4):956–68.

Sanbonmatsu, Kira. 2002. "Political Parties and the Recruitment of Women to State Legislatures." *Journal of Politics* 64(3):791–809.

———. 2006. *Where Women Run: Gender and Party in the American States.* Ann Arbor: University of Michigan Press.

Sapiro, Virginia. 1981–2. "If U.S. Senator Baker Were a Woman: An Experimental Study of Candidate Images." *Political Psychology* 2:61–83.

———. 1982. "Private Costs of Public Commitments or Public Costs of Private Commitments? Family Roles versus Political Ambition." *American Journal of Political Science* 26(2):265–79.

Schleicher, David. 2007. "Why Is There No Partisan Competition in City Council Elections: The Role of Election Law." *Journal of Law and Politics* 23(4):419–73.

Schlesinger, Joseph A. 1966. *Ambition and Politics: Political Careers in the United States.* Chicago: Rand NcNally.

Schlessinger, Laura. 2009. *In Praise of Stay-at-Home Moms.* New York: Harper-Collins.

Schroeder, Pat. 1999. *24 Years of House Work . . . And the Place Is Still a Mess.* Kansas City, MO: Andrews McMeel.

Schunk, D. H., and M. W. Lilly. 1984. "Sex Differences in Self-Efficacy and Attributions: Influence of Performance Feedback." *Journal of Early Adolescence* 4:203–13.

Schwindt-Bayer, Leslie A. and Renato Corbetta. 2004. "Gender Turnover and Roll-Call Voting in the U.S. House of Representatives." *Legislative Studies Quarterly* 29(2):215–29.

Schwindt-Bayer, Leslie A., and William Mishler. 2005. "An Integrated Model of Women's Representation." *Journal of Politics* 67:407–28.

Seligman, Lester G., Michael R. King, Chong Lim Kim, and Roland E. Smith. 1974. *Patterns of Recruitment: A State Chooses Its Lawmakers.* New York: Rand McNally.

Seltzer, R. A., J. Newman, and M. Voorhees Leighton. 1997. *Sex as a Political Variable.* Boulder, CO: Lynne Rienner.

Shaw, Catherine. 2004. *The Campaign Manager: Running and Winning Local Elections,* 3rd ed. Boulder, CO: Westview.

Sigel, Roberta S. 1996. *Ambition and Accommodation: How Women View Gender Relations.* Chicago: University of Chicago Press.

Simon, Stefanie, and Crystal L. Hoyt. 2008. "Exploring the Gender Gap in Support for a Woman for President." *Analyses of Social Issues and Public Policy* 8(1):157–81.

Smith, Eric R. A. N., and Richard L. Fox. 2001. "A Research Note: The Electoral Fortunes of Women Candidates for Congress." *Political Research Quarterly* 54(1):205–21.

Solowiej, Lisa, and Thomas L. Brunell. 2003. "The Entrance of Women to the U.S. Congress: The Widow Effect." *Political Research Quarterly* 53(3):283–92.

Squire, Peverill. 2000. "Uncontested Seats in State Legislative Elections." *Legislative Studies Quarterly* 25:131–46.

Statistical Abstracts from the United States. 2008. http://www.census.gov/compendia/statab/ (June 30, 2009).

Staton/Hughes Research Group. 1992. "To Be Continued: A Study of Democratic Women's Races for the House of Representatives in 1992." Prepared for EMILY's List. San Francisco: Staton/Hughes.

Stevens, C. K., A. G. Bavetta, and M. E. Gist. 1993. "Gender Differences in the Acquisition of Salary Negotiation Skills: The Role of Goals, Self-Efficacy, and Perceived Control." *Journal of Applied Psychology* 78(5):723–35.

Stone, Pamela. 2007. *Opting Out: Why Women Really Quit Careers and Head Home*. Berkeley: University of California Press.

Stone, Walter J., and L. Sandy Maisel. 2003. "The Not-So-Simple Calculus of Winning: Potential U.S. House Candidates' Nominations and General Election Prospects." *Journal of Politics* 65(4):951–77.

Stone, Walter J., L. Sandy Maisel, and Cherie D. Maestas. 2004. "Quality Counts: Extending the Strategic Competition Model of Incumbent Deterrence." *American Journal of Political Science* 48(3):479–95.

Swers, Michele L. 1998. "Are Congresswomen More Likely to Vote for Women's Issue Bills Than Their Male Colleagues?" *Legislative Studies Quarterly* 23(3):435–48.

———. 2002. *The Difference Women Make*. Chicago: University of Chicago Press.

Swint, Kerwin C. 2006. *Mudslingers: The Top 25 Negative Political Campaigns of All Time Countdown from No. 25 to No. 1*. Westport, CT: Greenwood.

Teixeira, Ruy A. 1992. *The Disappearing American Voter*. Washington, D.C.: Brookings Institution.

Theriault, Sean M. 2005. *The Power of the People: Congressional Competition, Public Attention, and Voter Retribution*. Columbus: Ohio State University Press.

Thomas, Sue. 1994. *How Women Legislate*. New York: Oxford University Press.

———. 1998. "Introduction: Women and Elective Office: Past, Present, and Future." In *Women and Elective Office*, ed. S. Thomas and C. Wilcox. New York: Oxford University Press.

———. 2002. "The Personal Is the Political: Antecedents of Gendered Choices of Elected Representatives." *Sex Roles* 47(7–8):343–53.

Thomas, Sue, and Susan Welch. 1991. "The Impact of Gender on Activities and Priorities of State Legislators." *Western Political Quarterly* 44(2):445–56.

Thompson, Seth, and Janie Steckenrider. 1997. "Gender Stereotypes and Decision Context in the Evaluation of Political Candidates." *Women & Politics* 17(4):71–92.

Tolleson Rinehart, Sue. 1991. "Do Women Leaders Make a Difference? Substance, Style, and Perceptions." In *Gender and Policymaking: Studies of Women in Office*, ed. Debra Dodson. New Brunswick, NJ: Rutgers University Press.

Verba, Sidney, Key Lehman Schlozman, and Henry E. Brady. 1995. *Voice and Equality: Civic Voluntarism in American Politics*. Cambridge, MA: Harvard University Press.

Weddington, Sarah. 1993. *A Question of Choice.* New York: Penguin Books.

Weikart, Lynne A., Greg Chen, Daniel W. Williams, and Haris Hromic. 2007. "The Democratic Sex: Gender Differences and the Exercise of Power." *Journal of Women, Politics & Policy* 28(1):119–40.

Welch, Susan. 1978. "Recruitment of Women to Office." *Western Political Quarterly* 31(2):372–80.

Whitaker, Lois Duke. 2008. *Voting the Gender Gap.* Champaign: University of Illinois Press.

Wigfield, A., J. S. Eccles, and P. R. Pintrich. 1996. "Development between the Ages of 11 and 25." In *Handbook of Educational Psychology*, ed. D. C. Berliner and R. C. Calfee. New York: Macmillan.

Williams, Shirley, and Edward L. Lascher. 1993. *Ambition and Beyond: Career Paths of American Politicians.* Berkeley, CA: Institute of Governmental Studies.

Wilson, Marie C. 2004. *Closing the Leadership Gap: Why Women Can and Must Help Run the World.* New York: Penguin Group.

Witt, Linda, Karen Paget, and Glenna Matthews. 1994. *Running as a Woman.* New York: Free Press.

Wolfinger, Nicholas H., and Raymond E. Wolfinger. 2008. "Family Structure and Voter Turnout." *Social Forces* 86(4):1513–28.

Woods, Harriet. 2000. *Stepping Up to Power: The Political Journey of American Women.* Boulder, CO: Westview Press.

# Index